SUBLIME POUSSIN

MERIDIAN

Crossing Aesthetics

Werner Hamacher
& David E. Wellbery
Editors

Translated by
Catherine Porter

Stanford
University
Press

Stanford
California
1999

SUBLIME POUSSIN

Louis Marin

Sublime Poussin
was originally published in French
in 1995 by Editions du Seuil under the title
Sublime Poussin

Assistance for the translation was provided by the
French Ministry of Culture

Stanford University Press
Stanford, California

Printed in the United States of America

CIP data appear at the end of the book

Contents

Illustrations and Tables

Illustrations

Tables

SUBLIME POUSSIN

Introduction

"Art history and art theory are inseparable. . . . [A] history of art can be achieved only through the simultaneous construction of a theory of art, just as a theory of art can be achieved only as a history of the theory [of art]." Thus for Louis Marin, who wrote these words in 1983 (see Chapter 4, note 12), the paintings and the writings of Nicholas Poussin, painter and theoretician of painting, were an enduring source of food for thought.

The studies that make up the present volume appear in two groups. The first has to do with describing or "reading" pictures, and it takes its title—"Read the Story and the Picture"—from the letter Poussin wrote to his friend and client Chantelou about the 1638–1639 painting *The Israelites Gathering the Manna.* The second presents Poussin's paintings as the development, enactment, and exposition of a theory of painting; its title—"Great Theory and Practice Allied"—comes from another letter from Poussin to Chantelou, on "modes." We have also included a 1984 article devoted to the tempest, a major figure of the sublime in Poussin's work, and the text of a lecture on the sublime Louis Marin gave in the United States in 1985.

This collection of essays makes no claim to be the book Louis Marin intended to write. He had envisioned the project as closely related to his major study on Philippe de Champaigne, and it was to include significant extensions of the work presented here (in particular, it would have dealt with *The Four Seasons*, the topic of a protracted seminar in the 1980s, and with other aspects of the Poussinian sublime, such as monstrosity and violence).

In appendices, we have provided Louis Marin's draft summary of the book he planned, along with the two letters from Poussin to Chantelou that gave us the titles of the two major parts of this collection.

Daniel Arasse
Alain Cantillon
Giovanni Careri
Danièle Cohn
Pierre-Antoine Fabre
Françoise Marin

PART I

"Read the Story and the Picture"

§ 1 Reading a Picture from 1639 according to a Letter by Poussin

We read letters, poems, books. What does it mean to read drawings, paintings, frescoes? After all, the term "reading" is immediately applicable to books; can we say the same for pictures? How valid or legitimate is it to extend the term's meaning and speak of reading in connection with pictures? And yet, even if we are using "reading" as a simple figure of speech, and thus in a sense misusing the term, the fact remains that a written page offers both a text—a reading—and a picture—a viewing. The legible and the visible have common spaces and borders; they overlap in part, and each is embedded in the other to an uncertain degree. In the present essay, I propose to explore those borders and spaces, through the implicit comparison that the expression "reading a picture" entails.

The enterprise, as I see it, has three distinctive features. First, it posits the operational nature of a comparison between reading a page of text and reading a picture. This means not only that the comparison may be valid in certain respects, but also that it has something to tell us about pictures as objects of viewing and, further, that it can tell us something as well about what it means to read a page or a book. In particular, the comparison allows us to take into consideration those aspects of the written or printed page that go beyond reading itself owing to elements and effects of visualization or iconization that, however "marginal" they may be, are by no means innocent.

The second distinctive feature of the undertaking is that it aims to institute theoretical levels and fields in which resemblances and differences between the two readings are pertinent. From a simple "manner of speaking" that is commonly encountered in criticism and discourse about art (the lexicon of a painter, the syntax of a picture, pictorial language, and so on), the intent is to move toward a method for carrying out research on the relations between literature and painting and, more precisely, on the legible and visible elements in pictures and texts, by establishing the levels of a given discourse and the fields to which it pertains.

The third distinctive feature of my enterprise, finally, entails speculation about the dimensions in which resemblances and differences between reading a page and reading a picture are played out in different ways, the dimensions in which the legible and the visible aspects of a picture are variously linked and contrasted.

With these three perspectives as my point of departure, I should like to indicate here, quickly and programmatically, the questions and problems that the very notion of reading raises when it is applied to the work of painting, starting with the fundamental problem: Are there aspects of a picture that can be read? Of what do they consist? Do they consist of signs, in the sense of discrete, identifiable elements from which one could construct a system, an articulated and structured set made up of a finite number of units? If there are signs in a picture, are they "readable"? Can we not ask whether these elements—forms and/or figures—are units apart from the proposition in language that states them, or, to use Peirce's language, whether the iconic *representamen* has the quality of a sign apart from the verbal interpretant that it determines? The problem would then be to inquire into that relation of determination, to assess its strength and its validity.

The second problem, even broader in scope, derives from the aforementioned methodical approach to research into the theoretical levels and fields pertaining to the notion of reading as applied to pictures. Reading is not a simple activity. In a dictionary alone, without even turning to work in applied or experimental psychology, we can find three meanings of direct import to us here that take us in three different directions. To read is first of all to recognize a signifying structure: to recognize that a given form, figure, or feature is a sign, that it represents some other thing even though we may not necessarily know what the thing represented is. This is the way we usually look at pictures, as the Port-Royal logicians remark in connection with their definition of a sign. For Port-Royal, this way of looking at pictures is "immediate" reading, and this is so given a double definition, presupposed and implicit: (1) of the idea of signs as representation and (2) of painted pictures (or geographical maps) as the idea of a thing that impresses itself on the mind only insofar as it represents the idea of something else.

In the second place, to read is to comprehend what one is reading, to assign meaning to the operation of re-cognition of the signifying structure. We may well habitually look at pictures as signs, as one thing representing another; still, do we necessarily read those signs? Do we grasp their meaning? Are paintings pictorial "statements" comparable to sentences, propositions, or judgments (to use the language of the classics)? If the answer is yes, is there some element in painting that plays the role of verb, subject, or predicate?

Finally, to read is also to seek, to decipher, to interpret, and perhaps to divine the meaning of a discourse. Is painting, then, discourse? By inciting us to read, does it not take on a properly discursive status? Is painting a discourse consisting of images whose figures should be analyzed, if not as signs, then at least as tropes?

These last remarks lead me directly to the third problem I should like to raise, and to which the present discussion will be limited, a problem that grows out of what I have called the historical and cultural dimensions of "reading" pictures. Does reading a painted picture not amount, at least from late antiquity to the eighteenth century in the West, to reading, in the picture, the narrative that the artist sought to translate into a "visual image"?[1] By the same token, are not all the problems raised by the expression "reading pictures" more or less insidiously formulated on the basis of this tradition, if only to emphasize the gaps, the distances, the breaks that exist with respect to the tradition itself?

According to this tradition, we have to say that the artist himself, in order to produce a picture, has read a text, and that the viewer, in order "really" to see the picture, has to read the picture as if it were that text. If the painter had to read a book, a text, words, sentences, in order to paint, in order to make the viewer see, the viewer has to "read" the picture in order to see what the text is talking about (to see what the picture translates, what it refers to).

My discussion will be situated within this historical field. More precisely, it will be a commentary on a letter by Poussin that has already caused a lot of ink to flow, my own in particular.[2] I shall comment on Poussin's text itself, in an effort to understand it, but I shall also use it as a heuristic instrument, sometimes looking closely even at its ambiguities and its obscure passages in order to put into place the historical problematics of a scholarly practice: that of reading pictures.

I should like to add that a commentary of this sort, an annotated reading of Poussin's letter, does not strike me as out of place in a meeting devoted to reading and its practices, since I am dealing with a letter written by a painter about one of his own pictures; the letter constitutes the explicit reading protocol for the picture, as it were, given the full complexity of the term "reading" indicated above. Furthermore, the question of the relation between reading and seeing, between legibility and visibility, between "text read" and "picture viewed," is raised in a remarkable formula at the heart of Poussin's letter: "Study [read] the story and the picture." I shall attempt to maintain the historical force of Poussin's formula as a theoretical and practical program for painting, even as I highlight its ambiguities.

We have before us, then, a letter from the painter to his friend and client Chantelou, a letter announcing the delivery of a picture, *The Israelites Gathering the Manna* (see Figure 1), to Chantelou. "I shall not bore you with a long discourse; I shall only inform you that I am sending you *your* picture of *The Manna* via Bertholin, the Lyon courier. I crated it carefully and believe that you will receive it in good condition" (emphasis added). The letter

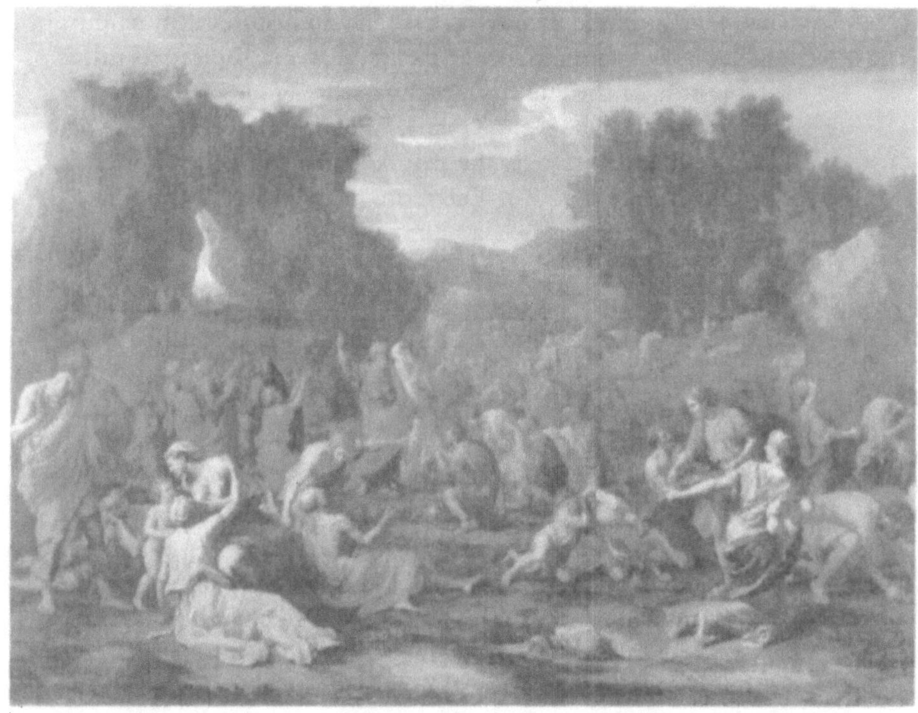

FIGURE 1. *The Israelites Gathering the Manna.* Courtesy Photographie Giraudon.

is thus a stand-in for the picture. Its text stands in for the image, announcing and articulating its transmission from a sender to a receiver as an object of value; Poussin, subject, painter-author of the picture, is writing the letter to Chantelou, privileged viewer, client, the person who ordered the picture, henceforth its owner, and reader of the letter. All the terms of our problem converge here, and especially, from this point on, the double splitting of painter and viewer into writer and reader. However, it is not entirely true that the letter stands in for the picture. The letter does not accompany the picture: it precedes and announces it. It speaks of the picture, and first of all by stating its name, *The Manna*, the proper name that gives the picture its title and constitutes it in its pure singularity. But the name of the picture is also its subject; its title is also the title of the story the picture tells. "Your picture of *The Manna*" means "The picture that I, Poussin, have painted for you, Chantelou, and that tells the manna story" (in other words, "a story you already know"). The term "manna" is thus simultaneously a proper name, a title, a noun phrase, the statement of a subject, and the abbreviation of a narrative that stands, once Chantelou has read it, in place of the absent picture. To read the picture is first of all to read a name and a title, that is, an author and a subject.

Paul Klee asked a remarkable question: How does a picture come by its name? How does a name come to a picture?[3] In this initial or ultimate meeting with language, the picture constitutes itself as subject. It is not a coincidence that, for Poussin, the proper name of the picture is itself a name—a proper name. But this name that names the picture in its singularity refers it at the same time to a series, a genre, a class: the series of all the *Mannas* painted before Poussin's, the genre of religious painting, the class of historical painting. By the same token, with this first reading of the picture as a name, all viewings are announced and preempted. Every viewing is invited to become a reading: the reading of a narrative (the name of the picture declares itself as the name of an episode in the history of the Jewish people), the reading of a religious narrative (the Old Testament), and the reading of a picture of a narrative from sacred history, thus the reading of a history of painting as much as of a painting of history. In contrast, we may ask what viewing and reading effects arise from contemporary pictures that bear the name, the title, "Untitled," or from pictures that have no title except the name of the painter or his signature: no longer "your picture of *The Manna*," but "your Pollock."

Poussin's picture is first of all a name that he writes in the letter he addresses to Chantelou, a name that Chantelou reads, and this name stands for an absence and for the reader's desire to see. For Chantelou, to *read* Poussin's letter and the name of his picture is in "some way" already to see it, that is, in a certain way, already to possess it. The letter, the *text* of the letter, its writing, thus appears as the deferred contemplation of the picture, and if to contemplate the picture is to delight in it, as Poussin would say, then to read the letter and the name of the picture is to have the benefit of a supplement of pleasure by way of the text, *in addition*. Thus, often (it can be necessary to generalize, while introducing nuances and specifications), the discourse that relates the picture, that speaks it, even in its "presence," the discourse that by that very token relates a reading of the picture by bringing it into language, has no function except to compensate for an absence, a lack in the image itself, or to make up for a defect that is consubstantial with the image.

As a kind of confirmation through conjunction and contrast, I should like to cite an interesting text with which Poussin was familiar and which was very widely read in the seventeenth century, Father Louis Richeome's *Tableaux sacrés* (1601).[4] The author evokes just such a confrontation of image and discourse: "Mute painting is for the eyes; the narrations are for the ears; and the exposition of each is for the spirit." Writing to the queen, Marie de Médicis, Richeome underscores the benefits of his book, which is illustrated with images, making it "a triple picture done with brush, words, and meaning." The book's privileged recipient is placed by the preface between an image she sees—the image illustrates the narrative by its material presence in the text to which it is linked—and a narrative she hears—as we have seen, the recipient does not *read* the narrative herself but listens to it *in praesentia*,[5] so that, during the interval, she can appropriate a spiritually useful meaning.

But at the very end of his book, Richeome, who seeks to link the "figurative" with the "literal," the better to explain the mysteries of the Eucharist,[6] adds a cautionary note: "If there is anything in the engraved pictures [the *images*] that does not correspond to the speaking pictures [the *narratives*], the reader will compensate for what the picture lacks, if he wishes, correcting the picture with the words of the text, which he will follow in all respects as the best guide to the meaning of the story." Let us note, in this admonition, the preeminence of the text read (the words of the text, its *parole*) and heard—the preeminence of the text's living word and the process of listening to it—over the picture, whose deficiency is at once a lack (hence the compensation for this lack by the reader of the text) and a mistake, an error (hence the correction of the error by the words of the story). Let us also note that images and narratives are called *pictures* (*tableaux*), but pictures in which painting is a sort of writing (engraved pictures) and writing a sort of speech.

This last point is important both historically and culturally. Written texts have a *visual* presence like that of images: the printed page is envisioned as a picture on a par with the image, if not comparable to it, in many texts that serve as prefaces or forewords up to the end of the century and doubtless beyond. But conversely, as it were, images are *graven* pictures, whereas texts are *speaking* pictures. To be sure, the first term designates engravings and etchings on wood or copper and so on, but by that very token a picture is a form of writing, or at least of inscription, with characteristics and properties that set it apart but that nevertheless also relate it to the written text, or rather to the read or readable text. For its part, a written text is a speaking picture: it is unquestionably read, and we shall not lose sight of the visual nature of the printed page; still, the distinguishing feature of a written text is that it is not so much an operation of sight as an operation of speech and hearing.

Let us note, finally, that if the words of the text are the best guide to meaning, that is because there is a hierarchy between reading the text and seeing the image: reading takes precedence over seeing. Nevertheless, filling in the gaps in the image is left to the reader's discretion. The search for the meaning of the story is not an absolute requirement; or to put it more precisely, no truth is posited that would govern the hierarchy—no truth to which the written text would be closer than the image. But we may also suppose that the deficiency of the image seen with respect to the text written and read stems from the very nature of the visual medium and its constraints as compared to those that govern graphic form and substance. Here we can recall Le Brun's response to certain academicians who criticized Poussin's painted image *Manna* for its lack of faithfulness to the text of Scripture. "Monsieur Le Brun," according to the report of a colleague, André Félibien,

> replied that it is not the same with Painting as it is with History. It is all very well for a historian to make himself *heard* by an arrangement of words and a sequence of discourses that form an image of the things he wants to say and that represent successively whatever actions he pleases. But the painter has only an instant in which he must seize the thing he wants to figure; in order to represent what happened in that moment he sometimes has to combine many earlier incidents in order to make the subject he is exposing understandable; without this, the viewers of his work would be no better informed than if the historian were satisfied to give only the end of his account.[7]

To return by way of Le Brun and Félibien to Poussin's *Manna* and his letter to Chantelou, it may be said that, if one of the functions of the letter is to please the client by allowing him to anticipate the pleasure of contemplation, another is to foresee, prepare, and even control the client's contemplation in order to bring it into contact with the truth of painting: emotional value on one side, cognitive value on the other. For Poussin's letter not only discusses delivery of the picture; it discusses the picture itself. But—in what is perhaps one of the letter's most remarkable passages—it deals, first of all, not with the picture's subject, with what the picture represents or relates, namely "manna"; rather, it deals with the picture as the object of a contemplative gaze. The picture is in fact a *name* and a *frame*, a readable and a visible entity in a state of reciprocal interaction as minimal conditions of possibility for a reading and a viewing. "When you have received yours [your picture], I beg of you . . . to provide it with a small frame; it needs one so that, in considering it in all its parts, the [rays of the] eye shall remain concentrated and not dispersed beyond the limits of the picture by receiving impressions [?] of objects which, seen pell-mell with the painted objects, confuse the light." The letter even ends with the following reminder: "Before you exhibit your picture, it would be highly appropriate to embellish it a little."

The text Chantelou reads formulates a double appeal, then: one by the painter to his client—"I beg of you"—and the other on behalf of the picture—"it needs one." And the painter is the spokesperson expressing what the picture requires: a frame. The text first constructs the picture as a frame for an absent picture. But the missing picture, the void, is what requires a frame to satisfy its own particular need. The frame may be an embellishment, but it is a necessary one: what serves to embellish is also what occasions (or enables) seeing. By means of the frame, the picture is fulfilled in its ultimate goal of being seen, hung, or exhibited, as Poussin also writes. When the printer's eye is replaced by the viewer's gaze, a frame is necessary, because the artifact considered in the process of its production is replaced by the picture considered in the process of its presentation, its exhibition, its staging as a spectacle.

Thus, to the readable element that is the name of the picture, Poussin joins its frame as the condition of its visibility. We can note, then, that if painting does not have access to a language in the Saussurian sense of the term—to a repertory of signifying units on which painting would draw in order to bring itself to fruition in its works—it nevertheless has access to means that are specific to it for showing, for making the viewer see, what it presents. These means are not discursive or even iconic in the mimetic sense of the term; they include the framing, the placement (Poussin concludes his letter by writing that the picture "must be hung very little above eye level, if not a little below"), the lighting, and so on: the form of presentation may be produced (may be shown, even though it cannot be described) by means available to the image itself. With the frame—a nonmimetic, nonsignaletic, nondiscrete element of the icon—we have an element that plays the role of integrant (in the linguistic sense) in representative painting. It is that element, and others of the same nature, that modern and contemporary painting will eventually dissociate from their function in the constitution of the image.

With the framing of the picture, Poussin posits a semiotic condition for its visibility and likewise, as we shall see, for its readability. For the frame concentrates the rays of the eye and, by neutralizing the perception of objects located nearby in the perceptual field (their optical simulacra), focuses them on the picture. Establishing boundaries for the picture, for representation, then, the frame is not a passive agent of the icon: instead it operates to constitute the icon as a visible object whose whole purpose is to be seen by the eye that sweeps over it with its rays while considering it in all its parts. Here it is noteworthy that Poussin speaks of the eye and not of eyes, of rays and not of gazes. The letter constructs a sort of geometric and optical schema, an abstract mechanism that comes into play to regulate visual perception. To look at a picture is not to perceive an object. It is not simply to see.

Three years later, Poussin theorizes this brief notation when he makes a distinction between aspect and prospect: "There are two ways of seeing objects: one is simply to see them, the other is to consider them attentively." The frame is one of the processes that conditions the passage from vision to contemplation, from the visibility of the picture to its readability. With a frame, a picture requires its own theory, that is, it requires that it be presented theoretically *itself* if it is to represent something. But this condition of possibility for the readability of the work of painting is neither discursive nor mimetic in nature. It is an element of the iconic metalanguage, one that the icon, the image, and the picture require as a necessary embellishment in order to present themselves to view. "Simply to see is nothing other than to receive naturally in the eye the *form* and the *resemblance* of the thing seen. But to see an object while considering it means that beyond the simple and natural reception of the form in the eye, one takes special pains to find a way to know that same object well" (emphasis added). Such is prospect: an "office of reason that depends on three things, the eye, the visual ray, and the distance from the eye to the object."[8] Such are the enabling conditions of "pictorial" knowledge; such is the theory of painting. To read a picture: the term "reading" has not yet appeared, but what turn out to be defined by the picture itself as conditions of its showing are a framework and a mechanism of perspective, nonmimetic elements of the icon that, for the time being, in the letter to Chantelou, provide a setting for a simple name: *Manna.*

In the letter, Poussin uses the term "consider" and the expression "consider the picture" three times. First in order to define what the frame and the prospective make possible: the office of reason, the act of coming to know the thing depicted. Next—and we shall come to this in a moment—he employs these terms in reference to a previous letter, in order to deal with the examination of iconic-narrative figures: "Furthermore, if you can remember the first letter I wrote you concerning the movements of the figures which I promised to depict, and if you consider the picture at the same time, I think you will be able to recognize with ease which figures languish, which ones are astonished, which are filled with pity, perform deeds of charity, are in great need, seek consolation, etc." Finally, in order to evoke the pleasurable effects the picture has on its viewer: "And if after having studied [considered] the picture more than once, you find some satisfaction in it, write it to me if you please, without hesitation so that I may be happy to think that I had been able to please you."

Three modalities of contemplation are specified here. The first in chronological terms, but also the most important, is that of a traversal, undertaken by means of the gaze, in which the picture is assimilated as a totality of parts, a traversal governed by the double mechanism of framing and prospect, a traversal internal to the pictorial representation by which the painted work is constituted as a closed system of visibility. The second, based on the first, is that of the constitution of the picture as a *readable* text in which it is a matter of the gaze *recognizing*, in the figures it is shown, the figures of an already familiar story; the gaze "re-marks" the picture as a double process of iconization of a written text and textualization of a figurative mechanism.

With the third and last modality, contemplation becomes a diversified repetition of the traversals accomplished by viewing and those accomplished by reading, a repetition in which the desire to see is brought to fruition in the theoretical delight in the work, in which viewing and reading, visibility and readability, are harmoniously conjugated, and in which the picture, a closed system of visibility, opens itself up to the happy, satisfied repetition of traversals by a gaze that contemplates and reads at the same time. Here it is important to stress the fact that Poussin's entire text is not primarily, and not simply, a description of the viewing-reading of the picture; rather, it constitutes a sort of theoretical schema for reading images in general, a schema whose discursive modality in the letter to Chantelou is simultaneously one of instruction, injunction, and persuasion. The text is thus highly revelatory of an informed, scholarly conception of the reading of the picture. Just as *Manna* could be taken as a manifesto-picture in Rome in 1639,[9] similarly Poussin's letter, without being of the same nature, reveals its desire to institute a certain new type of relation to the work of art.

The moment for reading the picture has thus arrived. It is noteworthy that in order to approach the represented content of the work, the story that the picture depicts through its own particular form of narrativity, Poussin refers not to a written narrative (here, to Exodus 16: 4–5), but to a letter he had written Chantelou earlier, a letter that was presumably at once a contract between the painter and his sponsor, a statement of the subject of the picture (the name *Manna*), and also a definition (in the optical, visual sense) of the image, that is, of the picture as a work that presents its subject in the form of images. The text from Exodus describing the Israelites' gathering of manna in the desert is thus not indicated explicitly by the reading suggestions Poussin offers Chantelou. The position of the biblical passage on the horizon of the letter is like that of the vanishing point of the text that Poussin gives Chantelou to read in place of the picture: a reference as absent from the letter as the picture is, a vanishing point occupied by a name, *Manna*, which names both the picture and the narrative that the picture stages.

> Furthermore, if you can remember the first letter I wrote you concerning the movements of the figures which I promised to depict, and if you consider the picture at the same time, I think you will be able to recognize with ease which figures languish, which ones are astonished, which are filled with pity, perform deeds of charity, are in great need, seek consolation, etc. The first seven figures on the left side will tell you everything that is written here, and all the rest is much to the same effect: study [read] the story and the picture in order to see whether each thing is appropriate to the subject.

This passage is central to the letter, but it is also central for the problems of reading and the readability of the painted picture. First of all, what is the alternative system of enabling conditions for reading the image, a system inscribed within that of the enabling conditions for its contemplation-viewing? The minimal unit of the picture's readability in its represented content is the movement of figures, or rather the representation of movement: not characters in the narration of the story, not figures in the images that tell the story, but movement. The figures in the picture that present to view the narrative of the story staged by the picture are first of all complexes, aggregates of movements.

In his memoirs, Félibien reports something Poussin had said: "Just as the twenty-four letters of the alphabet serve to form our words and to express our thoughts, in the same way the lineaments of the human body serve to express the various passions of the soul so as to produce outwardly what one has within the spirit."[10] Reading the picture thus consists in recognizing the movements of the figures the letter mentions as emotive figures of languor, admiration, pity, and so forth. Between the definition of the figures' movements, the naming of the passions these movements express, and the picture as exhibition or figured presentation, is one and the same act of recognition: the movements and gestures are *like* the letters of the alphabet. The figure that totalizes them is like both the noun and the verb of a passion (a nominal sentence), and the figures taken together are like a narrative statement of the story, like a narrative sequence. But this act of recognition on the part of the viewer's and reader's gaze presupposes the existence of a natural and universal language of the body whose movements and gestures would be signs representing the passions of the soul, passions designated by specific names; it also presupposes that the design of the figures as aggregates of movements and gestures is absolutely explicit, that the design should offer the eye a clear and distinct representation, that is, an immediately nameable representation. It is on these presuppositions that the recognition of narrative figures depends.

From such presuppositions, is it possible to construct a theoretical schema that would be—as some have claimed—the "Cartesian" conception of the passions of the soul? This is debatable, for it would amount to identifying Poussin with Le Brun in terms of pictorial theory and practice, and identifying Le Brun with Descartes where the philosophical and psychological underpinnings of those theories and practices are concerned. To challenge the first identification, we need only take a close look at Poussin's important "letter on musical modes," dated 24 November 1647;[11] to challenge the second, it suffices to examine the twenty-three categories of expression illustrating Le Brun's 1668 lecture on general and particular expression.[12] In this, Fréart de Chambray is perhaps a more obvious referent than Descartes.

Let us simply consider whether the set of presuppositions I have articulated might constitute not so much the enabling condition for reading the historical picture as the implicit background for the prescriptions and instructions for reading that Poussin offers Chantelou. From this standpoint, reading the picture amounts both to discerning what elements in the picture constitute signs, and to stating, declaring, what these signs signify. Correctly stated, that is, properly ordered, the series of meanings (whose names Poussin puts in Chantelou's mouth or ear) would form a sequence within the story of the distribution of the manna that the Israelites gathered in the desert. But it is just as noteworthy that Poussin does not speak of reading the picture at this stage; he simply emphasizes two *concomitant* operations. One involves memory: "if you can remember the first letter I wrote you concerning the movements of the figures . . . "; that is, it involves reading something written. The other is an operation of attentive vision: "and if you consider the picture at the same time. . . . " The concomitance or simultaneity of these two operations is what guarantees the act of ready recognition through which the contemplation of the gaze at once makes an icon of the text (painted figures are indeed in question) and makes a text of the icon (the figures are declared to be in languor, in admiration, and so on); it is a double process, at once inverted and simultaneous, that constitutes the picture's first level of readability: an enumeration of the "figures" (aggregates of gestures) and an enumeration of "names" corresponding to them.[13]

Still, an enumeration does not yet constitute a narrative, or even a narrative sequence of *Manna*. Poussin goes on to add a crucial indication: "The first seven figures on the left side will tell you everything that is written here, and all the rest is much to the same effect." A first remark: Poussin has just enumerated seven sets of figures—those that languish, those that admire, and so on. Each emotion is expressed by a *plurality* of figures, and all the characters in the picture fall within one of the seven sets. Here Poussin is suggesting to his viewer-reader the existence of a system of intermediate roles between the deep narrative structure and the surface narrative manifestations. A second remark: the first seven figures on the left *speak*, visually, within the picture; they each *express* one of the seven sets of figures that Poussin has just named. A third remark: these figures are "first" three times over, as it were. First of all, they are the first ones *seen* in the space that the picture represents; they are in the foreground.[14] Next, they are the first ones *read*, simply because they are on the left, and we read a text from left to right.[15] Finally, they are the first ones *heard*, for they express, they *state* or *declare*, they *exhibit* or *show*, each one in particular and through its group, all the other figures of the picture and all that can be said about them: a second level of readability of the picture is indicated in which considering or contemplating and reading or articulating are closely conjugated with what might be called the written-verbal statement of an attentive gaze.

The group of seven figures in the foreground at left offers, first of all, a grouping that is maximally readable, owing to its compositional rigor (Diderot will say that it "groups") and owing to the figurative density that makes it possible to recognize all the rest of the figures in the picture: each figure *expresses* a *passion* and *represents* one set of figures in the picture. Furthermore, this group functions as the narrative matrix for the rest of the picture: it constitutes the picture's scenario, which needs only to be *developed* in figurative sets in order to *produce* the entire narrative whose story the picture will tell. In this sense, one might say that the group of figures in the foreground constitutes a kernel of readability that generates the overall reading of the work according to rules that remain to be spelled out (syntactic and semantic rules establishing norms for the space of the classical representative painting). Finally, if this analysis is correct, it follows that the picture as a whole is represented by one of its parts, since a group of seven figures is the *iconic* synecdoche of the totality constituted by the seven sets of figures. By the same token, it also follows that one of the parts of the whole represents both the whole and itself: it represents itself by representing the whole. In other words—and the observation is important—it represents what is produced at the very beginning of the process of viewing or reading the picture (in which, from foreground to background, the arrangement of the figures as gestural-emotive complexes unfolds the linearity of the narrative within the space represented by the picture).

Within this "reflexive loop" a symbolic dimension (and here I am using the term "dimension" literally) is inscribed, inviting us to decipher its meaning, to interpret its numerical value, and to divine its intention.[16] Thus at the very point where the picture's narrativity is articulated in and by its figures—a readability ordered according to the *narrative* of the emotive-gestural series itself—a symbolic dimension to be *interpreted* opens up in the narrative. The narrative is accomplished iconically only in the symbolic. The symbolic—allegory, or "mystical" exposition, in Richeome's terms—is the reflexive dimension of the iconic representation of the narrative that it offers transitively to view by the arrangement of the figures on the stage of the represented space: this is the third level of the picture's visibility-readability.[17]

From this point on, can we not consider that "all the rest," which, as Poussin writes, is "much to the same effect," is in a way the "frame" for the group consisting of the first seven figures on the left? Just as the border of dull gold that the picture so badly needed was the initial enabling condition for its *visibility*, along with the mechanism of prospective (of which the frame, moreover, is one element), in the same way the set of figures of the picture in their space of representation, insofar as it is reflected in the seven of them that form a group, "frames" them and, in the very process, constitutes the fundamental enabling condition for the interpretation of the picture, that is to say, its maximum *readability*. Conversely, the border-frame may be considered as a *self*-reflecting mechanism of the object perceived or to be perceived (to be seen), constituting it as an object to be contemplated, as a "theoretical" object; in the same way, the matrix group of seven figures on the left is constituted as a *self*-reflecting mechanism of the statement of the picture (of what the picture represents), endowing the painted artifact with the highest meaning

Thus we have to proceed to what may be considered the principal narrative and symbolic statement of the picture, an arrangement of seven figures in the foreground on the left that simultaneously articulates the first sequence of the narrative, the first narrative signification, that of the Jewish people's wretched state *before* the manna falls (or at the moment when it begins to fall) and the fundamental meaning of the entire narrative of *The Manna*, its symbolic value. This is the group that must be considered attentively, the one that requires contemplation and meditation. Now, what does it offer to view? First of all, it comprises a plastic and figurative composition that is rigorous in its complex unity. Two pairs of figures, at once united and contrasted by their gestures and their movements, by their attitudes and their behavior, surround three other figures which form a pyramid of bodies at the center of the entire group—bodies interconnected by gesture and gaze. The three central figures—the young woman nursing an old woman at her breast and withholding her breast from her child, on whom she gazes with mingled love and sorrow—is a topical motif known as "Roman charity."[18]

This group is contemplated by an upright man, who is the *first* left-hand figure in the entire picture and the *first* in the group of seven figures on the left. This man, as Le Brun writes in his lecture-reading of *Manna*, clearly represents a person who is surprised, overcome by admiration; the gesture of his hand, palm outspread, makes this especially clear, like the slight backward movement of his legs and feet, an interrupted motion, so to speak.[19] He sees, contemplates, and admires the *marvel* of an act of human charity, an act that is admirable only because it transcends the natural order of maternal love (a mother for her son) through a daughter's devotion and love for her mother. He sees, contemplates, and admires this act of human charity shown on the stage of the picture, in the foreground at left, just as the viewer will see, contemplate, and admire the miracle of divine charity constituted by the falling of the manna, which will be exhibited and staged by the picture as a whole. In other words, the leftmost figure in the foreground indeed represents admiration, as Le Brun says, but it also represents Chantelou, the viewer of the entire picture, even as it models the emotive modality of the gaze that he is expected to have or will be obliged to have with respect to the picture.

As I see it, this rigorous construction, at once complex and subtle, might explain a somewhat mysterious expression Poussin used in a letter to Jacques Stella in 1637, about eighteen months before the letter we are examining.

> I have found a certain distribution for M. de Chantelou's picture and certain natural attitudes *that make visible*, in the Jewish people, the wretchedness and hunger to which they were reduced and also the joy and gladness in which they find themselves; the admiration they feel, the respect and reverence they have for their lawgiver; there is a mix of women, children, and men of varying ages and temperaments, which will not displease those who are able to read them correctly, I believe.[20]

The natural attitudes make certain things visible, but the complex distribution of the emotive figures, their variety, and their variation are a source of aesthetic pleasure only if one is able to read them; familiarity or knowledge, the condition for a correct (deep) reading, is identified more or less with the pleasure taken in the visual contemplation of the picture.

Perhaps we need to go further still: just as the totality of the figures in the picture is reflected in the group of the first seven figures on the left and constitutes the enabling condition for the picture's maximum readability, the symbolic level of interpretation of the narrative that the distribution of the figures relates, so the prospective mechanism (framing and point of view of the eye) is reflected by the leftmost figure in the group of the first seven figures on the left. As a delegate of the viewer who is the enunciatory recipient of the picture on the narrative stage, this first figure shows the viewer—offers to his gaze—the emotive affective modality that will inform his view of the entire picture, namely, admiration. Or we might say (and here a new relation of reflexivity and exchange would be established between reading and viewing) that the leftmost figure *makes* the viewer *read* the nature of *true vision* (admiration).

Let us imagine for a moment that the figure in the foreground on the far left is not an Israelite overcome with admiration before a marvelous act of charity observed during the crossing of the desert, but, rather, the viewer of a picture representing an instance of "Roman charity." The narrative that this viewer *would read* in the group of two women and a child would be a kind of duplicate of the narrative in book 4, chapter 4, of Valerius Maximus's *Dictorum factorumque memorabilium libri*, a somewhat misplaced duplicate in which a prison gives way to a desert and a compassionate jailer is replaced by a young child excluded from the maternal breast. Chantelou, too, will read this narrative, just as his admiring delegate reads it within the *Manna* picture; however, Chantelou will read it within another narrative, the one drawn from the Book of Exodus in the Old Testament. Here, then, is a marvelous example of pagan morality representing a miraculous episode in the history of the chosen people and representing itself in the first sequence of the sacred narrative: the sequence of lack and deficiency. From this point on Valerius Maximus's *exemplum*-narrative and the miracle-narrative of the Old Testament constitute for the viewer of Poussin's entire picture—and for that viewer alone—the two poles of a figurative relation in the rhetorical sense of the term, a relation whose meaning he still has to guess in and through the picture itself.

If we develop the figurative synecdoche constituting the relation between the entire set of figures in the picture and the foregrounded group on the left, we find, at the center of the picture, the double figure of Moses and Aaron. Moses is pointing upward with his forefinger to indicate the source outside the frame, outside the representation of the miraculous food, while Aaron, his hands folded and his eyes lifted toward the heavens, is giving thanks to God for his infinite charity. This double figure again echoes both the figure of admiration and that of the young mother performing an act of charity, but it has the effect of positioning the object of admiration and the origin of the food outside the field of visibility, outside the picture: an unrepresentable iconic element that is suggested only by a gesture, positioned only by a gaze, but one that Chantelou will read, in his memory as a Christian, as the eucharistic mystery in which the Father through Jesus Christ his son has eternally provided spiritual food for the soul to those who believe in him. The sacrament instituted in the narrative of the New Testament is in a way the invisible vanishing point of readability for an ancient, pagan *exemplum*: the marvel—displaced into sacred history—of a miracle befalling the chosen people.

The displacement of the allegory in the "Jesuit" or "baroque" sense of the term into the Poussinian "classical" symbolic dimension is explicitly marked, according to this view, by Poussin's suppression of Moses' identifying marks: the horns and the staff, the rod of commandment. The case of the horns is particularly clear as far as the reading and the viewing of the image are concerned.

Moses' horns are, to be sure, the result of a Latin misreading of the Hebrew term meaning "to radiate," an error committed by St. Jerome and corrected by St. Thomas.[21] But this correction has had virtually no impact on either the "popular" or the "scholarly" tradition of representations of Moses. Horns on the forehead of an individual signify "Moses" or "Here is Moses." However, let us note that the acquisition of horns by Moses, that is, the "radiance" of his forehead, occurs after the manna story in Exodus. The sign of the identification of the character with his name is thus also a sign anticipating the moment of acquisition of the Law. The horns, by narrative prolepsis, are the *pre-vision* of the Law in the representation of the episode, thus the indication (with the rod of commandment) of a divine order—simultaneous authority and commandment, power and design or plan—of which the Eucharist is the distant accomplishment: manna (material nourishment fallen mysteriously from the sky), Law (divine order fallen miraculously from the sky), and Eucharist (spiritual nourishment, the enduring miracle of the New Law) are at once in a relation of temporal succession and in exegetic figurative correspondence.

When Poussin eliminates Moses' horns and his rod of commandment, he is, by correcting the literal tradition, simultaneously eliminating Moses' two identifying signs and the figurative and narrative prolepsis of the representation: he eliminates the "reading" of the name *in* the figure of Moses and also the "reading" of meaning in the story. He must therefore recuperate this dual reading in his picture: if the "name" of Moses is read both through the arrangement of the figures, including that of the Moses figure, and through the circumstances represented (for someone who already knows the story), the "reading of the meaning" will be given on the contrary only to those who know how to read *well*, to those who are familiar not only with the Exodus narrative but also with Valerius Maximus and his collection of *exempla*—in short, the scholarly Christian humanists who ally knowledge of the ancient texts with biblical exegesis. Compared to the engravings found in popular or scholarly Bibles between 1520 and 1614,[22] Poussin's picture displaces Moses from the left foreground to the center of the middle distance, putting Valerius Maximus's "Roman charity" in his place while displacing his reading from Rome to the Sinai desert and from pagan texts to the Christian Bible. Hence the crucial function in Poussin's picture of the "admiring" character who is an "operator" for reading *and* for viewing the entire picture.

"Study [read] the story and the picture in order to see whether each thing is appropriate to the subject." Here we are back at the heart of the letter by the Master with which we began. Standing in for the absent picture, as a supplement to the painted work that is in the process of rejoining its owner (its recipient), the author (the painter) has constructed and described a complex discursive mechanism in the form of a written statement in order to have it read by the person who will receive the letter, the one who ordered the picture, its future viewer; but this mechanism also puts itself on stage as one of the characters in the play being performed. It is a matter, in short, of putting the reader in the position of a viewer of the picture. Poussin's letter does this three times. First, the viewer is an eye whose rays are confined by the frame and not scattered outside. Next, the viewer is a gaze directed toward the picture, where it re-cognizes a painting project and verifies the accuracy of its execution; this gaze sees the picture and, in what it contemplates, reads what it sees; the visible is exchanged with the readable and vice versa. Finally, in a third staging whereby the reader of the letter is positioned as a viewer of the picture, the viewer now becomes the receiver-listener for a discourse of narrative figures, a discourse that the painter, writing his letter, can only repeat; a discourse that is nothing other than epideictic discourse, an admirable *demonstration*, the marvelous *monstration* of the picture through its figures.

Put on stage as a viewer of the picture, the reader of the letter is, moreover, introduced onto the stage of history as a metafigurative figure (if I may use such a term) who, through a gaze of admiration and a gesture of surprise, gives the viewer—that is, himself—the exact key to the true reading of all that the picture represents while designating the mystery of what it does not represent and the rigorous manner appropriate to the perfect *viewing* of the work of painting. And yet in writing his letter the painter says none of this to his reader: he leaves the reader to comprehend it, that is, lets him wait to see, to contemplate, to read the work and divine its highest meaning. Thus it is that in the text of the picture, on the canvas of its representation, the readable and the visible are interwoven at all levels, in a tissue whose weft would be the trajectories of the gaze, and whose warp would be the discourses of the picture.

"Study [read] the story and the picture in order to see whether each thing is appropriate to the subject." The painter gives the future viewer an order in the form of a challenge. Read the story in the Old Testament for which the picture offers a narrative sequence—the manna falling in the desert—to your gaze, but while you are contemplating the picture, while you are considering it in all its parts, you will see *another* story in the front left-hand corner, an *exemplum* from paganism, and it is because you have admired the visible example of Roman charity that you will be able to meditate on something the picture neither shows nor tells, something that nevertheless defines the precise rule of appropriateness of each thing to its subject, the rule for reading, the eucharistic sacrament.

Thus the highest meaning operates in the gap between the visible—that which is shown, figured, represented, staged—and the readable—that which can be said, stated, declared; this gap is at once the place of an opposition and that of an exchange between the two registers, a gap on the basis of which it is appropriate to raise the question of the picture, of this picture, *Manna*, if indeed it is the case that "manna"—*mann-hu*, "what is that?"—was the question the Hebrews asked when they saw the whitish, sweetish, granular stuff, if this indeed was the word they used to name the thing, the word through which they read the miraculous event.[23] "Manna," "what is that?": a thing unknown, unnameable, unreadable, but visible in the picture, a question to which the invisible answer, outside the picture, "this is my body," replies, in mystery, words to be eaten; the invisible that can be recognized only if the viewer entering into the picture manages to figure himself at the far left in the foreground, like the character who contemplates and admires in silence.

§ 2 Description of the Image

Concerning a Landscape by Poussin

In an earlier study, I sought to analyze the principles of an intersemiotic transposition through a study of the relations between pictorial and mythic narrative in Poussin's work.[1] Given a narrative for which we possess the text(s) that constitute the literary "referent" for a painting, how is that narrative "transposed" onto canvas? Can the general rules of transmutation be defined? What types of transformation are imposed on a linguistic configuration by the transfer to a visual configuration? And so forth.

Problematics

In this essay I should like to raise a related but different question. I do not propose to analyze an intersemiotic transposition that has already been carried out in order to identify the general conditions that made it possible; rather, I propose to examine, in its relation to a given painting, the first and most immediate type of discourse produced about that painting, namely, descriptive discourse. At the level of language, what is description insofar as it "belongs" to the painted image? What is the status of the spontaneous "telling" of the painting that is the first evocation of meaning provoked by the image and that takes place, by design, at the level of the pictorial surface? We need to question the apparent innocence of such a "telling," its illusory immediacy, in order to discover the multiple investments—cultural, social, affective—that inform it and that by the same token transform the object described. Once described, the painting loses its status as an object and becomes a text on which successive readings are deposited. These readings displace the painting's elements, modify their relationships, create zones of intense visibility and also blind spots, blanks; they make a given element stand out or fade away, take on more or less importance, in relation to the other elements. Are these successive readings—which constitute the pictorial text-object itself, at least to a certain extent—infinite in number? Or—to ask a more relevant and more precise question—are they, in their open succession, "interminate," linked by some form of coherence? Are they articulated within a system that is not characterized by any degree of closure? If so, does this system not constitute the painting's "structure," understood as the articulated set of its readings? And does the meaning of the painting not lie in this ordered displacement of discourse throughout its readings?[2] If so, what is the status of the painting, the text-object, as it is read? In one sense the painting disappears in its readings, since there is no such thing as a virgin pictorial surface, untouched by any reading-gaze—if only because the surface is offered to view in order to be seen. The reading of a painting has no starting point that would be the painting as it exists prior to any reading, for the painting is, through and through, a *legendum*.

In another sense, paintings are constituted in the reading process: through readings, a painting is defined as a place where meanings begin, though for these beginnings there is no ultimate end point that would be the painting's *meaning*. There is a simple reason for this: the painting is not first and foremost an object of knowledge; it is not the supporting structure or the stimulus for conceptualization. It is a pleasure-producing entity, but one whose processes of production conceal themselves by borrowing the paths of readings, that is, the paths of the meaning that is being constituted by those readings. By that very token, the pleasure of reading is never fully realized; rather, in the temporary satisfaction it produces, it designates the force of which the text-painting is at

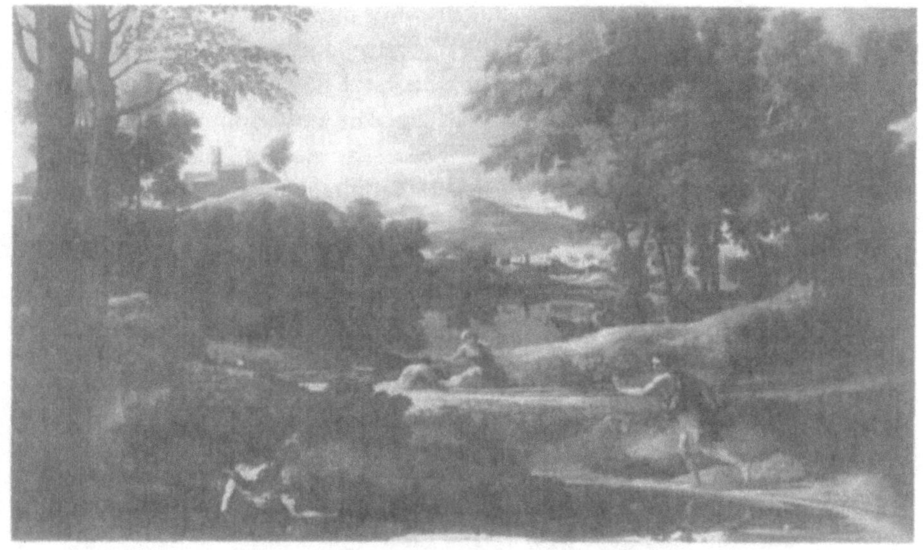

FIGURE 2. *Landscape with a Man Killed by a Snake.* © National Gallery, London.

once the trace and the figurative matrix, the desire. The painting is a trace or mark left by the "creative" gesture that is signified in it; it is a figure that displaces and engenders itself in the course of successive readings; it is desire's way of exposing itself to view in its figures without ever realizing itself in them. Hence the impossibility of ever concluding the reading of a painting, since what is being read is a visible element of desire that displaces itself in the reading process and of which the reading perceives only the surface turmoil, the traces, as it evokes them. This intermingling of the readable and the visible in a painting is what produces the painting's meaning or meanings; its "interweaving" is what I should like to follow, or undertake.

To make the analysis purer and more detached from the problematics suggested earlier, I have chosen a painting by Poussin (Figure 2) that is known with virtual certainty not to be the result of an intersemiotic transposition in the narrow sense of the term as I have used it above.[3] This does not mean that painting (or the painting in question) is not a narrative, and it certainly does not mean that the painted picture does not bring to light, in the "diagram" of pictorial readings that it allows and requires, a possible, unheard-of narrative with the distinctive status of narrative "matrix," productive of different and simultaneous narratives whose proliferation would simply be the *readable* face of the *visible Gestaltung* of the painting. This would be another way (while extricating ourselves from the narrowing imposed by the transposition of a narrative text into a painting) for us to rediscover the tissue of visible and readable elements that our general problematics posits as the basis for pictorial semiotics. The painting might then appear as a producer of narratives that are all derived from a single matrix form drawn on its surface by successive readings. Anthony Blunt, in his *Critical Catalogue* of Poussin's works, calls the painting in question *Landscape with a Man Killed by a Snake*.[4]

Descriptive discourse is discourse that records the painting one portion at a time, and transposes into language that which appears to be "written" on the canvas. This discourse is what I should like to interrogate—with reference to the figurative canvas that belongs entirely and in its extreme limits to the ideology of representation. In this discourse, language and image are primordially intertwined, at an insertion point that might appear to be the point of departure for all pictorial metalanguage. The fact that this point seems to me unassignable has major theoretical consequences. Any description is from the outset a reading in each of its two aspects: it is a visual traversal of the plastic surface following the order or orders of the reference points deposited on it, and it is a mental and perceptual deciphering of those same signals as signs within a discourse.[5] In other words, it seems to me difficult to distinguish between two phases in the approach to a painting, one descriptive or "factual," the other interpretive or "signifying," the second being constructed on the basis of the first and acquiring from the first its own objective limits and empirical conditions of possibility. Description is interpretation; but that assertion does not turn description over to the relativity and uncertainty of a proposition in the "grip" of its contexts and determined by them. Description is actually the first reading; or rather, the term covers the open set of possible readings, readings that converge on the painting in their plurality and construct the *system* of the differences that are constitutive of the painting's text. If description designates the open system of readings, it also names the objective coherence of the text in its radical independence from any particular process of interpretation: it refers, as it were, to a constant surplus of meaning, but on condition of understanding, through surplus, the openness of the system of readings in which meaning is initiated in its plurality.

Description

Let us take a close look at several descriptions, in their differences, of Poussin's *Landscape with a Man Killed by a Snake.* These descriptions vary considerably in quantitative terms. The shortest, the title stating the subject of the painting, is a sort of description-definition. The longest is found in Fénelon's *Dialogues des morts* along with a fictional exchange between Leonardo da Vinci and Poussin. In between, we find three texts by André Félibien from the sixth and eighth *Entretiens sur les vies des plus excellens peintres,* as well as the legend found in the Wildenstein collection for Etienne Baudet's engraving of Poussin's painting.[6] The first operation therefore consists in putting these texts "in perspective": the perspective converges in a vanishing point that is the painting itself; its order or arrangement is one of increasing reduction.

We may observe that, from Fénelon's text to the title Anthony Blunt gives the painting, a certain oppositional structure remains unchanged: that of landscape versus story (or description versus narrative), which constitutes a sort of general schema of readings, but which our systematic reading may have to interrogate and thus to transgress. Once it is referred to a determined historic and cultural dimension, the term "landscape" defines the painting's sphere of belonging to a "genre" within a hierarchy of genres that is itself subject to historical variation: for the "landscape" genre, it is possible, at least in a first approximation, to give the rules that spell out its limits and the lexicon that supplies its elements.[7] But at the same time, the subject of the painting given in its title as landscape—an indication that the painting belongs to the genre—is specified by a second subject, a subject within the subject that defines a subclass of landscapes. These are in fact known as "landscapes with a subject": here, it is "a man killed by a snake," an anecdote, event, or narrative referring to a different genre that is itself defined, historically and aesthetically, in its variations, as a story. For the time being we cannot determine to what subgenre or type of story the story of the man killed by a snake belongs: mythological, historical, contemporary, or generic.[8]

Let us note as well that, in its opposition to the landscape, the story is reduced to a few essential marks that constitute it in its specificity: the man, death, the snake. Thus the title does not tell the story; it only indicates the story's central, "pivotal" moment, the killing of a man by a snake. The title articulates two genres, or superimposes two "codes," that are themselves subject to variation, that is, to restructuring, to reorganization, in later periods along different lines. These genres circumscribe a second-degree code in which finer and more complex articulations are latent. Simultaneously, however, we encounter an opening up of meaning characterized by the binary oppositions "landscape *vs.* story," "nature *vs.* man," on the level of content; or "description *vs.* narration," "figurativity *vs.* discourse," on the level of expression. Let us note, finally, that the story and its marks will serve to individualize the painting within a series of subjects, a list that constitutes a veritable paradigmatic field in which a process of commutation is at work:

1. Landscape with a man killed by a snake.
2. Landscape with a man pursued by a snake.
3. Landscape with two women (nymphs) and a snake.
4. Landscape with a woman washing her feet.
5. Landscape with a man washing his feet.
6. Landscape with a boy drinking.
7. Etc.

To be sure, this list was constructed by Anthony Blunt for an annotated catalogue; still, the art historian chose the terms for the title according to a certain number of logical rules related to Leibniz's rules for constructing a nominal definition, "which is nothing but the enumeration of sufficient marks" with the aim of arriving at the "distinct concept which assayers have of gold; one, namely, which enables them to distinguish gold from all other bodies by sufficient marks and observations."[9] This reference to Leibniz, and especially to the example the philosopher uses to illustrate an effective nominal definition, or title, in "Meditations on Knowledge, Truth, and Ideas," is significant: for here the word "title" applies not only to a painting or a book, but also to a coin. It establishes a right by inscribing a mark in the substance treated, the mark that "a worker puts on the face of every piece he makes"; it also designates "the degree of fineness of gold and silver coinage."[10] The painting's title is thus the nominal definition of the painting through the enumeration of its marks, that is, through description. By means of the title, the painting is catalogued or grasped in its generalities; it is the expression of a code, or of several overlapping codes; it is an element in a series, at the heart of which it acquires its own value, the difference that (en)titles it, or "cashes" it, a title that is its name, more than and in a quite different way from the painter's signature, which is ordinarily hidden in it. If Blunt, abandoning the excellent reasons that made him name or title the painting in this way, had, for example, taken up the old title, sometimes still used, of *Landscape with Cadmos* or *Landscape with Cadmos and the Snake*, the canvas would then have joined the series "Landscape with Hercules and Cacus," "Landscape with Orion," " . . . with Orpheus," " . . . with Polyphemus," and so on, and it would thus have acquired a different value, being caught up in another differential network of substitution—"Landscape with a mythological subject, with a narrative of the founding of the city-state"—hence another signifying opening adjacent to the one we have explored.

Félibien's three descriptive texts, like Fénelon's and like the legend accompanying Baudet's engraving, also use the oppositional structure "landscape *vs.* story," but they bring to light two new differences with respect to the description-definition of the title: all these texts develop the narrative, tell the story, expose the event that is taking place "in the foreground of the painting." None of them, except Fénelon's lengthy text and one notation in Félibien's eighth *entretien,* emphasizes the landscape; none *marks* it in a distinctive way.[11] Here is the beginning of a new departure for meaning, a possible new codification of the painting. If in more extensive descriptions of the painting the landscape is mentioned in the text only under the generic term "landscape," whereas the subject-narrative is spelled out by the notation of new episodes, does this not signify that discourse in language has an immediate affinity with actions and drama, that is, with a *succession* of events of which human beings are protagonists? Is not the possibility of producing a discourse, of speaking of something in general, based on a temporal succession of instants or moments? On the other hand, do not the enduring quality of nature in the landscape, its immutability, and even more its full and immediate visibility, in their simultaneity, challenge the chain of words, even if the words in question are not narrative but descriptive?

In other words, when it is a matter of speaking briefly and precisely of a painting, of describing it in terms of its distinctive features in relation to the other paintings in a series, it is the subject-narrative that is recounted, not the landscape that is described—a signifying facility marked in Blunt's annotated catalogue by the invariant "landscape" and by the variant character: "with a man," "two women," "a child," and so on. At bottom, the narrative recounted is what makes it possible to distinguish one painting from another, and however precise the description of the landscape may be, language drowns the singularity of the visible—as it is given in its "figures"—in "abstract" generality.

Hence the new opposition between a landscape defined in its abstract generality as decor and a narrative described in its concrete specificity as drama. Although the significance of this opposition appears only at the level of the form of expression (the number of words produced under one rubric or another—landscape, story), its consequences on the level of content quickly come to light. Is it not the disappearance of the narrative-subject in still life or in pure landscape that condemns discourse on painting to the verbal, poetic analysis of visual, sensory impressions? It would no doubt be fruitful to study the processes and metaphors of this new form of intersemiotic transposition (for example, the Goncourt brothers speaking about Chardin). With the opposition between decor and drama, we are introduced onto the theatrical stage, and it is this new codification whose starting point is indicated by the opposition between "landscape" and "story": we have an immobile, immutable, always visible decor that surrounds and limits the space of the stage on which the episodes and peripeties of the drama are exposed in turn. From the outset, the descriptive discourses read the painting as a theatrical performance through which a drama is represented in a place whose entire function is to offer it to view, in the diachrony of its moments: nature is henceforth defined functionally as the decor for human action, and man as the actor in a drama that puts him on stage. And if the theater constitutes one level of codification of the painting, it will then be appropriate (and this comes to light, in quite a remarkable way, in Fénelon's text) to distinguish between the *ground* (*l'aire*, or "area")[12] on which the story unfolds—and which is, properly speaking, the immobile stage serving as the local infrastructure for visibility, as a platform for representation—and the *decor* that provides the story with both its backdrop and side walls. In the decor, there is no human action; it simply represents "the place where the thing is acted."[13] Nature will thus take two forms: in one, it is the ground, the *locus standi et representandi* for human action, while in the other it is pure decor, the environment from which man is excluded. As Fénelon indicates astutely, certain accidental features of the ground constitute an incident or accident of the action in this painting: this geology or geography is at the same time a topology or a topic of the dramatic discourse in its traversal of the surface of the painting. And perhaps this is what Félibien means, in a less stereotypical fashion than may appear to be the case, when he talks about a situation of the "place": there is the place that is the very

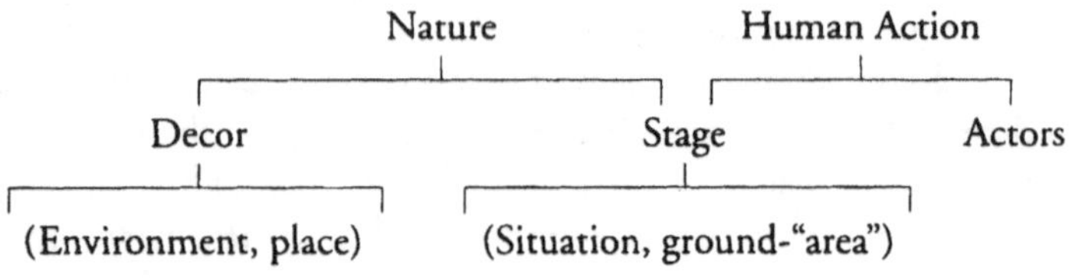

FIGURE 3. Theatrical oppositions in the painting.

space of representation, and there is its situation, which is the topic of that place—the stage itself.

Thus the absence of marks on the landscape that would contrast with the pronounced character of the narrative-action in the description has led us to unlock a new code, that of theatrical representation, where a new opposition is constructed at the very outset: "landscape *vs.* story"; "nature *vs.* human action"; "decor *vs.* stage." These oppositions are expressed more precisely in the schema shown in Figure 3. The schema brings to light the crucial importance of the stage or *scene*, a complex middle term between human action (the narrative, the story) and the decor (nature, the landscape described). The import of this opposition between a marked and an unmarked term is taken up again by Fénelon in his discussion of the opposition between marks.

"The zero-degree landscape" that is presented simply as "landscape" in the other texts has a signifying value in its pure opposition to the narratives. Fénelon's text confirms that value, although with a new inflection, as it confirms the inception of meaning identified above. Indeed, in the dialogue between Leonardo and Poussin, it is noteworthy that the latter, describing the "organization of one of his paintings," integrates the elements of the ground, that is, the stage, with the narrative, and contrasts them, as marked terms, with the decor. Furthermore, he moves into the decor figures and actions that our own descriptive reading will identify within the environment of the representation; this means that the properly ideological cleavage between decor and action, which is no doubt essential to the notion of "theatrical" representation, will be modified from one reading to the next. The modification begins in one of our texts, the legend accompanying Baudet's engraving: from one description to the next, the limits of the decor and the stage, insofar as these constitute the topical situation of the action, are displaced. Fénelon relegates the figures of play and work to the environment. The counterdisplacement of our own reading corresponds to this rejection, whose meaning we shall need to interrogate; in our reading, these figures move onto the stage, and so, perhaps, do those of the castle and the city.

The whole first part of Fénelon's description combines accidents of the terrain with incidents of the action: "a *rock* [on the] left side of the painting. *From this rock there flows a spring of clear, pure water.* . . . A man had come to draw water from the spring. . . . *Close by is a broad path on the edge of which* there appears a woman who sees the terrified man but who cannot see the dead man [because of] *a low spot . . . a sort of curtain between her and the fountain*" (emphasis added). Even the *curtain* (of earth), concealing death, functions as a machine for dramatic action. On the other hand, "the background" of the painting combines all the elements that can "refresh [the gaze] from all the horrors [it] has seen. . . . In the water there are various objects diverting to view: in one place young people bathing and playing while swimming; in another, fishermen, one pulling in a net, two others rowing, . . . others are playing [the game of] *mourre*," and so forth, back to the "distance" where mountains of a "bizarre" appearance produce a varied horizon. The marks indicating opposition here are complex. They are developed on several levels: the essential index is the opposition between the horror of the action, the drama that links the human actors in the narrative, and the charm, the sweetness, the pleasant variety, the peacefulness of the decor, to which numerous human figures belong, tracing the graces of a pastoral like silhouettes against a natural background. Thus it is not going too far to suggest that a new code feature appears at this point in Fénelon's description, namely, the signifying correlation of two pictorial-theatrical genres, drama and pastoral, opposed/juxtaposed in the representation as the place of the staging is to the environment of the decor.[14] But Fénelon's description is permeated by delicate and subtle correlations that trace a play of correspondences on the surface of the painting, one that we have not yet finished examining: "leisure *vs.* work" (swimming parties, walks, the game of *mourre vs.* the fishermen, the three peasants); "age *vs.* youth" (the big trees *vs.* the fresh and tender woodland), "the sacred *vs.* the profane," the castle *vs.* the city," and so on.

In this deployment of signifying correlations, as we can see, Fénelon's description, with its "zero-degree landscape" inflection, is charged with interpretive values of reading. However, the point has to be made more specific: it seems difficult to speak of connotation in the linguistic sense of the term, for the simple reason that the level of denotation has been absent from the very beginning of our analysis. It is of course true—and to become aware of this it suffices to read Fénelon's text and to look at the painting (and in so doing to obey the precepts Poussin set forth for Chantelou: "read the story and the painting")—that nothing in Fénelon's description goes beyond the painting's boundaries; Fénelon does not describe anything that is not painted. What is more, on several points his discourse alone makes it possible to see certain features today: the *mourre* players in the middle ground on the left, for example, become visible only after the text has been read. Indeed, description becomes reading only to the extent that it leaves certain features unmentioned, effacing or displacing them—to the extent that it articulates the continuity of the pictorial surface in a particular way. Establishing relations of contiguity between certain elements perceived as discrete, it distances other elements that weave other relations among themselves and function as poles of opposition.

To articulate, in short, means to link together, but also to disjoin, to oppose: these terms can be "properly" applied to the surface of the painting. They mean that the interval between two terms marking their oppositional relation in the painting is insignificant in its materiality, in its continuity. Contiguity is not the same thing as continuity, for it presupposes an interval, a blank space between two elements.[15] Now, this distance which allows the contiguous to subsist within itself cannot be a pure and simple gap in the painting, a gap that is fundamentally space. This distance, rather, is the insignificance of the continuous which the analytic discourse articulates in meaning. To be sure, Fénelon's text, in comparison with the catalogue title, covers the painting with a much denser network of relations, but the discursive net will always have holes, and they will allow parts of the pictorial surface to pass through it as insignificant. It is fortunate that this is the case; otherwise nothing would have any meaning. Other descriptions, by displacing the network on the surface, will allow these parts to signify by extracting them and retaining them in the play of relations. Hence displacement of the figures occurs in the surface of the painting from one reading to the next, provided that we understand figures not as objects in the world, insofar as they are represented in the painting, but as relationships that are exhibited, extracted by the description on the surface of the painting.

From this standpoint, Fénelon's description brings to light a second set of correlations, one that corresponds to the major dichotomy between landscape and story but that also initiates meaning in "the form of expression"; these correlations involve the dimensions of the surface of a painting, or the spatial zones on which the figures articulated by the descriptive discourse are inscribed: on the one hand, for example, "the foreground *vs.* the background *vs.* the middle distance," zones that correspond to the lower, middle, and upper bands of the painting's surface; and, on the other hand, "the left side *vs.* the right side" of the painting, zones that are determined in Fénelon's text in relation to the viewer's position in front of the canvas. The conversion of the terms of the description that we have just produced warrants an observation: these terms are in fact drawn from the ideology of representation that my own analytic discourse must at once *conserve*—paintings are representations, and the most general system that links their signs is that of representation—and *dismantle*, by reconnecting the "ideologized" terms with their ideology, by making it clear that they translate that ideology. The terms "foreground," "background," and "distance" refer to a space of representation that brings an illusionist depth into play within the frame of the painting; "left side" and "right side" are defined only with respect to the sovereign gaze of the viewer toward whose eye the perspective appearances flow.

For the purposes of Fénelon's description, the story unfolds at the front of the stage—right on the proscenium of this theater—or at the bottom of the painting in "that part of the Stage where the Histrions did both act and speak."[16] The background is the intermediate zone of the environment, the place where characters and human constructs are integrated with the decor, and the distance is pure decor: in the opposition and correspondence of those three terms we discover once again the binary organization with which we began, the foreground being reserved for the narrative-drama, the background and the distance for the scenic environment, the decor-landscape that is described. As for the left and right sides, in the description they mark something like zones of alternation between movement and rest as the eye traverses the painting's surface. It is indeed significant that the gaze of the viewer, Fénelon, leads him to begin his discourse at the bottom left, with the rock, the spring, death, and the snake, and then to move rightward to the man advancing toward the fountain, after which, in a return to the left, it reaches the frightened woman. The same sweeping motion, zigzagging from left to right and bottom to top, is pursued in the "decor," but there it is accelerated, as if the gaze were to perceive it in the form of a natural totality enveloping the scene with a simultaneous environment. In a single movement the left and right sides define the poles of Fénelon's gaze as it encounters the surface of the painting and the polarizations of descriptive discourse in his text; the places of articulation of the viewer's traversal of the painting and his discourse on the painting are conjoined. But they also bring to light, in the play of figures within the painting, an "I" to whom the gaze belongs, an "I" that is both anonymous and constantly present as absence in the representation. That "I" *literally* and *visually* articulates the figures of the painting through the trajectory of its gaze, whatever the order of that trajectory may be and even though the order, displaced from one descriptive text to another, is itself meaningful.

In the unified movement of his description, Fénelon connects the dimensions of theatrical representation (foreground-background-distance or proscenium–intermediate decor–pure decor) and the order in which the figures enter (left-right), an order that determines their orientation with respect to one another. Indeed, the figures come on stage in an order that varies according to the trajectory-discourse. Like any viewer, Fénelon is the stage director who enters into the painting through its figures; present, he acts through his absence, from the first moment the painting is seen, from the moment it is, in fact, a painting. Thus the stagings performed by the viewer, in the succession of descriptive readings, are signifiers of the "I," each reaching a trace of that "I" designating it as absent from the painting.

Finally, we must note the lack of correspondence between the dimensions of the pictorial surface and the quantitative measures that ought to result from them. The foreground of the painting occupies half of its surface, and Fénelon eliminates from his description the central area between the left and right sides, even though this area is delineated by two figures: the woman in front and a building in the background. And my own descriptive discourse indeed constructs these figures as fundamental relations for the painting: they link the left-hand section to the right-hand section. Fénelon's description, since it does not mark the woman's central position, gives the figure it exhibits in this trajectory-discourse a different orientation and value. Because of the effacement of the center, the woman is one pole in a bipolar relation; she does not play the role of generating figures and relational differences that she plays in my description.[17]

The Problem of Narratives

For Fénelon, the story is articulated in three sequences that constitute three distinct and related pictures within the narrative, centered, as it were, on three characters. We are obliged to speak of pictures internal to the narrative, for in the narrative process Fénelon inaugurates a description that is no longer merely a description of nature as decor or scenic ground; it is, rather, also a characterization or an aspect of the action itself—an all-the-more-necessary characterization in that what is at stake allows the action to be *seen* through discourse. This multilayered construction through which a painting unfolds within the discursive sequences is characteristic of descriptive discourse about painting, whether action or decor is at issue; such discourse is always preceded by its object, the painting. However, the painting itself signifies only through the descriptive reading that is produced of it. Thus we have a sort of paradox of reading in general and of descriptive readings of a painting in particular: the painting already precedes the reading that nevertheless constitutes it as a painting in its signifying capacity. But this first observation leads to another, more fundamental question: How can discourse tell a painted story without being necessarily unfaithful to the represented aspect of the painting? This question in turn raises a third: How can a story be painted, that is, transposed to a picture, a painting?

If we analyze the first "picture" in the narrative, we note that the multilayered construction takes imbrication to a vertiginous extreme, since in this "minipicture" Fénelon inaugurates a narrative ("A man . . . *had* come to draw water from the spring. [He] *is in the grip of* a monstrous snake. . . . This man is *already* dead . . . his flesh is *already* livid") whose unfolding is marked throughout by tense changes and by the adverb "already." In the painting, *already*, before he came to draw the water, the man was dead. In other words, the painting represents a dead man, a man killed by a snake, and that is what the discourse of description has to say; but that discourse can only say so if, in making the observation, it inaugurates a sequence that is no longer in the painting but in the discourse, a sequence owing to which the "character" in the painting begins his metamorphosis into a *figure* and becomes a signifier.

The same process is repeated in the other two "minipictures" that constitute sequences of the action. In all three cases, the narrative that is opened with the painting is closed on a mark (of death, horror, or fright), a symptom-sign inscribed in the painting itself, referring the narrative to the painting and making it disappear within the painting. By this mark, which is the only "thing" in the painting that is actually described, the narrative-discourse finds its anchor point in representative spatiality, entering and disappearing there. Therein lies the value of these marks or figurative signs: not only do they serve as symptoms of death, horror, or fright, not only are they understood in a rhetorical and psychophysiological coding of which the theory of *affetti* is the expression, but they are also a signifying condition for the characters in that they allow the narrative-discourse to be proffered, allow it to enter into the painting and thereby to transform the characters into figures, to articulate relations within the plastic surface. Through them the painting becomes a text, by absorbing discourse.

Thus in this type of painting, known as "representative" and characterized in particular by the unity of the space of representation, there is no pictorial narrative, properly speaking. Perhaps this is what Poussin meant by his pointed yet enigmatic formula: "Read the story and the painting."[18] The temporality that comes into play in Poussin's painting is not successive and linear. It entails the expansion of a moment represented by discourse, by the story that enters the painting—owing to the marks laid down on the plastic surface—in the characters or objects represented. The temporality proper to the painting is signaled in it by an oscillation of the descriptive discourse that describes only to open onto a narrative and that narrates only to close on a description. The most obvious manifestation of this temporality is constituted by the trajectory of reading within the overall viewing, and its "determinist" sequencing of affects is the representation and the illusion in Poussin's painting. Indeed, the painting never represents anything but a unique event taken as an indivisible moment in time. In the represented elements of the painting itself, events only seem to occur in succession. This appearance of sequentiality is created by the diversity of the simultaneous psychophysiological effects associated with a single event that remains identical with itself in the instant of its representation. The diversity in question is not pure and incoherent dispersion: it is signaled by certain representable external signs arranged in a certain order *within the space* of the painting according to the differential representation of the sign's intensity or power. The spatial order of the marks (the affects) and, within that order, the distribution of the intensities represented create, through the trajectory of reading implied in the overall unitary viewing of the painting, a sort of representative illusion of duration, of successiveness. The marks are indeed what convey this illusion inasmuch as they are signs or symptoms, but beyond this, in the plastic surface they come to articulate the properly descriptive-narrative discourse through which the painting is transformed into a text and the characters into relational figures. Our task now is to pin down this representative illusion of time, both theoretically and historically, and to show that it stems from the general ideology of representation. In the seventeenth century in particular, time is envisioned in spatial terms, because time is reduced to its representation.[19]

Let us note the differences among the various texts that narrate the central scene (Table 1). In three of them (Fénelon [Fén] and Félibien II and III [FII, FIII]), this scene includes three sequences. In the other three, the narrative is articulated in a single sequence (the catalogue [C]), in two sequences (Félibien I [FI]), or in four (the legend accompanying Baudet's engraving [L]). Moreover, the order of the sequences varies from text to text.

These descriptive variants modify the figurative network of the painting in a remarkable way, for each figure turns out to be displaced in the same stroke. In Fén, FII, and L, the figurative network is a chain that starts at 1 and arrives at 3 or 4, whereas in FIII we are dealing with a sort of irradiation $\begin{array}{ccc}2 & \rightleftarrows & 1\\ & & \downarrow\\ & & 3\end{array}$. Similarly, by adding a fourth sequence to the narrative, L initiates the liquidation of the decor as such, a liquidation that our own discourse will systematize by bringing to light, as an ideological presupposition, the theatrical bias that is essential to all figurative art, but that, once it has been thought and expressed, moves the decor into the scene. Finally, FI and C, by leaving out most of the sequences, highlight the narrative's "characteristic feature," the essential figure that will be the model for all the others in the painting: the fatal relation.

TABLE 1. *Sequential readings of the central scene*

	Fénelon (Fén)	Félibien II (FII)	Félibien III (FIII)	Félibien I (FI)	Catalogue (C)	Legend (L)
1	the man killed by the snake	the dead body encircled by a snake	a man approaching a fountain remains frightened	a dead man encircled by a snake	a man killed by a snake	a dead man with a snake wound around his body
2	the man who is moving forward and stops, frightened	the man who is fleeing with a frightened look	a dead body with a snake nearby	a frightened man who is fleeing		a man is fleeing, troubled glances, hair standing on end
3	the woman surprised and fearful	the woman astonished to see him running	a seated woman completely horror-stricken			a seated woman, horror-stricken
4						fishermen are turning their heads toward her

But that relation is also the distinctive figure that differentiates this painting from the others in the same series, a title-figure that establishes the painting's value. Moreover, through the differing order of sequences, these variants reveal a difference in the trajectory of the gaze, as if a choice were proposed at the outset: left or right, "the dead body encircled by a snake" or "the man who is fleeing with a frightened look." This vagary of the viewing trajectory is obvious in FI and in C, which give us the minimal possible narratives necessary for setting this landscape apart within the series of landscapes "with a subject." It also indicates the painting's basic figure, the relation "dead body–snake" ⇄ "man fleeing horror-stricken." This is the starting point from which the description can be pursued and on which it is based. But this base is not a certainty for the reader, nor is it self-evident to the viewer. The choice of trajectory is once again multiplied. To see this, let us undertake a simple examination of the variants involving the character on the right (from the viewer's standpoint):

L and FI	the frightened man *is fleeing*: variant 1
FII	the frightened man *is fleeing*—but *not as fast* as he would like: variant 2
FIII	the frightened man *remains*—but the woman is horror-stricken at the sight of the terror with which the man *is fleeing*: variant 3
Fén	the man *stops* suddenly—but only in the disequilibrium of his walking toward the fountain: variant 4

It is remarkable that, concerning a character as "obvious" as the man on the right in the painting, three different readings should come into play, each one tracing the man's figure beneath its representation, and precluding any immediate reference to a denoted level of the painting. It is our analysis of the readings and their differences that initiates the constitution of such a level, even as it initiates the meaning of the painting. In the end, the three readings play on three implicit sequences, under the represented character—which shows once again that description can be accomplished as such only in the narrative mode, but that narrative can be inscribed in painting only through what is described: (1) the man is walking (moving forward) toward the fountain (spring, stream); (2) he remains immobile (while seeing the frightful spectacle); (3) he is fleeing (frightened). FI and L have chosen terminal sequence 3—the only one inscribed in the painting. FII has chosen 3, but evokes sequence 2 as a potential one: the man's expression is not a "grimace of flight," but he is not fleeing as quickly as he would like. FIII chooses 2 and 3, but it grasps 3 in the painting only through reflection of another character, the woman: the man is seen *remaining* in relation to the dead body and the snake, and is seen *fleeing* in relation to the woman, who is horror-stricken at seeing him flee.

This analysis of FIII confirms in another light the schema of irradiation obtained in the global analysis of the narrative (description). Thus the character at right, having become a figure, is drawn into a dual relation, with the snake and with death on the one hand, with the woman on the other. These relations are contradictory, since the one implies immobility and the other flight; they are marked in the painting by the gaze directed toward the dead man and the movement directed toward the woman, and they are translated by Félibien in the complex psychophysiological notation of blocked flight, a veritable race, but an arrested one, a synthesis evoking the phrases "to take to one's heels" and "to be nailed to the spot." As for Fén, it chooses the first two sequences: "the man is moving forward toward . . . he remains immobile." It obtains the same result as FIII, a synthesis of movement and immobility, but the figure in the painting is articulated differently: it loses its relation to the woman and retains just one relation, albeit a reciprocal one, between left and right. The man moves from right to left (he is advancing toward the fountain): this is a place that attracts him, marked by "a spring of clear, pure water." He notices the frightening scene and is thereby immobilized, caught off balance as he walks (left-right effect: the terrifying power of the death of the man suffocated by the snake keeps him from moving forward). FIII takes the character in the state where the Fén figure leaves him and sets him back in motion toward the woman: it displaces the figure from the Fén position into a new FIII position. Thus our meticulously, tediously analyzed example shows the transit of the figure in representation.

Clearly, in the painting itself, nothing has moved. There has been no need, as there is in certain pedagogic films, to animate the character in the painting in order to transform him into a figure. The simple play of readings has sufficed: *from the horrifying event* (a man "with a snake wound around his body") *grasped by the gaze*—a scene of fright—to *the flight, dynamic gesticulation* toward the woman with outstretched arms who is responding to his terror with a cry, the simple superimposition of five readings (texts) furnishes "a beginning of meaning"[20] in a displacement of the figure. This figure is the slippage of one dual relation into another, a rearticulation of the network of relations, where no particular orientation of the slippage is privileged. The reading can go in the other direction: the tension toward the woman's response is blocked by the sight of the mortal embrace. The initiation of meaning is the same, but it has a negative nuance not found in the preceding position: thus a double meaning is effected that *is* its two complementary variants, a duality that is the meaning and not a variation on a hidden theme. Such is, let us note in passing, the polysemy of the figure.

This polysemy is not, as it is in Koulechov's experiment, the mark of the isolation of the figure with respect to the semantic field, which, by "overdetermining" it, reduces it or causes it to disappear; quite the contrary, because it is in the "semantic" field that the element becomes a figure and then immediately displaces itself as a figure. The polysemy of the figure is the figure itself, inasmuch as it accedes to meaning. It is the opening of meaning as figure—in its lability—*onto* representation, *through* representation.

Let us go back once again to the example. When we read FII, FIII, or Fén, we are well aware that the man on the right poses a problem: he is fleeing and not fleeing. Hence the echo of criticisms revealed by Félibien's text: it is not a "grimace of flight," but a sort of "slowed-down" movement, of which Fén, FII, and FIII give us a psychophysiological explanation, that manifests the articulation of the character into a figure. The movement is slowed down because it is complex—it is composed of two forces, one being a force of inertia or immobility, the other a kinetic force. But the explanation as such—as pure manifestation—is interesting in its own right, for, if we depart from the painting itself, if we go beyond analysis of the simple description, it signals the interference of two stylistic codes. The first, which is Poussin's inspiration and which Fénelon exhibits at the end of the dialogue, is the formal and stylistic code of the ancient bas-relief.[21] Hence the sculptural aspect, struck in stone, of the character who is fleeing; hence, too, his immobility in flight, an immobility that is awkward in terms of the second, naturalist code of representation. One way of resolving the conflict between the two codes on this particular point consists in justifying the first by an explanation drawn from the second. The character frightened by the death scene is turned into a "statue" by his fright: we are witnessing either a movement petrified in one of its instants (the Fén solution) or the first instant of a movement of flight undertaken in an attitude of horrified fascination (the FII solution).

The interference of two stylistic codes—a commentary that, in its explicitness, is transcendent to the descriptive discourse—is taken up again, found again, rearticulated in the descriptive discourse itself, that is to say the discourse in and on the painting, insofar as the painting is an object read and seen. This affirmation is an important one, and in its overall thrust it relates two opposing methodological orientations that must nevertheless be kept together. On the one hand, the only readings we have are readings of the painting: this painting is their origin and their end. The readings are developed on it and in it, and they constitute it as a signifying object; its meaning is the interminable recapitulation of its readings. On the other hand, these readings refer beyond the painting, to other paintings, to painting in general, to the culture in which painting is one of the signifying systems, a system in which the painting in question is absorbed and disappears. The readings offered by Fénelon or Félibien put into play reading codes for painting in general. And yet, as pure descriptions, we superimpose them on the surface of *this* painting, which they articulate as displaced figures, initiations of the *meaning of this painting and a meaning that is proper to it.*

"The Effects of Fear"

The analysis of the variants among the descriptive texts may be considered on yet another level. Here it is a question of their essential semantic investment, which one of the painting's early titles expresses quite clearly: *the effects of fear.* In five texts out of six (and

Fén. FII. FIII 1. *FI*

Frightening → Frightened Frightening → frightened...
(1) Frightening → astonished... indifferent
(2) (3) (4)

FIGURE 4. The sequential effects of fear (a).

L.

Frightening → Frightened (3) (4) (5)
(1) Frightening → astonished
Astonishing → attentive... indifferent

FIGURE 5. The sequential effects of fear (b).

even the sixth, C, provides the causal point of departure) we encounter a chain of affects characterized by two features: (1) the decrease or softening of an emotional force that is transmitted from character to character through gazes and that gives rise to movements; and (2) the ambivalence between active and passive in the intermediate sequence(s). Consider, for example, the explanatory schemas shown in Figures 4 and 5.

It is noteworthy that this affective-emotional space coincides both with the spatial grid of the painting's surface according to the categories of left-center-right and foreground-background-distance, and with the general opposition between narrative (story) and decor (nature). Figure 6 presents the most complete description, L.

Thus we note that one element in Fén, FII, and FII operates on the border of these assorted semantic (affective or "literary") and expressive spaces: the woman on her knees at the center of the painting on the second level. She is the "marked" end point of the emotional chain, but at the same time she is situated on the border between scene and decor, story and landscape. The woman on her knees is thus the point of articulation for several of the topics presented in the painting.

In text L, however, the fishermen occupy the pivotal position.

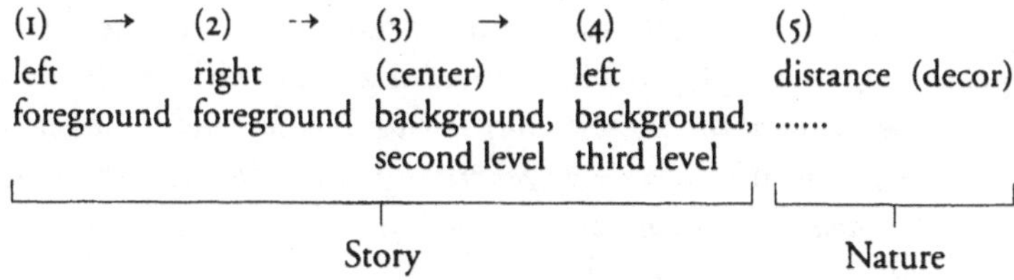

FIGURE 6. The use of space and basic narrative oppositions.

This variation brings to light a new example of displacement of figures in the painting: in her relation with the characters that precede her in the typical spaces, the woman becomes a figure and shifts, in L, toward a relation with the fishermen, "who turn their heads toward her." Which fishermen—those on the right or on the left? Text L says nothing more. My own reading cuts through the ambiguity in favor of the (fisher?)men on the right who are playing *mourre*. But a diagrammatic analysis of the texts has to maintain the ambiguity that results in integrating an element of the decor into the scene. The ambiguous relation between the woman and the fishermen (on the right, on the left?) then constitutes an essential element of the reading, since this relation is situated on the border between the three figurative topics.

The second feature of the chain of affects is the ambivalence of the intermediate sequential elements, which are at once active and passive (frightening and frightened, astonishing and astonished). Within the narrativity of this pictorial "narrative," they could be viewed as complex terms that allow an active-subject term to be reversed, turned into a neutral term that is neither subject nor object, neither active nor passive: in short, to merge with the decor, with the landscape. But if we bring this ambivalence into play with respect to the displacement of the central figure of the woman, a figure doubly articulated at (1) and (2) and at (4) and (5), we are heading toward paradox, for the active subject is *death (and the snake)*, and the neutral term in which the affect is weakened and the transformation of the positive is accomplished is *the living (at work or at play)*. In this view, death takes on positivity while life has a neutral aspect; put differently, under the dual aspect of work and play, life has something to do with death. *Analysis of the figure of the woman may not be able to teach us what that "something" is; still, if only by generating numerous relations among the other figures, analysis can uncover it for us in a plurality of meanings that* is *the meaning.*

Before we begin to analyze this figure in all its signifying richness, two prefatory remarks are in order:

First, our diagrammatic reading-analysis of the descriptive texts was entirely devoted to the "syntagma" of the painting, whether we were concerned with the "representing" surface of the space of representation or with the semantic investment in what is represented. Now, it is important to stress that, on the level of the plastic surface, breaks in contiguity necessarily exist on the various syntagmatic levels. The existence of such breaks, already articulated in signifying relations, is marked both in the painting and in the texts. For example, let us consider the very indication, evoked earlier, that Fénelon gives when he describes the "path on the edge of which there appears a woman who sees the terrified man but *who cannot see the dead man because she is in a low spot, so that the terrain forms a sort of curtain between her and the fountain.*" This is a crucial descriptive remark, for it has allowed us to notice how elements of the decor, inasmuch as they are accidents of the terrain, *come into play* as elements of the scene. Their role is to define the affective chain in linear fashion, from the "dead man with a snake wound around his body" to the woman or the fishermen; it is thus a signifying element that allows the articulation of a figurative relation. Yet it is important to note that this element should be defined as a "break" in the represented space (and not in the representing space, which is perfectly continuous, and within which the unity of the painting as such is manifested in the plastic surface, or in the equally continuous plastic space, as is shown by the uncertainty of the notion of background).

The break is situated on the level of the gazes and grounds that are marked, in Fénelon's text, by the difficulty of naming the break ("a low spot," "a sort of curtain"); it is an element of the decor that becomes an element of the scene by fragmenting it, by constituting a scene that is doubled through unevenness or indentation. The first includes the nocturnal water that is scarcely lighted by the luminous central spots (the footlights), the dead man encircled by the snake, and the frightened man who advances, remains, and flees; in the second, situated at a higher level, the woman appears on her knees, crying out, her open arms outstretched. In the first scene, the frightened man sees "the scene of horror," but not the woman, though he is running toward her; in the second scene, the astonished woman sees the frightened man and greets him but does not see "the scene of horror." The double negation in the gazes repeats the break in the scene and in the grounds, a rupture of contiguities in the represented space. But an additional break affects the represented characters and thereby helps to draw in a figure. In the text of L, the woman attracts the attention of the fishermen through her cries, though she has her back turned toward them; she is looking only at the man who is running toward her but who cannot reach her since he is separated from her by the embankment. These breaks in the continuity of what is represented, breaks that "work" it in depth and respect it in appearance, contribute to the articulation of the figures of the painting, but in a different mode: relations of interdiction are posited among the characters in the represented space. The unevenness of the terrain and the position of the woman's face keep her from seeing the scene of horror or the fishermen, and these interdictions contribute to her figurative significance: they are positive interdictions that define new relations in which the woman is displaced as figure.

The second prefatory remark concerns another type of relation that appears in Fénelon's descriptive text but that no attentive description can fail to note: it involves the relations of similarity among a certain number of elements in the painting, relations that are formal and also undoubtedly semantic. To be sure, these relations cannot be justified or described in the pictorial syntagma, they cannot be borne by the figures' articulation in contiguity; and yet they operate, and can only operate, within the syntagma, for the painting exists only in the global presence of all the elements that compose it and in the unity of its surface as limited by its frame.

The "narrative" sequences are three in number, and they are polarized, at least in Fén, FII, and FIII, by the dead man suffocated by the snake, the frightened man, and the astonished woman: a figurative triangle traced in the painting itself with the woman at the summit and the two men, one dead and one living, at its base. Now, this triangle is repeated twice, in a reduced mode, on the one hand because of the distance—the "low spot" in the space of representation—and on the other hand because it echoes or "rhymes with" the central triangle that constitutes the *subject*. For Fénelon, it is a reminder of the subject in the decor; for the legend accompanying the engraving, it is the beginning of an interpretation of the decor in the subject. It is repeated with the three fishermen at the right of the painting—"one is leaning forward and seems about to fall as he draws in a net, the two others, leaning backward, are rowing strenuously"—and with the three *mourre* players—"one is thinking of a number to surprise his companion, the other appears attentive for fear of being surprised"; the third is not described by Fénelon, but he is described in the legend: stretched out on his stomach, propped up on his elbow, he has his head turned away from the game toward the woman who has her back to him. These two figurative triangles, while they echo the first one, are in opposition to it, and they are in opposition to each other as well, even as each evokes the other through the arithmetic and gestural disposition of the characters. The drama in the foreground is contrasted with the peace and tranquillity of the background, as the repetitive rhythmic activities, the gestures of work and play, are contrasted with the linear chain of affects triggered by the fatal accident.

Thus the group of three figures in the dramatic scene is reiterated metaphorically (but what are the meaning effects of this metaphor?) by the "decorative scenes" of work and leisure-play, secondary scenes that repeat in the decor—in nature—the drama that is taking place on stage and give it endlessly renewed signifying resonances, all the more so in that the elements of these triangles are in a relation of correspondence that varies from one group to another: the fisherman who is pulling in the net seems to be falling into the water; the dead man has fallen into the water, caught in the snake's "net"; one of the players lying face down is turning away from the game; the dead man lying face down is "turning away" from life; or the dead man is in the water, the frightened man and the astonished woman are on earth, the players are on earth, the fisherman on the water; and so on.

The similarities appear to multiply from this point on, and in so doing they appear to produce multiple meanings, or at least the beginnings of meanings, endlessly working the figures, making and unmaking them, displacing them across the painting while multiplying their relations. It may not be possible to pinpoint them all. In any case, one function of metaphor is undoubtedly to multiply meanings while multiplying ambiguities.[22] Thus in this first descriptive pinpointing that deals only with the lower half of the painting we already encounter an actional code (work-play-death) with its philosophic and mythic subcodes, a sexual code (man-woman-snake), a geological code (water-earth), a numerical code (3), and a zoological code (snake). I shall offer a detailed analysis of this code elsewhere.

But the diagrammatic reading of the painting must, at this point in its discourse, work to recover contiguities in the painting by means of the similarities that the description indicates. These similarities are located on the painting; they articulate the figures in different ways by moving them into the painting's surface. They do not constitute, in the painting's background or private world, a second, hidden meaning, a secret semantic level that would have to be discovered, uncovered, as the painting's essence. The integration of similarities into the contiguities that the reading in its discursivity brings into play *after the fact* is *already* accomplished at the outset in the totality of the painting that is read and seen. We can also note that this integration defines the poetics of the painting, inasmuch as it is constructed by the descriptive analysis: "The poetic function projects the principle of equivalence from the axis of selection into the axis of combination."[23] Thus for the surface

TABLE 2. *Similarities and contiguities in the painting*

	left	right		
Earth	the three *mourre* players	the three fishermen at work	water	top
	x			
Water	the dead man encircled by the snake	the frightened man frightening	earth	bottom

dimension (left-right/foreground-background, bottom-top), we would have the arrangement shown in Table 2.

In what I have labeled *x* (Figure 7), a central place between left and right and between top and bottom that is defined as a second stage, intermediate and indented between the *scene* (stage) and the decor and the scenes that are integrated with it, is articulated the figure of the woman who is truly, by virtue of her position and her function alike, a knot of meaning, a figurative "matrix," a fertile source of relations in that portion of the canvas.[24] The woman is a source of articulation, at one and the same time in the representing space, in the represented space, and in the text of representation: she is situated exactly at the intersection of the painting's median vertical line and the horizontal line, in its lower third. She thus occupies an intermediate position in all directions of the plastic space and the surface of representation. In the descriptive text, or text of representation, she is the destination and end point of the narrative, its figure of resolution, but also the point at which the decor is articulated with the narrative: a figurative place in which the narrative is completed and in which the space of description opens up.

On the level of semantic investments, the chain of affects, variant L points toward a reading of the figure that is not tied to the psychological signified insofar as it is represented by the characters; it thus allows us to rediscover the pure, manifestly signifying description. This is the end point of the weakening of emotional force, a pure object figure. If in L the woman refers to the fisher-

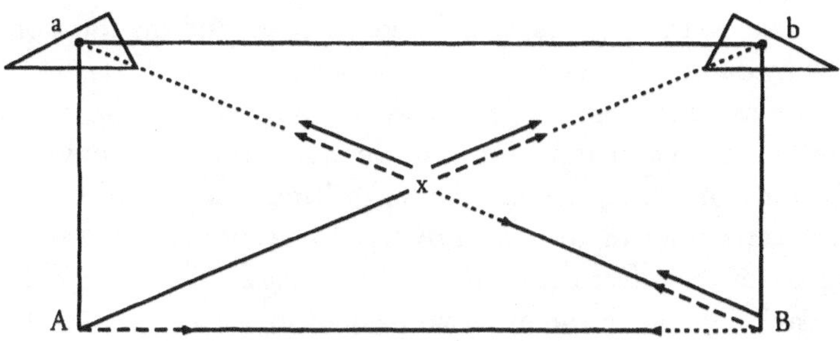

FIGURE 7. Polar oppositions in the lower half of the painting.

men by crying out, she also refers to them through her internal articulation: she is looking at the man who is fleeing toward her without looking at her, but through her outstretched arms she designates the game players and fishermen at whom she is not looking. This play of oppositions between gazes and gestures has to be spelled out: in the reading, the gesture is split into a "representor" of a psychological signified (surprise and fear) and a plastic "indicator" pointing to fishermen and players.

The necessary schism in which the figure is realized—or initiated—is marked by representation even as it contains representation. In other words, the figure is realized in relational polyvalence only if the integrating representation is dissociated and if a "plastic" level appears in its significance: the figurative polysemy arises from this dissociation that constantly works the pictorial representation, that simultaneously threatens and maintains its integrity. Thus the kneeling woman—in the pictorial representation—is turned away from the fishermen and the players, and by her gaze she designates the fleeing man. But her figure indicates them (outstretched arms pointing right and left) just as, in a negative relation (noted by Fénelon), she indicates the snake wound around the dead man, "behind the curtain of earth." Figurative contiguities are reestablished where representative ruptures had intervened, and vice versa. On this basis we can construct a first schema of the lower half of the painting, in which the gazes are expressed by dotted arrows, the gestures by unbroken arrows, and the force of affect by dashed arrows.

A is the fatal pole: the dead man is looking at nothing, his eyes are closed, an arm and a leg lie in the water; the sense conveyed is the force of inertia, weight. The snake "wraps" around him tightly, suffocates him: there is no privileged direction, other than the power of the affect that strikes B in his gaze. This is the pole of passivity, in which the maximal passion that is the source of the maximal action is "death" in the active and passive senses of the term.

B is the reactive pole: its movement toward *x* is only the reaction to the gaze at A, to the scene of horror. To be sure, the movement and the gaze are the most intense in the painting, but these are reflex intensivities.

Even as *a* and *b* echo the triangle *ABx*, each repeats the most apparent characteristics of *A* and *B*: *a* is a pole closed onto itself in the gestures of the dialogue of the game, which refer to one another, or in the repose of the third player, who turns away from it passively; *b* is positive and reactive like *B*, in the maximal tension of the movement of effort—the boat is about to move forward; one fisherman is pushing on the pole, the other on the oar, with gestures whose inversion is effective.

Finally, x puts the four poles into relationship in all desirable directions: this is the matrix figure for an exchange of figures, the center of a figurative transit in which the diverse relations are knotted together and evoke one another, namely, the combinations *a/Ax*, *b/B1*; *a/bx*, *A/B2*; *a/Bx*, *A/b3*, whose signifying proliferations would be worth pursuing. It is out of the question to do so within the limits of this text, or even to begin an inventory, in its opening, all the more so because we are dealing only with the lower half of the painting and because as a hypothesis we could observe the displaced repetition of the same in the upper part. Indeed, we find the opposing figures of the "celestial" castle on the left and the city on the right, beyond a great mirror of water in which the representation represents itself in its reflection. An indication of the signifying character of that figurative proliferation will have to suffice: each figure *A*, *B*, *a*, *b* turns out to be engaged by *x* in a certain number of relations in which it finds meaning: it gathers up meaning and puts a face to it. Thus *x* is a figurative matrix that, like the other figures, has no meaning in itself, but in figuring the others it gathers up the multiple floating meanings in the numerous relations that the representor causes to appear in its space of visibility. The problem here is to establish the meanings through the descriptive discourse in its repetition. The controlled setting into relation of the four figures *a*, *A*, *b*, and *B* by *x* (combination, syntagmatics) in the representing-represented space is what has to allow us to extract the appropriate term from the semantic field and constitute a signifying reading every time. Is each of the readings necessary and, as it were, requirable in the descriptive discourse? Such does not seem to be the case. With this acknowledgment, we rediscover the figurative proliferation that is difficult to stop, but that is concentrated in *x*, a center of transit, a place of exchange. What is in question is a working woman (a washerwoman?) in a moment of repose, at once immobile and gesticulating, a character in a state of pathetic repose confronting a character who represents death for her, someone she does not see: she is the only woman in the painting, situated between the entertainment of the game being played and that other game that is death in the form of the man encircled by the snake, and so on.

Unquestionably, the foregoing indications go beyond analysis of the descriptive discourse, in its variants, though not without revealing a number of its reference points. My remarks have been intended only to interrogate the signifying polyvalence that the painting contains hidden in its reiterated description and that is perhaps only the reading of the painting by a viewer in a state of "delectation," to use Poussinian language, a viewer who reads the figures of his own desire in those that the painter's desire, in representing, traces and displaces in the surface of the painting.

Appendices to Chapter 2

I. Fénelon, *Dialogues des morts*, vol. 3: Leonardo da Vinci and Poussin, Description of a landscape made by Poussin.

(Fénelon, *Oeuvres complètes*, vol. 19 [Paris, 1823], pp. 342–345)

POUSSIN: Picture a rock on the left side of the painting. From this rock there flows a spring of clear, pure water, which, after bubbling a little as it falls, flees across the countryside. A man who had come to draw water from the spring is in the grip of a monstrous snake; the snake wraps itself around his body and encircles his arms and legs several times; it squeezes him, poisons him with its venom, and suffocates him. This man is already dead; he is lying stretched out; one sees the weight and the stiffness of all his members; his flesh is already livid; his frightful face represents a cruel death.

LEONARDO DA VINCI: If you present no other object, here is a very sad painting.

POUSSIN: You are going to see something that only increases the sadness. Another man is advancing toward the fountain: he notices the snake wrapped around the dead man, he stops suddenly; one of his feet remains suspended; he lifts up one arm, the other drops down; but both hands are open, they mark surprise and horror.

LEONARDO: This second object, although sad, does not fail to animate the painting, and it gives a certain pleasure similar to those tasted by spectators of the ancient tragedies in which everything inspired terror and pity; but we shall soon see if you have . . .

POUSSIN: Ah! ah! you are beginning to be a little bit human, but wait for what follows, please; you will judge according to the rules when I have told you everything. Close by is a broad path on the edge of which there appears a woman who sees the terrified man but who cannot see the dead man, because she is in a low spot, so that the terrain forms a sort of curtain between her and the fountain. The sight of that frightened man produces in her an aftereffect of terror. These two frights have the qualities that pain is said to have: a big one keeps silent, a small one speaks out. The man's fright renders him immobile: the woman's, which is the lesser, is more marked by the grimace on her face; one sees in her a feminine fear that can hold nothing back; she expresses her full alarm, gives way to her feelings; she falls to a seated position and forgets what she is carrying; she extends her arms and seems to cry out. Is it not true that these different degrees of fear make a sort of game that touches and pleases?

LEONARDO: I agree. But what is this drawing? Is it a story? I do not know it. It is rather a caprice.

POUSSIN: It is a caprice. This sort of work suits us very well, provided that the caprice is controlled and that it does not deviate in any way from actual nature. On the left side one sees some large trees that seem old, like those ancient oaks that sometimes passed for the divinities of a country. Their venerable trunks have a harsh, bitter bark, which repels the tender young woodland placed behind. The woodland has a delicious freshness; one would like to be there. One imagines a scorching summer that respects this sacred wood. It is planted along a clear body of water, and seems to be reflected inside it. On one side one sees a deep green, on the other pure water, in which one discovers the somber blue of a serene sky. In the water there are various objects diverting to the eye, refreshing it from all the horrors it has seen. In the foreground of the painting, all the figures are tragic. But in the background everything is peaceful, gentle, and laughing. Here one sees young people bathing and playing while swimming, there, fishermen in a boat: one is leaning forward and seems about to fall, because he is pulling in a net, while two others, leaning backward, are rowing strenuously. Others are at the water's edge, playing *mourre*:[25] the faces suggest that one of them is thinking of a number to surprise his companion, who appears attentive for fear of being surprised. Others are strolling beyond the water on a fresh and tender lawn. Seeing them in such a beautiful place, one almost envies their happiness. Fairly far away, one sees a woman who is going to the neighboring village on a donkey, and who is followed by two men. We immediately imagine that we see these good people, who in their rustic simplicity are going to carry to the cities the abundance of the fields they have cultivated. In the same lefthand corner there appears above the wooded area a rather steep mountain on which there is a castle.

LEONARDO: The left side of your painting makes me curious to see the right.

POUSSIN: It is a little hillside that comes down in an imperceptible slope to the river's edge. On that slope one sees a profusion of bushes and shrubs on uncultivated ground. In front of the hill big trees are planted; between them one sees the countryside, the water, and the sky.

LEONARDO: But how did you make the sky?

POUSSIN: It is of a fine azure, mingled with bright clouds that seem to be of gold and silver.

LEONARDO: You have made it thus, no doubt, in order to have the freedom of disposing of light as you see fit, and to shed it on each object according to your designs.

POUSSIN: I admit that; but you must admit, too, that this makes it clear that I am not at all ignorant of your rules, of which you speak so highly.

LEONARDO: What is there in the middle of the painting beyond the river?

POUSSIN: A city I have already mentioned. It is in a low area where it fades from view; a hillside full of greenery hides part of it. One sees old towers, crenellations, large buildings, and a confusion of houses in deep shadow; this brings out certain places illuminated by a gentle and lively light that comes from on high. Above this city appears what one almost always sees above cities in good weather: smoke is rising and obscuring the mountains in the distance. These mountains, bizarre in appearance, make for a varied horizon, so that the eyes are contented . . .

II. Félibien, *Entretiens sur les vies et ouvrages des plus excellens peintres anciens et modernes* .

(London: Morties, 1705, vol. 4, 8th *entretien*, pp. 119–120)

The landscape that is in M. Moreau's Cabinet produces a contrary effect. The situation of the place is marvelous, but in the foreground there are figures that express horror and fear. The dead body lying stretched out at the edge of a fountain and encircled by a snake; the man fleeing with a frightened look; the seated woman, astonished to see him running and so frightened—these figures create emotions that few other Painters have been able to represent as worthily as he. One sees that the man is truly running, so well is his bodily equilibrium arranged to represent a person who is fleeing with all his might; and yet it seems as though he is not running as fast as he would like. It is not, as one of our friends said some time ago, the grimace alone that shows he is fleeing; his legs and his whole body indicate movement.

III. Excerpt from legend accompanying Baudet's engraving.

(Georges Wildenstein, "Les graveurs de Poussin au XVIIe siècle," *Gazette des beaux-arts*, July–August 1955)

A young man, dead, near a fountain, has his whole body enveloped by a serpent of enormous size. His frightful appearance causes another man to flee. The latter's troubled looks and hair standing on end terrify a woman farther away, seated at the edge of the path. Her cries cause some fishermen to turn their heads.

IV. Félibien, vol. 3, 6th *entretien*, p. 160.

I do not believe one could better represent the state in which one finds oneself on this occasion than M. Poussin has done in a landscape that he painted earlier for his friend M. Pointel. One sees a man who, seeking to approach a fountain, remains in a state of total fright upon seeing a dead body girdled by a snake; and, further on, a woman seated and wholly horror-stricken, seeing with what fright the man is fleeing. One discovers in the man's countenance and facial features not only the horror that he feels at seeing the dead body stretched out at the edge of the fountain, but also the fright that gripped him at meeting that terrifying snake, from which he fears similar treatment. Now, when the fear of evil is joined to the aversion one feels for a disagreeable object, it is certain that the expression of it is very much stronger. For the eyebrows go up, the eyes and mouth open wider, as if to seek asylum and ask for help. The hair stands up on the head, the blood recedes from the face, leaving it pale and distraught, and all one's members become so impotent that one can scarcely speak or run: all of which one sees perfectly represented in this painting.

V. Félibien, vol. 4, 8th *entretien*, p. 51.

Around the same time, he did two large landscapes for the same Pointel: in one there is a man who is dead and girdled by a snake, and another man, frightened, who is fleeing. This painting, which M. du Plessis Rambouillet bought after M. Pointel's death, is presently in the Cabinet of M. Moreau, the King's first Valet de Garderobe, and it must be considered one of the finest landscapes Poussin ever did.

§ 3 Description of a Painting and the Sublime in Painting

Concerning a Poussin Landscape and Its Subject

From Giorgione to Poussin, from *Tempesta* to the three "tempests" by a master rediscovered after a detour through the Academy: my own detour and return have no guiding thread, no signposts, no justification beyond the blinding flash, here and there, of an identical stroke of lightning. And even the lightning stroke exists (?), is inscribed, in only two of the three tempests. In one of the two, to be sure, there are two strokes of lightning. Perhaps the absent stroke, suppressed (?) in *Landscape—A Calm*—but present in Chatillon's engraving of that painting—has been transported into *Pyramus and Thisbe* as a double for the one that falls on the city in *Tempesta* (Figures 8–10).

It is not a matter of comparing the *Tempesta* of the one with the tempests of the other: the similarities and differences encountered would have no ground, no basis, whether historical or stylistic. Only for that comparison would the accident of a fortuitous encounter come into play, the wholly aleatory contingency of two moments of my own history (which interests no one but myself) meeting in this phenomenon of painting, the vagary of the flash of a lightning stroke in the background of a painting: the stroke of a meeting of several strokes, a repetition of this same painterly motif or occasion, a recurrence of something like a subject of a painting, and, with that meeting, that repetition, that recurrence, the same question: What is the status of the sublime in painting? And if

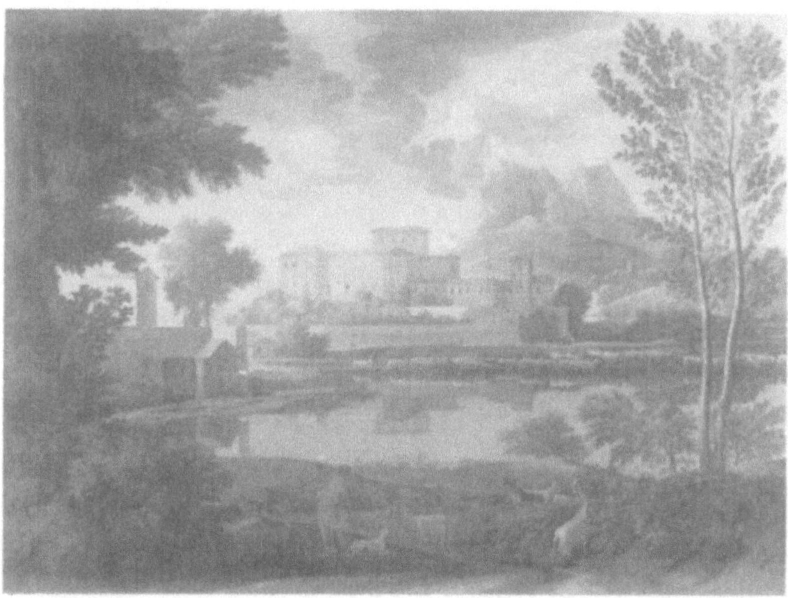

FIGURE 8. *Landscape—A Calm.* Courtesy Photographie Giraudon.

storms are instances of the natural sublime, what is the status of painting of the sublimity of tempests?

The question invites us to approach and interrogate the limits of representation in painting while positioning ourselves at those limits: the order (but is it an order?) of the unrepresentable, something that is external to the entire enterprise of painting and that nevertheless would orient it, tempt it, exert fascination over it as its internalized other. The question elicits a desire to paint, to represent, to display, to make visible something that by itself, in itself, resists that desire, that intention: the invisible through which the visible meets the condition of its visibility.

Or again, with that representation, with that intention, the gaze of the painter, the gaze of the viewer in the painter's stead, active and technical contemplation on the painter's part, receptive and learned contemplation on the viewer's, the gaze attempting to recover blindness by a dazzling flash, precisely at its outer limit and

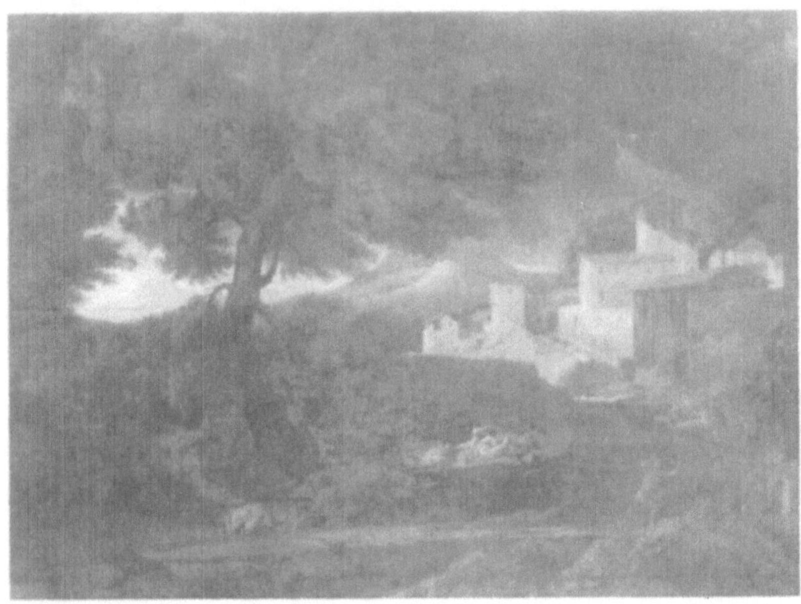

FIGURE 9. *Landscape—A Storm*. Courtesy Photographie Giraudon.

even just a bit before, where it would surprise itself at the instant of seeing, where it would see itself see. The tempest (and the lightning stroke that is its signature) would be the figure of that attempt, the primitive figure, the archifigure, in art, in the painter's *technē*, its origin and its end, an origin that would precede itself, an end without end, the sublime figure of the sublimity of painting and its truth.

Or the question of description, of the scription-(de)scription of the painted picture by its viewer when the painting shows the limit on which it founds its desire-to-display, or with which, rather, it aims to appropriate that desire to that intention, an intention of intention in which the foundation is found only in its "unfounding." How to write, how to (de)scribe the painted picture when that painting is in question, at the sublime altitude of that attempt, of that temptation, that fascination with painting the sublime?

That question, through which I had begun with Giorgione's

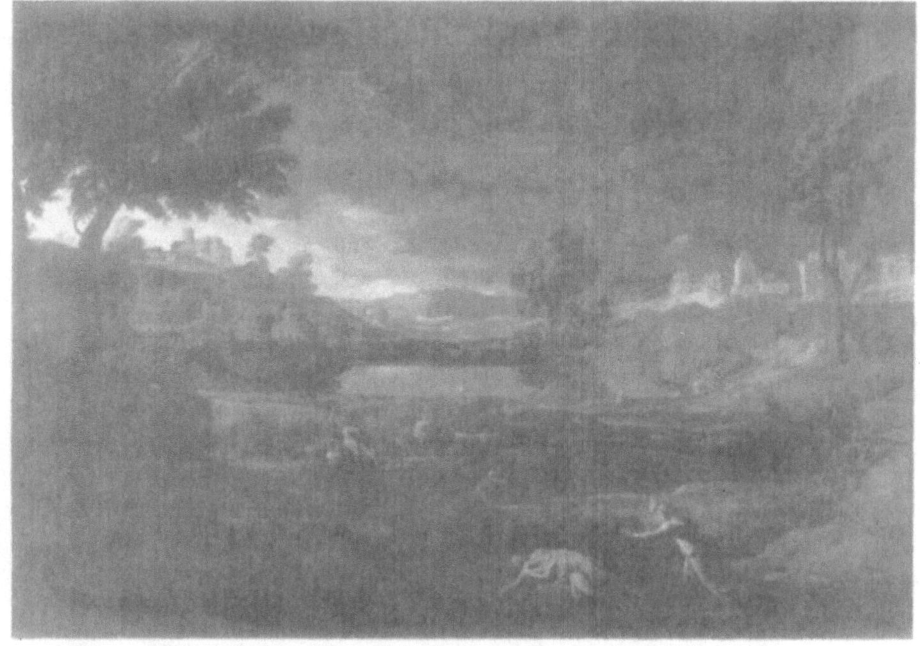

FIGURE 10. *Landscape with Pyramus and Thisbe.* Courtesy Städelsches Kunstinstitut. Photograph by Edelmann/Artothek.

Tempesta in Venice while asking myself where to begin to write, to (de)scribe, had been answered by a woman's figure, or at least the figure had given me the opportunity for a beginning; while contemplating the painting, I simply fixed my gaze on her and referred it back to my theoretical eye. In an instant, in a flash, everything at stake in the work of painting, in the work of presentation and representation—Narcissus instantaneously transformed, in the mirror of a fountain, into a painter—had found itself presented-represented at the chance event of an inscription, a scription, a (de)scription, at the very instant when a lightning bolt flashed in a stormy sky above a city in which a white bird kept watch at the top of a tower, at the very instant when the sublime burst out dazzling, blinding in a streak of yellow paint.

A Poussinian *Ekphrasis*

Today Poussin has his descriptive pen in hand. In 1651, he writes a letter to Jacques Stella that André Félibien will reproduce in his *Entretiens* (vol. 4, 8th *entretien,* p. 127):

> I have tried to represent a tempest on earth, imitating to the best of my ability the effect of an impetuous wind, air full of darkness, rain, lightning bolts and flashes falling in several places, not without creating a certain disorder. All the figures one sees there are playing their roles according to the weather; some are fleeing through the dust, in the direction of the wind that is driving them along; others, on the contrary, are going against the wind, walking with difficulty, covering their eyes with their hands. On one side, a shepherd is running, abandoning his herd, seeing a lion that has downed a number of cowherds and is attacking others, some of whom are defending themselves while others are prodding their cattle and trying to escape. Amidst this disorder, the dust is rising in great whirlwinds. A dog some distance away is barking, his fur abristle; he does not dare approach. In the foreground of the painting, one sees Pyramus lying dead on the ground, and near him Thisbe, who has succumbed to grief.

At this point Félibien adds: "This is how he was able to paint perfectly all sorts of subjects, and even the most extraordinary effects of Nature, however difficult they may be to represent; accompanying his landscapes with appropriate actions or stories, as in this one, which is unpleasant weather, he found a sad and lugubrious subject."

On the Sublime of Tempests

From the outset, everything has been said, or seems to have been said—from one painter to another. Starting with the first sentence, the intention to represent, the desire-to-display on the painter's part, is expressed, written, to another painter, as if it were an infinite task always incommensurate in its realization with the project in which it originated. With this intention to represent, the subject of the painting arises twice: the painter-subject who has tried—in a recent past, a past still pregnant, still poignant, since it is owing to its present impetus that he takes up his pen to write—to represent; and the subject of the painting, a constant motif throughout the enterprise, which has guided it, directed the work and the effort. The painter, subject of the subject of his painting and the invention of the subject of his picture: a tempest *on earth*. And here indeed we have the subject of all painting, its definition: "It is an imitation made on a surface with lines and colors of everything that one sees under the sun. Its end is to please."[1] On earth, everything that is seen under the sun, on earth, a tempest.

But the painter does not say everything, does not write everything to his friend Stella. The invention of the subject of his painting (and Stella too knows this perfectly well), the intention to paint, is not found one stormy day in the Roman countryside, or in the secret meditations of the Master in the studio on the via Babuino. It is found in the one *and* the other, first within the closed field of painting. Leonardo da Vinci wrote a description of a storm in his *Treatise on Painting*; thus he painted a storm in and through a *text*—Leonardo, the rival, one of the greatest. Poussin, in turn, writes a storm on earth, but by describing his finished painting, the painting that represents a tempest. And, before Leonardo, there was Apelles, a mythical painter, the very myth of the painter. Pliny says in his *Natural History* that Apelles enjoyed painting things that cannot be painted, such as lightning, thunder, and storms: the impossible subject of painting through which the act of painting is nevertheless consummated. Apelles painting the unpaintable is not only the myth of the painter or the paradigm of his perfected science, but also the myth of painting, in the absence of all works, painting in its impossible perfection, the unknown masterpiece that exceeds anything the *technē* of painting can do: the storm, or the sublime in painting, a subject that can take form with lines and colors only in a written text, a scription, a (de)scription, Pliny's, or Leonardo's. In a word: "I have tried to represent the unrepresentable, the sublimity of a tempest on earth." I have tried . . . : the intention of painting *that*, the invention of this subject of a painting, the position, in this intention and this invention, of the painter-subject, myself, Poussin, necessarily, ineluctably failing in something, since this subject cannot be painted, and that is perhaps why he writes, why he (de)scribes. An impossible wager, an absolute risk, that is to say disconnected from everything in the art of painting that can be ensured by the means and the ends, the rules and the norms, of that art, an excess over itself of the intention to represent, since it is a matter of representing the unrepresentable—the act of painting (*le "peindre"*) is *realized* there through its very failure, since on this subject, this very special subject, it *indicates by default* the end of the art of painting in its entirety: that which cannot be painting. Not said, not written, but no doubt secretly intimated, by one painter to another, we understand each other: a counterdefinition of painting, or rather the opposite of the one Poussin will offer fourteen years later in writing to M. de Chambray: "It is an imitation made on a surface with lines and colors of everything that one sees under the sun." With a tempest on earth, there is no more sun, and nothing is seen except on the basis of a different principle of visibility: nothing is seen except by virtue of a different visibility.

Persistent, this motif of the impossibility of "presenting-to-view," of "desiring-to-display," returns in the very process of mimesis in which the art of painting finds its means: "Imitating to the best of my ability. . . . " But the best of this ability, this ability at its highest technical power, this ability on the Master's part to paint, does not suffice to carry out the intention, to realize the wish, for the end point of the intention, the objective of the wish, its aim, is precisely that which is without end point or end, without goal or target, something incommensurable with such an intention and with such a wish, the sublimity of a tempest on earth. Moreover, one does not represent a tempest on earth, at best one imitates, to the best of one's ability, the effects of its incommensurable forces: "an impetuous wind, air full of darkness, rain, lightning bolts and flashes falling in several places, not without creating a certain disorder." The effects? No—but the unique effect of all the many forces in manifestations dispersed here and there, the singular effect in which all that disorganized diversity of forces is concentrated and compressed. At the very moment when the painter once again notes the impossibility of painting while remaining true to his intention, at that very moment he discovers the ruse, the *mēchanē* of his *technē* of painting: find the unique effect of the scattered forces of the tempest and stick to that, concentrating on it all the forces of mimesis.

"When the sublime succeeds in bursting forth where it should, it is like a tempest: it scatters everything in its path." And yet, "from the outset, it shows the multiple forces of the orator concentrated together." Such is the ordering principle of mimesis, its order in the sublime disorder of the forces of the tempest: a unique effect to be imitated, the ordering principle of representation itself even if the unique effect is in the represented, disorder.

Poussin names this unique effect twice in characterizing wind and air, a terrestrial tempest being nature's *pneuma* or lung: the wind is impetuous and the air is filled with darkness and flashes of lightning. The dual qualification is contradictory. A tempest is wind and air; wind is the *impetus*, the movement of a force that is visibly graspable only in its movement and its traces on things and beings; air is night and rain, whose lightning bolts and flashes are, as it were, the signatures that make them visible. In the impetus of the wind there is an *effect*. In the atmospheric obscurity there are meteoric *signs* that, even as they show the weather's invisible opacity by way of a blinding light, indicate only random disorders stirred up here and there: a multiple effect that the effect of the wind's force will order, even if the force is that of a gust of wind.

But in so doing, in stating the subject of his painting, his intention, as subject, to paint, and his means for representing the unrepresentable sublime, Poussin writes, (de)scribes, it seems, what is at the "back" of the painting, the background of landscape and nature that was to have the function of decor for the actions and passions of the human figures. Henceforth (and we have to believe Poussin on this point), the work—the intention of painting, the subject of painting, the desire to display—has passed into its decor; or conversely, the frame has become a subject and the space of the painting's ultimate depth in its surface, its very subject. Or, to put it differently, the effect of the tempest's impetuous wind organizing the effects of disorder among the flashes and bolts that trace the darkness of the air is the subject, that is, the story that the painting aims to tell, a tempest on earth, and all the figures that can be seen in it across the deep surface of the painting right up to the foreground will only be the various actors of that event, the bearers of affects of the unique effect of the violent breath of the sublime: "All the figures one sees there are playing their roles according to the weather." The fate of the narrative is assigned here: the painter aims to represent an unrepresentable event of nature, by imitating as best he can the ordering effect of his impetuous wind, in all its effects of disorder, night, and blinding, in all its figure-effects, of which Pyramus and Thisbe, in the foreground, are the ultimate figures.

Thus our first task, using the Master's pen and starting at his own point of departure, is to describe the upper half of the canvas, which is the only place where the intentions of the painter and the demands of his subject are expressed and realized, in their impossibility, the portion of the letter to Stella in which no viewer has yet been posited as subject of the gaze for the painting, as if, in this exact correspondence between the beginning of Poussin's letter and the upper portion of his work of painting, the domain reserved to the painter alone were unfolding, the painter in his painterly struggle, his infinite unrealizable task, the sublimity of painting the sublime itself.

A double scene is juxtaposed horizontally, from one treetop on the left to another on the right, separated by a tree at the edge of the lake—a tree that lightning strikes. In the center, a plain, in the distance, illuminated by an absent sun, with its river, its hills, and a mountain chain closing off its horizon: a central place that is also the centered place of the gaze, the median point of the horizon line, the vanishing point for the optic architecture of the painting and the geometrical center of the rectangular surface of the canvas. The task is to learn—by sharpening the gaze—to unlock this central place from the figured appearances that cover it, invest it, and indicate it, between a far-off hill and an enormous building crowned by towers and pierced with monumental arcades, a blend of ruined Colosseum and unfinished Tower of Babel, a colossal vestige and a nonaccomplishment of the infinite project. There, at the edge of the site hiding the place toward which all appearances fade away and from which, at the same time, they originate and invade the canvas, a colossal architecture arises, twice interrupted, in its past and in its future—both present—to which I attach the name Babel, Babylon.

Sky first of all, before earth, sky where day and night, light and shadow, meet: daylight above the left-hand scene, a luminous fringe between the foliage of a tree in the foreground and the summit of a hill crowned by a castle and trees bent by an impetuous wind and a road tracing a path—a solar interval that continues and ends above the mountains on the horizon; night fills all the rest of the "air," night traversed in the center by a flash of lightning, an undulating serpent realized in its fall by a perfectly rectilinear line of fire, coming down to strike the main branch of the tree at the edge of the lake that marks the boundary of this first scene. Amid all this accumulating night, a second flash of lightning strikes above the city on the right and falls with its thunderbolt at the top of a mountain, on a fortress, illuminating it instantly. The task is to write, to (de)scribe the city made visible by a streak of light coming from the left (from the "fringe") and progressively fading away: the ancient noble edifices, reminiscent of others found in the Master's backgrounds. The time to make an inventory of these edifices has not yet come. For now, we need to re-mark, with the (de)scriptor's pen, the effect of the impetuous wind against this background of unequal opposition between day and night: the trees, bent over by the storm, popping back up violently from left to right, blending in with the immobile architecture, stably resisting the unleashed hurricane and the double signature of darkness and rain, the two flashes of lightning and the thunderbolt striking a tree and breaking off a large branch, striking the fortress rock that stands erect on the horizon on the border between heaven and earth. How to imitate as best one can the effect of "an impetuous wind, of air full of darkness, rain, lightning bolts and flashes falling in several places," except by exposing to view all that bends and yields to the order of the unique break, to the imperious "government" of the wind *and* everything, immobile and stable, that resists: the tree and the dwelling, marks and re-marks of a wider struggle, the cosmic drama, of the solar light that abandons the field of the painting, even as it projects itself in the interval to illuminate, to expose to view, marks and remarks of the nocturnal powers that invade it to produce the invisible that a double flash of lightning only displays.

The Actors of the Sublime

Such is the question of painting in general: how to expose to view the invisible as such? How to paint the light of night? How to show the darkness that all light contains at its source? The sublimity of the representation of a tempest might well be one of the singular places of painting in which the "metaphysical" question of painting *itself* could be raised by the painter as painter, the *eidos* visible in a *pathos* that annuls it.

What is the fate of the narrative of painting, that unrepresentable event of nature? Poussin writes, (de)scribes his painting: "All the figures one sees there are playing their roles according to the weather; some are fleeing through the dust, in the direction of the wind that is driving them along; others, on the contrary, are going against the wind, walking with difficulty, covering their eyes with their hands."[2]

Here, finally, at the second level of the painting, we have reached the painting's reader-viewer: Stella, no doubt, and also the spectator in general. "One sees there . . . " in the painted picture, in the tempest landscape represented by imitation of the effect of an impetuous wind and of an air filled with darkness where it is nevertheless possible to see. A space of mimesis, a space of reading, of the production of narrative by the spectator on the basis of what the figures express, their affects, their passions as presented in and through their signs, immediately nameable indexes. But the viewer will produce a narrative according to the law or cosmic destiny of the tempest, whose mark or sign is the unique and ineluctable effect of the wind, the *meaning* of its force. The passions of which the figures are bearers, the passions that constitute them as narrative figures through their various and related affects, are, in the occurrence of the event of the sublime, merely the effects of that unique effect of a one-way force. These figures have no movements apart from those that determine this rigorously oriented motion. Like the tree and the dwelling noted a moment earlier against a background of day and night, some flee with the wind that carries them along; they obey the order of the wind, the unidirectional force of nature, the destiny manifesting itself in that instant; they cooperate with the necessity to which they are subjected, a necessity that surpasses any will of their own. Conversely, others oppose the movement, combat the tempest's effect of force; they go against the wind, they resist its power, and in order to do so, covering their eyes with their hands, they blind themselves to what is shown of destiny in the wind that traverses the entire field of the painting with its unique effect—owing to their contrary movement, these figures do not see what the painting makes visible. A simple polarity of a simple opposition between figures with contrary movements: here the *istoria* finds not its narrative—yet—but its schema and its law: two affects opposed to the effect of the wind.

Thus all the figures indeed play their roles according to the weather. The weather itself is singular here, a gust of wind, a prompt and immediate effect, a one-way natural force, while there are two characters, two roles between which all—truly all—the figures are distributed. There is only one law, one destiny: the duration of the tempest, whose unique effect the painter imitates as best he can; and there are only two characters, two roles, two affects: go with the movement that carries everything away, or else resist the movement, go against it and go blind; act in conformity with nature or, by apparently opposing it, be forgetful of its power.

> The duties (or the necessities) that grow out of situations impose themselves on us as a given role imposes itself on an actor. The actor is not responsible either for the character who has been entrusted to

> him or for the time granted him to play his role. All he is asked, and all that depends fully on him, is that he act as well as possible, at every moment and as long as the magistrate who has engaged him leaves him on stage . . . [3]
>
> Is it then in your power to choose the theme? A certain body has been given you, certain parents, certain brothers, a certain fatherland, a certain rank in that fatherland. And you come and tell me: "Change the theme for me." To resist the theme that life allots us [to resist the weather, the unique effect of the impetuous wind of the sublime which bursts forth here and now], and to refuse the argument of the dramatic poems, is to make the same mistake, and it is to close oneself off to the highest lesson of the tragedies, which is to "recall [to us] the events of life, and that they must thus arrive naturally."[4]
>
> The actor symbolically represents the sage in that he accepts his text and puts all his care into reciting it, even as he refuses, because he is only an actor, to take the events that he is performing "tragically"; as they are for the sage, these events are nothing to the actor; they are "indifferent."[5]

So here we have a remarkable textual movement in the Master's (de)scription of his painting. With "I have tried to represent . . . " he evokes the infinite task in which the incommensurability between the painter's intention and its realization in painting is disclosed and, along with this inequality, all the sublimity of a painting of the sublime: then, with the phrase "one sees there [in the painting]," emerges the interpretation by the spectator of the finished work in the present, the work's own presentation of a readable scene, of an iconic narrative: by its representation of the tempest, governed by cosmic law or destiny, in its signifying movement that makes it at once the "subject" of representation and the "means" of mimesis. This movement in the process of (de)scription is that of a withdrawal of the narrator-painter to a space outside the story that he has represented in the narrative of the figures that present it to the anonymous gaze. The representation speaks on its own to anyone who may be contemplating it: not at all a tempest of Nature itself, it is rather the painting of a tempest in which the painter has tried to represent the other by imitating it, that is to say, by discerning as best he could its effects on things and beings. From here on, in Poussin's letter to Stella, the painting describes itself, by exposing itself, presenting itself in its discerned figures. Hence a remarkable expression, in the text: "All the figures . . . are playing their roles according to the weather." One could write about this what Claude Imbert notes in his discussion of the prologue to Longus's *Daphnis and Chloe.* By uniting the heuristic function of the reduced model with the initiatory function of the sign in a lasting way, Imbert writes,

> the painting schematizes and prefigures the episodes of the novel, surveying the whole drama which Fortune will play out. . . . The novelist thus possesses a synoptic vision. . . . By its very nature, the painting is a repository of speculative activity; for it is unaffected by the delays and the linearity which the temporal ordering of events imposes on discursive consciousness. Indeed, it enjoys a God-like vision of the succession of events: *divinitati omnia praesens.* Anyone who has seen the whole picture knows more than its heroes whom misfortunes have blinded.[6]

This is all the more true when the "theme" (the *hypothesis*, the argument of the drama, the subject) is none other than the irruption of the cosmic sublime on earth in the power of a tempest. Thus the figures play their role in representation, as actors play their character on the tragic stage, in conformity with the order of destiny; but in reading the representation, in stating what it describes, the viewer alone enters into the initiation to wisdom that the sign proposes by schematizing the event in the simple polarity of the two roles—follow the movement of nature, or blind oneself by going against it—and by synthesizing the event in the present of an epiphanic presentation.

> If [descriptive-iconic] utterances get their meaning from the presentations which they analyze, then the intentions and the character of the speaker [painter] can be suppressed in favour of the presentation which he communicates. . . . A *lekton* [the iconic] carries no trace of a speaker [painter]—just as an oracle carries no trace of the soothsayer. A *lekton* is not a *statement* (*apophansis*), understood to include a

> reference to the act of uttering and to the process of linguistic expression [a function reserved for the first sentence of the letter to Stella]. It is *something stated,* which in its grammar and syntax as it were itself bears the responsibility of the assertion.[7]

An impersonal art, the represented lacks any trace of the process of enunciation-representation. As Imbert puts it, "*Deixis* . . . writes the character of the presentation into the grammar of the utterance, and recalls the conditions under which it was experienced. . . . The speaker is thus simply the interpreter of the presentation he conveys; his identity is lost in his message."[8] The tempest on earth, then, is the entire painting in its unique effect *and* especially its upper half, which opens up its depth in the surface of the canvas. Thus is inscribed, in the "grammar" of what is represented, the character of the presentation in its simultaneous planes. There is no need for a figure in which the painting would figure itself by figuring the process of representation that produced it and, by positioning in external space, the gaze that contemplates it. It is the "character of the presentation" alone that "recalls the conditions under which it was experienced," and the painter is abolished in his icon: "All the figures one sees there are playing their roles according to the weather; some are fleeing through the dust, in the direction of the wind that is driving them along; others, on the contrary, are going against the wind, walking with difficulty, covering their eyes with their hands."

The Master always (de)scribes his paintings with remarkable precision, as we have seen, for example, in his letter to Chantelou about *Manna* (see chapter 1). In the present case, as it happens, his description includes an interesting, if obvious, inconsistency. All the figures we see in the painting, he writes, either are fleeing, going along with the movement of the tempest, or else they are resisting, going against the storm, blinding themselves in the process. All—and yet only two of the figures are fleeing, one on horseback and one on foot, under the impetus of the storm wind, and only one, in the middle ground at the far right, mounted on a donkey, is going forward against the wind, his hands covering his eyes. All the others seem to be playing their roles not in response to the weather but in chronological coincidence with the hurricane; they are driven by other causes or events. The question raised by the inclusive in the description, the question that what the painting represents appears to answer in the negative, introduces us in turn to the status of narrative in general and to the status of narrative in this painting in particular.

Here we might recall Aristotle's well-known critique of historiography as opposed to tragic poetry: history is less philosophical than tragedy because it is attached to individuals. Unlike tragedy, which depicts general characteristics, history is obliged to narrate the succession of events circumscribed by a given period; thus history lacks the unity of action proper to tragedy and is rarely able to assign causes. By subordinating narration to the synopsis of an overall picture, Poussin's historical painting raises narrative to the level of *apodeixis*. "Like a blueprint for a simple machine, it shows schematically the conflicting forces involved, their tensions and their positions of equilibrium," and all the particular specifications of this schema, far from altering it, serve merely as exemplifying illustrations. "History," writes Imbert, "deals with sequences of actions in which individuals are the figures, and events the points of intersection. . . . A unitary vision alone can yield knowledge of true causes, by distinguishing them from the illusion of mere conjunctions: it mirrors the unity of action and the necessity of fate."[9] If all the figures, and not just three of them, are playing their roles according to the weather, it is because the weather in question is not merely the imperious effect of the wind that traverses the entire space of the painting, but also the chronological framework of the storm, the time when a cosmic destiny imposes itself as a shared necessity, the time when a common unity of action makes itself felt in the place, a time of which the meteoric event of the hurricane, and the animal event of the lion, appearing in its inexplicable occurrence, and the passionate event of Pyramus and Thisbe, imported from the myth, are only isolated illustrations, organizing a *demonstration* through the vectors and the modes of the figures that appear in the relief of the representation. Such is the painting with all its narrative-descriptive figures: the simulacrum of the sublimity of destiny through the sublime of a representation of the unrepresentable, the representation of a multiple and unique tempest.

A Narrative within a Description

> On one side, a shepherd is running, abandoning his herd, seeing a lion that has downed a number of cowherds and is attacking others, some of whom are defending themselves while others are prodding their cattle and trying to escape. Amidst this disorder, the dust is rising in great whirlwinds. A dog some distance away is barking, his fur abristle; he does not dare approach.

Here, then, apparently, is the anecdote, a pastoral scene, however dramatic it may be. Look at the painting and you will see, on the same vertical plane, a stroke of lightning and a lion leaping onto a white horse whose rider has been thrown to the ground. A story can be told here, beginning with its central moment in the very present of its occurrence. The action, or rather the event of the lion's attack, circumscribes and determines the present and its immediate circumstances: a confused struggle, three actors, a knot of bodies and gestures, the lion appearing suddenly from the left clinging to the mane of the rearing horse, the rider already on the ground and making useless gestures of self-defense, another mounted on a dark horse, his arm raised to attack the wild beast. But here we already have a third horseman fleeing on his mount while whipping up his cattle, and farther down the road a shepherd is running, his head turned toward the melee, driving his fleeing herd toward the right. This present, as we can tell from the brief description, is not a pure instant of abstract simultaneity, but a moment articulated by a single action. Thus who can say whether the third horseman is fleeing from the battle because he has already seen the lion's attack or because he is galloping off under the impetus of the impetuous storm wind without seeing the drama taking place behind his back?

The same question arises about the shepherd and his herd of sheep. Are we encountering quasi-simultaneous consecutivity, or a result closely linked to its cause? Only the overall view—the spectator's—reveals any unity of action; the actors in the story cannot perceive it themselves. This overview provides the schema of equilibrium and movement between forces in conflict. The narrative can then borrow "the weak linkage of the succession and conjunction of events." Only we who see the whole picture know that the lion is the tempest and that the figures who are yielding to the wind and following the force that is carrying them along may be under the illusion that they are fleeing the leaping animal, as those who are fighting the wind may be under the illusion that they are resisting the cosmic event of which the lion's attack is only an illustration. An animated animal allegory of nature, the lion's emergence onto the median stage is a natural tempest, the suddenness of its appearance specified by a figure representing force, and an anecdote-narrative can certainly be related, in the figures of the painting—it is and will always be *for us* just one particular representation of the cosmic tempest on earth. Poussin's description of the painting marks this with a reminder: "Amidst this disorder, the dust is rising in great whirlwinds." Do not give in to the charms of narrative, do not yield to the mirage of a singular history. The tempest of heaven on earth remains the painting's argument, its hypothesis, its theme, that of cosmic destiny, and the disorder of animal and human passions is just one case among others of Nature's sublime, which is disorder only for the characters the figures embody. Does the lion not arrive from the left in keeping with the order of the unique effect of the wind?

In the description, the only indication of the change of level and of the appearance of an accessory cause (the lion) that is exactly contemporary with the real and unique principal cause (the storm wind) in their similar and simultaneous effects is the "immediate" transformation of the hurricane's unidirectional movement into a whirlwind. The effect of the impetuous wind is the imperious governance of a rigorously oriented force in one place, the repetitive vortex of the dust-earth in the other. The great whirlwinds of dust in Nature that the written description underlines are given an image, in the world of animate beings, in the tangle of animal and human figures—lion, horses, and riders, intermingled—in which the narrative finds its moment. If the general schema of forces in conflict sets up a structural opposition between the figures that yield to the wind's effect and those that resist it, the whirlwind knot of characters and natural forces gives the particular narrative its anchor point. But the whirlwind is only the momentary and particular transformation, on the scale of animal and human actions and passions, of the one-way movement of the cosmic tempest, a circular movement in which the forces in conflict are exhibited dynamically in their repetitive succession. The whirlwind as the dynamic moment of the momentary equilibrium within the disorder, the conflict of the unresolved forces of which the barking dog—"some distance away" with its "fur abristle" that "does not dare approach"—is in its immobility the culminating figure, simultaneously embodying aggressive reactions of attack and passive reactions of flight.

The whirlwinds of dust are the random, particular, and momentary transformations (the metamorphosis) of the unidirectional effect of the wind, just as the narrative of the attack on the horsemen, cowherds, and shepherds by the lion is the transformation of the assent to cosmic necessity and of the illusory and blinding resistance to its omnipotence, through specification of the simple polarity of the two "characters." Thus we have a double transformation culminating in the short sequence of the fable that is exhibited by the two figures in the foreground on the right, where the movement effect of the cosmic destiny is transformed into a contrary effect, but in the error of human passion: "In the foreground of the painting, one sees Pyramus lying dead on the ground, and near him Thisbe, who has succumbed to grief."

The wind's taut force traverses the entire space of the painting: background, middle ground, foreground. But with the perpendicularity of the lightning flash where the darkness of the sky is signed, we have the luminous epiphany of the tower of Babel-Babylon, the whirlwind tangle constituted by the lion, the horses, and the men in the great swirling dust clouds rising up. However, from the point where the thunderbolt comes crashing down, tearing off the main branch of the central tree, a single vertical axis, in its fall, links the barking dog with bristling fur that does not dare approach with Pyramus lying dead on the ground. Next, we note that the second lightning flash, whose thunderbolt is striking the fortress-mountain in the background, links the horseman fleeing toward the city, driven by the wind, in the middle ground, with Thisbe succumbing to grief in the foreground. After the effect of an impetuous wind, here we have the effect of air filled with darkness, rain, lightning bolts and flashes falling in several places, not without creating some disorder; we have the bloody and absurd denouement of a lovely and unhappy love story told, in Ovid's text, by one of Minyas's daughters, who are so engrossed in weaving cloth in honor of Minerva that they forget all about Bacchus's festival.

An Ovidian Tale: The story of Pyramus and Thisbe, or how does a tree that bore white fruit spattered with blood now bear black fruit?

How can white (the universal color of light) become black (the non-color of darkness) through the mediation of red? This metamorphosis is an absurd story of unhappy love, but it is also a painter's problem, and as we shall soon see in listening to the tale, it is also the problem of signs, traces, or marks and their interpretation, in which error can lead to death.

"Pyramus and Thisbe," writes Ovid, "lived next door to each other, in the lofty city whose walls of brick are said to have been built by Semiramis": Babylon. "Pyramus was the most handsome of young men, and Thisbe the fairest beauty of the East." The two young people fall in love, but their parents oppose their union.

> No one shared their secret: they communicated by nods and signs. . . .
>
> There was a crack, a slender chink, that had developed in the party wall between their two houses, when it was being built. This fault had gone unnoticed for long years, and the lovers were the first to find it: nothing can escape a lover's eyes! They used it as a channel for their

> voices, and by this means their endearments were safely conveyed to one another, in the gentlest of whispers. Often when Pyramus stood on this side, Thisbe on that, when in turn they felt each other's breath, they used to exclaim: "Jealous wall, why do you stand in the way of lovers? How little it would be to ask that you should let us embrace or, if that is too much, that you should at least open wide enough for us to exchange kisses! Not that we are ungrateful—we admit that it is thanks to you that we have any way at all by which our words can reach our true love's ears."[10]

Passage of a single and dual lovers' voice across a crack in a wall, but no contact of bodies. Exchange without accomplishment, two breathing as one without physical consummation: here is the starting point for erotic initiation, a separation that does not prevent a primitive form of conjunction: a dash that hollows out a surface, a trace, but one deep enough—though it is infinitely narrow—to make a hole in a boundary; an inscription that is, in its hollowness, the breath of a double voice doubly harmonized. Thus, for example, the crack of lightning on the nocturnal wall of the heavens.

> At first, softly sighing, they lamented their sad lot. Then they determined that, at dead of night, they would try to slip past the watchment and steal out of doors; once outside their homes, they would make their way out of the city too; and in case they should miss each other, wandering aimlessly in the open country, they agreed to meet at Ninus' tomb, and to hide in the shade of its tree. For a tree grew there, a tall mulberry, hung thick with snowy fruits; it stood close by a cool spring. . . . The daylight seemed slow to depart, but at last the sun plunged into the waters, and from those waters came forth the night.

Passage of voices across a wall, flight of bodies beyond the shelters of home and the city into the open space of the countryside, owing to the vanished daylight and the sudden appearance of night: the site of the nocturnal meeting is the monument, the tomb, the sign of death, and the tree with white fruit close by the spring. The mark of conjunction, the signal of reunion has all the ambiguity of semes: black and white, chance wandering and dual signpost, death and life. The initiatory voyage is doubled by a necessary interpretation of the ambiguous marks and signs.

> Stealthily Thisbe turned the door on its hinges, and slipped out. . . . Her face hidden by her veil, she came to the tomb, and sat down under the appointed tree. Love made her bold.

Sudden irruption of the event:

> But suddenly a lioness, fresh from the kill, her slavering jaws dripping with the blood of her victims, came to slake her thirst at the neighbouring spring. While the animal was still some distance off, Thisbe saw her in the moonlight. Frightened, she fled into the darkness of a cave, and as she ran her veil slipped from her shoulders, and was left behind.
>
> When the savage lioness had drunk her fill, and was returning to the woods, she found the garment, though not the girl, and tore its fine fabric to shreds, ripping it with bloodstained jaws.

Aleatory irruption of the event and, at the various knotting points of chance, indices, traces, signs. The blood and foam on the lioness's muzzle, index of the slain oxen: Thisbe's fallen veil, trace of her flight and torn to shreds by the satisfied lioness, has become a sign of the beast's ferocity, a sign in which the ox blood marks the herd she has just devastated. But the veil has fallen *by chance* from Thisbe's shoulders, and the lioness has found it *by chance*, and *by chance*, with her bloodstained jaws, she has torn it to shreds. A composite text, made up of signs, indices, and marks, writes itself in this nocturnal place of death and the subterranean, a text of readable-visible space under the pale light of the moon, a text that its scriptors, the lioness and Thisbe, unwittingly, unwillingly, inscribe on their bodies and in things, irresistibly impelled by need and passion.

With the scriptors vanished or hidden, the reader comes on stage.

> Pyramus came out of the city a little later. He saw the prints of the wild beast, clearly outlined in the deep dust, and the colour drained from his face. Worse still, he found the veil, all stained with blood. Then he cried out: "This night will bring about the death of two fond

lovers, and of the two she deserved to live far more than I. 'Tis I who am to blame: poor girl, it was I who killed you! I told you to come, by night, to a place that was full of danger, and did not arrive first myself. Come, all you lions who live beneath this cliff, come and tear me limb from limb! With your fierce jaws, devour my guilty person. But it is a coward's trick, only to pray for death!" He picked up Thisbe's veil, and carried it into the shade of the tree where they should have met.

The traces of the beast are unmistakable to the eye of the late-arriving lover: accurate inference of the past passage of the beast on the basis of present indices. And the same holds true, apparently, for his lover's torn and bloody veil, the unmistakable indication of her killing by the lioness. But this is to forget that, by chance, the lioness found the veil without its mistress, it is to forget that a veil may fall, may detach itself from the one wearing it, and it is also to forget that blood soiling a veil may belong to slain oxen. For there are signs that are joined to the things they signify and signs that are detached from them, and it is not possible to conclude with full certainty and without further interpretive examination of the sign as to the presence or absence of the thing signified. Thus we have an erroneous inference on the part of Pyramus, articulated on the basis of a correct inference. What accounts, then, for the tragic error? Pyramus misreads because the passion of love carries him away and blinds him to the prudence of all reasoning about and on the basis of the effects, traces, marks, and signs perceived at a given moment and which offer only the truth of their presence. Passion blinds him, passion made up of hopes and regrets for having been unable to be content with the present, which is the only time man truly has at his disposal.

Weeping and kissing the garment he knew so well, he said: "Drink deep, now, of my blood too." And as he spoke he took the sword which hung at his waist, and thrust it into his side: then, with a dying effort, pulled it out of the warm wound. As he lay, fallen back upon the ground, his blood spouted forth, just as when a water pipe bursts, if there is some flaw in the lead, and through the narrow hissing crack a long stream of water shoots out, and beats on the air. The fruits of

> the tree were sprinkled with his blood, and changed to a dark purple hue. The roots, soaked in his gore, tinged the hanging berries with the same rich colour.

The lover's death is a necessary (true) event following from a false conclusion. And the intentions that preside over its accomplishment—human, all too human, rooted in passion—will also lead to error. Pyramus wanted his blood to impregnate the well-known cloth and to espouse Thisbe's in a double death. But the god takes pains not to confuse the blood of slain oxen with that of the fairest beauty of the East. Pyramus's blood spurts out and stains not the torn veil but the fruit and roots of the tree where the two were to meet. Red mixed with white—in the strange palette of metamorphosis—produces black or deep purple. Yet the fact remains that the *fabric* of the veil is not what, like the painter's picture, brings this blend to the viewer's sight, but rather the tree, its deep roots and its fruit, in its foliage. What occurs is ***natural metamorphosis*** of the colors white and black, the white of the luminous innocence of happy love turned into the funereal black of deadly night by virtue of the red of human blood, not a technical mixing of pigments under the painter's brush. A painter's dream: that the colored mixtures should not be devices and procedures to create illusions for the eyes, but rather geneses and metamorphoses of living material, or that the fabric, the canvas, should be like the tree where the lovers were to meet on the outskirts of Babylon—the place where universal language (universal as white is the universal color because it is that of the light of the unique sun) was dispersed into incommunicable idioms, if not into a meaningless mix (as heterogeneous colors can blend without ever returning to the universal genre of white even though they emerged from it through analysis), unless rules for translation are produced (unless the art of mixing pigments is elaborated, the entire art of painting). A painter's dream: that the canvas of painting should be like the tree—a signpost of the lovers' meeting, a space productive of poetic metamorphosis (but perhaps this is never possible except in death), a poetic metamorphosis that, unlike natural metamorphosis, is the transmutation of non-color (black) into universal color (the white of light). All the misfortune of the lovers in the tale originated in a rift: the crack in the wall that separated them and permitted only their voices to pass (here is the dash or cut on the support constituted by the painting), the bloody tearing of the lover's veil, not by her late-arriving lover but by the lioness, the wild beast; but the wall will keep its crack in the shelter of Babylon, and the torn veil will be stained only with the blood of slain oxen, and from the tear in Pyramus's side, a narrow opening in a flawed lead pipe, the spurt of blood will sprinkle the tree only to turn the white of its fruit to black.

> Now, though Thisbe had not yet quite recovered from her fear, she came back; for she was anxious not to disappoint her lover. She looked about for the youth with eager eyes and heart, impatient to tell him of the perils she had escaped. But although she recognized the spot, and the shape of the tree, yet the colour of its fruit made her uncertain; she was unable to decide whether this was the place or not.

To the tragic play of errors multiplied by the passions of hope and regret, fear and desire, the metamorphosis of color blurs the marks of recognition, makes the signs waver.

> As she stood in doubt, she saw the quivering limbs writhing on the bloodstained ground, and started back. Her cheeks grew paler than boxwood, and she trembled as the sea shivers when a soft breeze ripples its surface.

But "after a moment's pause, she recognized her love"—despair on Thisbe's part . . . :

> Wailing aloud, she beat her innocent arms, tore her hair, and embracing his beloved form, bathed his wound with her tears, mingling the salt drops with his blood, and passionately kissing his cold cheeks. "Pyramus," she cried. "What mischance has taken you from me? Pyramus, speak to me! It is your own dear Thisbe who is calling you! Hear me . . . !"

When she had recognized her veil and seen the ivory scabbard without a sword:

"Alas, your own hand and your love have destroyed you. I, too, have a hand resolute for this one deed; my love, as great as yours, will give me strength to deal the wound. I shall follow you in death, and men will speak of me as at once the unhappy cause and the companion of your fate."

The discovery of the dying body reestablishes in the immediacy of grief the truth of the recognitions and the narrative truth of the erroneous inferences: seeing the veil, seeing the scabbard without a sword, allows Thisbe to understand, *uno intuitu, tota simul,* the whole story in the present representation and allows her, at the same time, to make her decisive resolution. Far from being a definitive separation, death reunites the two lovers in a nocturnal marriage.

"Most wretched parents, mine and his, I beg this one boon for us both: since our steadfast love and the hour of our death have united us, do not grudge that we be laid together in a single tomb. And you, O tree, already sheltering one hapless body, soon to shelter two, bear for ever the marks of our death: always have fruit of a dark and mournful hue, to make men remember the blood we two have shed!" As she spoke, she placed the sword blade beneath her breast, and fell forward on the steel, which was still warm from Pyramus' death.

A double and common prayer to the parents and the gods, a prayer for the erection of a monument, a double monument in the place where the tomb of Ninus stands and the tree with snow-white fruit, at the place of the nocturnal meeting. A prayer heard, its ambiguity between death and life should restore the unity of the seme and join the uncertain anticipations together in the ever-present stability of a single meaning. Traces and marks of the somber story will be transformed into definitive signs, ever-present signs of the past gone by. "Only the present exists"; the only time existing is the present. As Victor Goldschmidt puts it in *Le système stoïcienne et l'idée du temps,* past and future

subsist but do not exist at all. . . . Past and future are predicates expressed by verbs but are not current accidents of the agent-subject. As

> the act indicated by these verbs is no longer or not yet present, past and future are only creatures of reason; are they absolutely without relation to the present? This seems to depend upon the perceiving subject. . . . In the expanse of the cosmic period, they remain offered to the gaze of Zeus. They are also offered to men who interpret signs. . . . "The present sign is a sign of a thing present" and not of a thing past or to come. A scar is a sign, not that someone has been wounded, but "that he *is* having been wounded"; a wound in the heart is not a sign that someone will have to die but that he *is*, having to die, in such a way that the present sign, in the grip of sensation, makes it possible to apprehend the signified, hidden and invisible in the mode of the present.[11]

This present sign: the tree, the tomb, the painting.

> Her prayers touched the gods, and they touched the parents also: for the berry of the tree, when ripe, is a dark purple colour, and the remains of the two lovers, gathered from the funeral fires, rest together in a single urn.

A Stoic Interpretation

"In the foreground of the painting, one sees Pyramus lying dead on the ground, and near him Thisbe, who has succumbed to grief." Poussin chooses to represent the moment in the tale when Thisbe discovers the dying body of her lover ("she saw the quivering limbs writhing on the bloodstained ground") and, more precisely perhaps, the instant of the recognition that the body is Pyramus's ("after a moment's pause, she recognized her love"), an instant that the painter composes, in a single presentation, with the movement of return to the obscure grotto where the girl had sought refuge upon the arrival of the lioness who had come "to slake her thirst at the neighbouring spring." It is a brief narrative sequence between a past death and a death to come, the moment of the burst of wind that traverses the entire painting, an instant of simultaneity featuring the two lightning flashes in the heavens and the thunderbolt striking the tree across the lake, striking the fortress-mountain in the distance.

The necessity of introducing this moment of the narrative into the foreground of the painting has to be examined within the general economy of the work of painting, in the context of the thought that subtends it, the "philosophic" intention that animates it.

"In the foreground of the painting, one sees . . . ": the Poussinian *ekphrasis* in no way yields, in its concluding sentence, to fascination with the "historical" reference. Representation itself generates its discursive description: what happens near the tree where the lovers were to meet, at the edge of the spring, happens in the foreground of the painting, and in the same genetic movement representation brings its anonymous viewer back both into the text and to himself. What you see there is not reality, these are not two wretched lovers for whom you feel pity because you identify with their passion, it is a painting, the foreground of a painting to be contemplated from a viewing site in which no tempest is agitating the space, where no passion other than that of seeing animates the spectacle of its phantasms. "All the figures one sees there are playing their roles according to the weather. . . . In the foreground of the painting, one sees Pyramus lying dead . . . " Imbert states, "'The term *phantasia* is used generally for anything which in any way suggests a thought productive of speech (*gennetikon logou*).' [Longinus] adds that . . . the term . . . designates that state of emotion or enthusiasm by virtue of which a speaker can *see*, and make his audience *see*, whatever he is talking about."[12] Once the structural schema of the narrative has been made explicit, once the anecdote that specifies the schema by exemplifying it has been related, the representation reaffirms in the discourse it engenders its spectacular character in the painting where what is stated, written, or (de)scribed is first of all seen; it is stated, written, or (de)scribed only because representation sets it before the eyes of those who, as they look, talk about what they are seeing.

This final sentence of the description (this final phase of the representation) is also the one in which all the figures in the painting find their proper names in the two figures arrayed on the forestage of the spectacle, where their generic anonymity and the plurality in which their dual role is distributed are focalized and synthesized in the singularity of two names, those of the two lovers, heroes of the fable. "Some are fleeing through the dust, in the direction of the wind that is driving them along . . . a shepherd is running, abandoning his herd . . . others, on the contrary, are going against the wind, walking with difficulty, covering their eyes with their hands . . . a lion that has downed a number of cowherds . . . Pyramus lying dead on the ground, and near him Thisbe, who has succumbed to grief." "Pyramus" and "Thisbe": these two names sum up both all the rest of the painted work and the set of figures that the painting exhibits to view and, through the reference to the "story" that the names presuppose (or knowledge of which they presuppose on the part of the viewer of the painting), that give the work its iconographic explanation, its moral exegesis, and its philosophical interpretation. On the basis of those names, set forth in the *ekphrasis*, declared in the painter's discourse, and contemplated in the representation, it becomes necessary to re-cognize the entire painting, to re-mark it in an inverse trajectory that would totalize the juxtaposed enumeration of its scenes, bringing them together in a new and higher unity; it becomes necessary to reread the painting in an overview that would discover its global meaning.

Thus the "absurd" appearance of the lioness, the chance event of her irruption on the middle ground of the painting, has its necessary explanation in the fable, even if the event of its irruption in the fable also remains inexplicable, as absurd as it was in the earlier description, a simple perception of the spatial distribution of the figures. Thus the city at right takes on its name, Babylon, and the colossal architecture at the edge of the place where appearances vanish is re-marked as the tower of Babel. Thus, too, finally, the darkness that is invading the background of the painting, as well as the great tree on the left and the water in the foreground, are explained by the fable. The result is a string of singular nominations attached to the names Pyramus and Thisbe, the constitution of a network of "signs" dispersed here and there in which "a lion," indefinitely named in the Master's *ekphrasis*, as in the perception of the figure, a simple immediate recognition of the represented, becomes the lioness of the fable, a city becomes Babylon, a tree becomes the mulberry tree that is the nocturnal meeting place, because the young woman making pathetic gestures of despair is said to be, is written as, "Thisbe," and the body lying prone in the repose of death is "Pyramus," while the sword lying beside him does not signify murder but rather violent death in a suicide provoked by love. The representation produced itself as a narrative text because in the last line of the letter to Jacques Stella the description spells out two proper names.

But on the basis of this network of names and a few of their predicates immediately recognized on the icon, on the basis of this nominal network with few elements and erratic units, the various planes that give the representation its relief and allow it to initiate its *apodeixis* take on the unity of an allegory, and with that unity comes a way toward a possible exegesis. Indeed, if we reread Ovid and the tale of Minyas's daughter, the night of the lovers' flight is not stormy, and, while a slender chink splits the wall that separates them, no lightning streaks across the sky. There are no clouds in the sky of Babylon, for Thisbe saw the lioness approach by moonlight. There are no gusts of wind, however brief. From here on, cannot the entire landscape of storm, wind, lightning flashes, thunderbolts, the meteoric night, whirling dust storms, in the picture, a work of painting, like the allegorical description of the drama of the senseless mistake and the deadly passions that it produced for the two lovers, the hour of their meeting and precisely in this moment of the tragic discovery of Pyramus's dead body and the sudden and immediate recognition by Thisbe, cannot all this be said to be the truth of the errors and misunderstandings that have marked the entire story? The impetuous wind of the hurricane becomes, in a moment of comprehensive catalepsis, the imperious governance of the violence of the passion of love, and the lightning flash in the dark, cloud-laden sky becomes the destructive instant of the *Augenblick*, in which the self-evidence of the truth of a senseless unhappiness dazzles. A figure at the confines of the first and second levels of the painting, on the vertical median of its surface, could well be, in the represented narrative in which it plays, to that effect, its character, the tropic(al) figure—in all the senses of this adjective—of the allegorization of the "landscape" through the narrative: head turned toward the lion leaping onto the white horse, driven by the violence of the wind toward the right, arm outstretched in flight, the figure initiates the landscape's metamorphosis into an allegory of the narrative, or else it refers the foregrounded narrative sequence, that of the dead Pyramus and Thisbe giving herself over to her grief, to the sequence of the sudden appearance of the lioness that was its remote cause. Carried away by the wind of the tempest that traverses the entire painting, this figure still does not fail—figuratively—to anticipate Thisbe's return, her being carried away by the force of passion and her succumbing, *against the cosmic wind,* to the grief of a tragic recognition. As for the background, the flash of lightning, as we have seen, instantly signs the stormy sky: an undulation, a serpent of fire in the clouds, it culminates in the immediate rectilinear trajectory of the thunderbolt that strikes the branch of the tree on the edge of the lake and pulls it down. But this same prolonged line comes down with a *luminous flash* to strike Thisbe, who is walking against the wind at the instant of her discovery of Pyramus's prone body; Thisbe herself is a lightning flash illuminating the body that has been torn loose, hurled to the ground, struck by the fatal blow, by the misreading of the meaning of the signs. Pyramus has been felled by a false inference, as the cowherd of the second level has been felled by the lion, as the tree branch has been felled by the lightning bolt: Thisbe is instantly illuminated by the background lightning, just as she herself immediately illuminates her lover in a flash of recognition; Thisbe is walking against the wind just as the figure in the middle ground on the far right is advancing with difficulty, his hands covering his eyes, obstinately blinded, even as Thisbe, instantly, sees Pyramus's blindness to the true causes.

Yes, to be sure, "all the figures are playing their roles according to the weather," but the weather is just as much the meteoric time of the wind and the sudden lightning flashes of the cosmic tempest as it is the time of passion-driven errors of hope and despair and the present of the tragic recognition of truth. Depending upon the order of viewing-reading, the first focalizes and synthesizes the second in the actions and passions of the characters of the tragedy, or else the second allegorizes and symbolizes the first by supplying the moral and philosophical meaning of the wind that traverses the entire space of the painting and of the lightning flashes that shine through the celestial obscurity here and now. Thus from the narrative forestage to the background of the landscape, or from the cosmic tempest to the tragic fable, a correspondence is instituted, that of a double representation through which the representation is raised to its own universal and singular comprehension.

The painting, in the presence of the represented, the painting as painting subjected to the constraints of representation that are its own, thus operates the integration of the cosmic time of nature and the moral time of personal existence. It places its viewer, provided he is capable of describing it accurately, that is, of contemplating it, in the position of sage or god.

Divinitati omne praesens. Just as the fragility of the illusory present was communicated to time as a whole, in the same way the cosmic present comes to communicate its density and its plenitude to the lived present. Marcus Aurelius, in *The Meditations*, writes:

> Reflect how many physical and mental processes take place at the same moment of time in each one of us; you will then not marvel that many more, or rather all things that come to be, are contained at the same moment in that over-all unity which we call the universe. . . . He who has seen the present has seen everything, all that from eternity has come to pass, and all that will come to be in infinite time. For everything is akin and the same. . . . Look back upon the past: so many changes of rulers. One can also foresee the future, for it will be altogether similar and cannot deviate from the rhythm of the present. Hence to examine human life for forty years is the same as to examine it for ten thousand years, for what more will you see? . . . The rational soul travels through the whole universe and the void which sur-

rounds it, and observes its form; it stretches into infinity of time and grasps and understands the periodic rebirth of the Whole; it observes that those who come after us will see nothing new, nothing different from what our predecessors saw, but in a sense a man of forty, if he has any intelligence, has seen all the past and all the future, because they are of the same kind as the present.[13]

Thus one gains a conception of instant happiness through which the sage rivals the gods, the crowning of moral philosophy and physics, the rigorous equivalence of an instant and eternity. "It is the sign of a great artist," writes Seneca, "to have confined a full likeness to the limits of a miniature. There is one point in which the sage has an advantage over the god; for a god is freed from terrors by the bounty of nature, the wise man by his own bounty."[14]

Remarks of Wisdom

Of this operation of integrating or converting cosmic time into existential time, and vice versa, or the operation of concentrating universal movement in the singular instant represented in proportion to the expansion of that moment (the instant of tragic re-cognition) to the infinite—sublime—dimensions of the tempest, but to the benefit, not of the figures that embody their characters in the scenes of the painting—the tree and the dwelling, the shepherds who are fleeing in the direction of the wind that is driving them and those who are walking blindly against it, Pyramus lying dead on the ground and Thisbe succumbing to her grief—but of the one who is contemplating all these spectacles *tota simul* in serene delight—of this operation, then, the Master's painting proposes two marks that he leaves to the wisdom of his anonymous general viewer to note, two marks to be re-marked in the form of a double paradox of time and space.

Let us return once more to the Ovidian narrative of the sudden aleatory arrival of the unexpected, the entry of the lioness onto the stage: "But suddenly a lioness, fresh from the kill, her slavering jaws dripping with the blood of her victims, came to slake her thirst at the neighbouring spring." And Thisbe, who has seen her, runs off to take refuge in the darkness of a cave, losing her veil, which falls from her shoulders during her flight. "When the savage lioness had drunk her fill, and was returning to the woods, she found the garment, though not the girl, and tore its fine fabric to shreds, ripping it with bloodstained jaws." And the lioness disappears from the narrative, leaving nothing in the dust but her unmistakable traces, fatal premises of Pyramus's mistaken reasoning. The succession of narrative sequences in Ovid is all the more clearly articulated in that it constitutes the proximate cause of the lover's error and, in this misunderstanding, the advent of the contrary destiny. At the instant of Thisbe's discovery and recognition of the dying Pyramus's body, the lioness's attack on the oxen, her arrival at the spring, her tearing of Thisbe's veil are past events.

Now, in the painting, the attack of the famished lioness is contemporaneous with the instant of discovery and recognition of the body near the spring where, her hunger satisfied, she has already come to slake her thirst, all the more so in that about halfway between the rampart of earth and bushes that marks off the foreground of the painting, one sees the veil Thisbe lost. If the present of the representation, the present represented moment, is that of tragic re-cognition, then the scene on the second level that is its remote cause in the narrative order, its past, must be declared to be simultaneous with this present, that old present simultaneous with the presence—the represented presence—of the present, the only time of representation. Either the master of representation is transgressing the rules that institute the only time that is proper to him, or else he is juxtaposing in a single painting at least two pictures, each of which represents two successive scenes in two separate places; but then he is transgressing the rules that institute a single space, the spatially homogeneous scene that constitutes the painting. Let us forget Ovid and conceive of the unity of "Pyramus and Thisbe" as unity through repetition: the storm, the lion, Thisbe, the lion repeating the cosmic tempest in its animal order, and Thisbe repeating both in her human order. But it is not possible to forget Ovid entirely, since the two figures in the foreground of the painting have received their names from him, and with them the tale he tells in the *Metamorphoses*, the tale whose two figures are playing out one scene in the painting, and since the lion on the second level is its remote cause . . .

Let us notice, rather, in this transgression of the rules of representation in painting, the formulation of the Stoic paradox of an abolition of all distance between cause and effect by the instantaneous perfection of movement. "But the coincidence to which he continually leads these two terms is in no way dissolved in an infinitesimal time. The present of movement is not distant with respect to itself, but it is actually an extended present." Movement does not reduce distance but possesses an extension, occupies an interval. Still, writes Goldschmidt, "that interval is not marked, ahead of time, by two immobile terms; it is marked, at each point in its trajectory, by the movement itself. . . . Movement does not fill the interval, it determines it." Henceforth the present measures the totality of the movement even as it is delimited by the extension of the movement. "The agent is the perfect cause of the movement of which, in its turn, the extension determines the present. The total perfection of movement, being due to the agent, is likewise perceived only by the agent." Thus it is that

> in the extension of a cosmic period "all things are present to God," who is from beginning to end their unique author. By him the successive linking of causes is perceived as simultaneity and as harmony. But for us, the simultaneity is given only in the *temporis traductio*; destiny appears to us as the reason in conformity with which the past, the present, the future unfold. . . . God is destiny. But the series of causes is an interweaving in which everything is present. Of this totality we shall never restore more than fragments.[15]

The lion's attack on the cowherds is in the successive series of causes and effects the remote antecedent cause of the death of Pyramus and of the grief to which Thisbe surrenders, but, understanding the events and wanting them to be in the order of the cosmic conflagration of the tempest and after the manner of God, the painter and/or the viewer of the painting, who presents *tota simul* the attack and the death and the grief, succeeds in including the singular and successive events in the same harmonic present in which they are all ordered in a common simultaneity. The painting, the representation in painting, owing to its own unsurpassable rules of presentation to view, is the privileged instrument of wisdom following the example of the divine unique cause. And the unrepresentability of the sublime of the cosmic tempest, which is the *subject* of the painter's intention to represent, this conflagration through wind, lightning, and thunderbolts that the Master introduces as a supplement to the narrative *subject* of the painting, which is also the tragic story of Pyramus and Thisbe, has perhaps no other end than to bring out in the representation itself, in the painting, the unrepresentable unity of all the singular events in the act of the god and their eternal repetition, even though the simultaneous representation of two successive events in the narrative marks the fact that in accepting the mutilated and fragmentary present from which we cannot exit, we still have the possibility of understanding the events in God's manner, as wise men do.[16] Indifference, then, with respect to the "matter" of the argument, with respect to the "text": this signifies simultaneously that the sage is the best of actors, that he tries to represent on stage as best he can the character that providential destiny is compelling him to play, and that he too is a mere spectator in the face of the world and the events that he is content to contemplate, whereas the common man identifies with the character and is overwhelmed by the passions whose signs the character exposes to view in the theater where he is put on stage.

Of this requirement, the representation of the tempest on earth with Pyramus dead and Thisbe succumbing to grief in the foreground of the painting gives the viewer a mark to re-mark. The impetuous wind traverses the entire painting with its imperious force; the trees, at the rear of the foreground, bow down under that force, bend and twist so that their leaves are turned the wrong way; dust here and there rises up in great whirlwinds; the figures follow the hurricane that drives them or walk into it with difficulty, blinded. From the dark sky, two flashes strike, and one tears off the main branch of a large tree in the middle ground at the edge of a lake. Thisbe advances against the wind and, in a flash, recognizes her lover's body lying prone on the ground, "and she tremble[s] as the sea shivers when a soft breeze ripples its surface." And yet in all this agitation of air, water, earth, and fire, in which all the elements mingle their multiple forces, the great lake in the middle distance remains immobile and calm, a clear mirror without a ripple to blur the reflections, sending back a serene image of the tree that the thunderbolt is striking and that the wind is shaking, and, along with that image, images of the buildings and of the sunlight that is abandoning the heavens to the stormy thrust of darkness. "I have tried to represent a tempest on earth, imitating to the best of my ability the effect of an impetuous wind. . . . " The lake, a pure unchanged mirror in repose: does it constitute a breakdown of the intention to represent the unrepresentable? An inconsistency in exact mimesis, manifested everywhere in its propriety except in this central place of the represented "landscape"? A flaw in the sublime tableau of cosmic sublimity, which envelops with its dynamics the characters embodied by all the figures, except the one that is presented on the middle stage by the figure of that peaceful body of water?

Or does the lake, as a figure of the painting, play in the painting a character other than those who cooperate with destiny or resist it, a different character, one that is no longer a character belonging to the painting but is rather the great eye of the viewer, of the sage who has been brought back to himself by the representation of the unrepresentability of the tempest and the human passions? This sage-lake would figure a reduced gaze, returned to its eye, after all the trajectories and all the readings of the places, spaces, and figures of the painting; it would figure a gaze that is now serene, since it is aligned with itself in the present presence of the instrument that has been the instrument of this return, the painting, that of Pyramus and Thisbe, that of a tale of two unhappy lovers reunited only by death in the monument of a tree with snow-white fruit metamorphosed into the fruits of night . . . that of a tempest on earth, the impossible sublime subject of painting at its most extreme altitude, which joins the universal effect of pneumatic *impetus* with the singular and punctual effect of a celestial fire.

Between the two lies a mirror of calm water, that of Narcissus—but in which, far from dying in it through the stupefaction of his own desire to see, the gaze of the sage contemplates itself in the figure of its eye, while contemplating, his mind at rest, the work of painting, "indifferent" in its presentation to what it represents.

Could it be, then, that a secret relationship is thus established between the *Landscape with Pyramus and Thisbe* (1650–1651), which can be seen at the Städelsches Kunstinstitut of Frankfurt, and the Master's two *self-portraits* (1649–1650), located in Berlin and Paris (see Figures 16 and 17)—especially the second one?

§ 4 Panofsky and Poussin in Arcadia

ET

Return one more time INTO that perfect surface through the crack that scores the double wall and the ground where it unfolds the scene.

Put the eye back in the O through a small gap and look from there at the other eye—across—dead, now, here. Again lose oneself in the tiny black hole in its center, made barely larger by the early-morning light.

Begin again: retraverse in an instant the path without distance from one *O(œil)* [eye] to the other *O(eil)*.

Lose everything each time and take it all back another time.

IN . . .

This is how the dead are conjured up on perfectly smooth surfaces. This is how they emerge from the other world. Such is the ritual of return to their own. Indefinitely, continually, then, purify oneself of the ancient crime, of the sacrifice of the child; of the ancestor's devouring the child to acquire the clairvoyance of the god.

Come back, as a couple, every morning, before the herds head out to the vain pastures, come back to face the tomb; look with the same dread at the signs inscribed in the stone; each time await the arrival of the goddess, the Virgin Mother, the Most Beautiful One; a gentle touch on the shoulder, the breath that passes over the thicket and into the cork oaks and subsides for a moment;

hear, wait for a voice—unheard (of)—long forgotten, the voice of the child, long ago, devoured as a sacrifice, in order to see. Arcas torn, dismembered, has returned, but, recomposed, he is a god or a star. He has come back; his elbows rest on the tomb from which his name has been rubbed out. Day after day he contemplates the two shepherds who come, each morning, to look at the signs, because they know only how to sing: they can neither see nor read.

Thus the tomb is guarded, invisibly, by the Most Beautiful One on the right and by the god, her son, on the left; these two hold the secret of the figures in the heavens and the secret of the signs in the stone. Guardians without eyes, but clairvoyant. A caress for the stone, a caress for the shoulder. Ever attentive—forever, because the son has long ago killed his mother, but sovereign pity has set them both here: angular statues.

ARCADIA . . .

Return one more time into the wall of smooth stone, if only it were not for the horrible crack, to rewrite the vanished name mine, yours, and perhaps also the blazon of a Roman cardinal or the unique letter, the first or the eighteenth, which—if I knew it—would surely give the code.

Put the eye back in the O and continue—rewrite. What name? Yours, mine, his, hers, perhaps even that of the buried god.

Place where the living lose their shadow despite the early morning light. M as in mortal, dead from the blows of crossed sticks.

Begin again. Put the eye back in the O to see the single shadow under the single letter: the blade of the scythe that amputates the living, cutting away their double.

This is the way I see it, the shadow reflected ON the perfect surface, the lovely shadows

No place, neither yours nor mine nor here nor there

Hand

EGO . . .

Holding.[1]

~

Erwin Panofsky dealt with Poussin relatively infrequently in his scholarly work. We can point to only five encounters between 1936 and 1961;[2] three of these dealt more or less directly with the painting in the Louvre known as *The Arcadian Shepherds* (Figure 11). In 1936, in a collective festschrift for Ernst Cassirer, *Philosophy and History*, Panofsky published an essay called "*Et in Arcadia ego*: On the Conception of Transience in Poussin and Watteau"; in the *Gazette des beaux-arts*, a two-page note, "*Et in Arcadia ego* et le tombeau parlant," expands on one particular point in the earlier study.[3] In 1955, in his well-known *Meaning in the Visual Arts: Papers in and on Art History*, Panofsky "revisited" the 1936 text; in reality, he completely rewrote it, under the title "*Et in Arcadia ego*: Poussin and the Elegiac Tradition."[4] These encounters, separated as they are by more than twenty years, suggest that the "theme" of Arcadia exerted a kind of fascination over Panofsky. The first essay, written less than three years after the author's definitive exile from Germany, is almost contemporaneous with his definitive appointment at the Institute for Advanced Study at Princeton;[5] the second is the last chapter in a book that brings together, as Panofsky points out in his preface, studies "chosen for their variety rather than for their consistency." Some of these texts, "*Et in Arcadia ego*" in particular, were "completely rewritten and, as far as possible, brought up-to-date by incorporating both the subsequent contributions of others and some afterthoughts of my own."[6] In the meantime—in 1939, to be precise—Panofsky had published a highly theoretical and methodological text, "Iconography and Iconology: An Introduction to the Study of Renaissance Art," as an introduction to his *Studies in Iconology*.[7] His essay "*Et in Arcadia ego*: Poussin and the Elegiac Tradition" (reprinted unchanged as the first chapter in *Meaning in the Visual Arts*) could easily appear to be an application of this powerful construction, which systematized a practice of art history and art theory begun in 1914.[8]

The play of the revisiting and "rewriting" of an experience of fascination with a Poussin painting and its "theme" is what I should like to evoke here, without studying it in detail. This play consists of displacements and after-the-fact reflections; the theo-

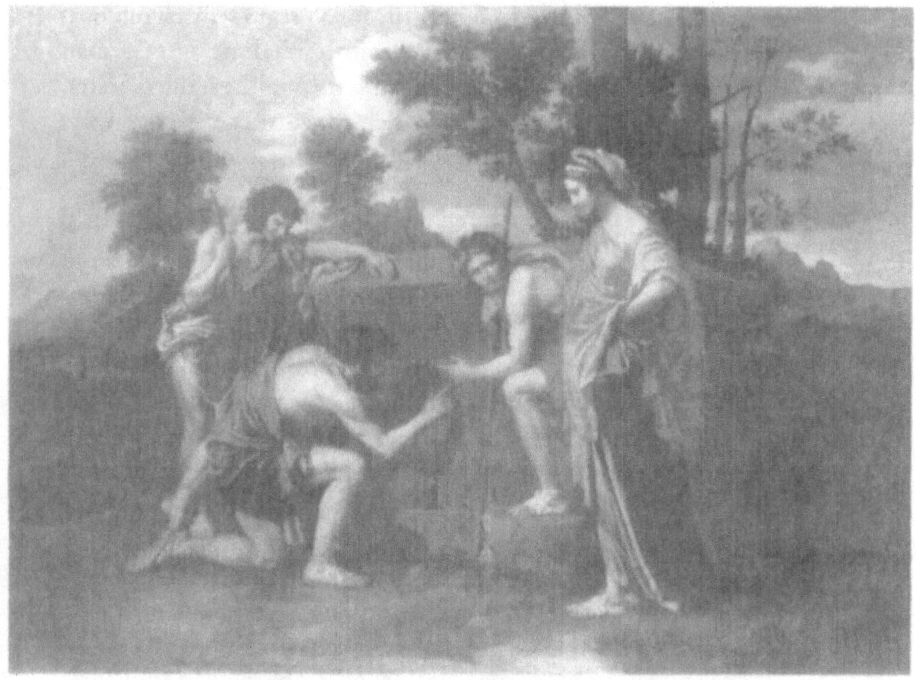

FIGURE 11. *The Arcadian Shepherds.* Courtesy Photographie Giraudon.

retical and historical model of "iconological" analysis could well provide its rules, constraints, and norms. Its background might be said to be "sociologically" constituted by the American "grafting" of an offspring of the Warburg School, through a crucial "epistemological moment," in the period between the wars, of art history and theory, and also by the place that Panofsky's work held and continues to hold for those who in France, in the 1950s and 1960s, came to art history and theory from philosophy, aesthetics, or cultural sociology.[9] In this adventure, it might seem that we are dealing only with displacements and revisitings: a text devoted to a French painter who painted in Rome, revisiting an earlier painting, a work on a *motto* invented by an Italian cardinal;[10] a text that marks the transition from a festschrift for a great German philosopher exiled in Sweden to a collection of studies done by a German art historian and theoretician who had settled in the United States, and whose very content ends up being rewritten, twenty years later, by way of a model of description, analysis, and interpretation of works of art.

The brief study I am undertaking here will be neither a funereal monument to Panofsky's glory nor a "displacement" onto a work by Poussin of a polemical interrogation of one of Panofsky's particular investigations. I would prefer that it be read as a critical theoretical and methodological reflection on Panofsky's work by way of a painting that readers can then go see again at the Louvre, and as a contribution to a history and a theory of art according to Panofsky: a contribution to post-Panofskyism, if one may use a barbarous neologism whose only justification is to acknowledge Panofsky's decisive importance for the constitution of a new theory-history of art, a new aesthetic philosophy that can conceptualize and develop its own novelty only on the basis of such a theory-history.[11]

Between 1936 and 1955 the principal object of the two studies remains unchanged. It is announced in their very titles, by the Latin expression *Et in Arcadia ego*. In the subtitles, too, the name of a painter, Poussin, remains unchanged. However, two noteworthy modifications affect the theme of the study and its field, respectively. In 1936, Panofsky sets out to analyze the notion or concept of "transience" (the transitory, the temporary, the changing) in Poussin *and Watteau*; in 1955, he focuses on Poussin's relation to "the elegiac tradition." Over twenty years, the philosophical or even metaphysical notion of the transitory or the temporary, of movement as flow and change, has become an expression designating the historical stability of a poetic mode of discourse and a poetic genre: a striking historical, methodological, theoretical, and philosophical "transition" from "transitory" to "tradition," but also to "elegiac." To be sure, one may wonder whether the very idea of an "elegiac tradition" does not make the philosophical conception of "change" explicit in developing it, since all tradition is a transmission of facts, doctrines, and legends through time, and since an essential element of the elegiac mode and genre, that is to say, of the discursive, poetic, and literary institution of the elegy, is the expression of feelings born of the flow of time and its mark on things and beings—in short, the expression of the sense of the transitory. But it still remains the case that from one title to another there is also displacement: behind the permanence of a Latin expression and a name, Panofsky has surreptitiously shifted from a notion that stems from poetic (or even philosophical) discourse to a metadiscursive notion that stems from a discourse *on* poetry.[12] Furthermore, when we note that, between 1936 and 1955, the field of inquiry is restructured and refocused on Poussin alone, to the exclusion of Watteau, we may well wonder whether we are not grasping, on the spot, as it were, the epistemological effects of the systematization, in a theoretical and methodological model, of an analytical practice, or more precisely of a certain "theoretical" gaze on the painter's work. In fact, only the attentive examination of Panofsky's writings on Poussin can allow us to answer these questions.

How, then, does Panofsky construct the problematic that subtends his 1936 essay? The first two pages are critical in this regard. He starts with a current use of the expression, "you, too, have lived in Arcadia" or "I, too, have lived in Arcadia," and goes on to discover its historical place and language: a tomb, a dead language, the Latin *Et in Arcadia ego*, a funereal inscription, and, proceeding from one tomb to another, from one inscription to another, he encounters Poussin's painting in the Louvre, *The Arcadian Shepherds*, the best-known interpretation of the theme of Arcadia. He then describes the work rapidly, concentrating on the four figures grouped around a half-effaced inscription, *Et in Arcadia ego*,[13] and the expressions on their faces: "It is as though the youthful people, all silent, were listening to or pondering over this imaginary message of a former fellow-being: 'I, too, lived in Arcadia, where you now live; I, too, enjoyed the pleasures which you enjoy; and yet I am dead and buried.'"

Panofsky's description of Poussin's work is precisely an *evocation*, the fiction of a voice from beyond the grave that is already the spectator's expression of the global (Poussin would say modal)[14] effect of the scene represented in his gaze. And indeed, Panofsky goes on, "*We* instantly perceive a strange ambiguous feeling which suggests both a mournful anticipation of man's inevitable destiny and an intense consciousness of the sweetness of life." Starting a new paragraph, he continues: "Thus *the inner meaning* of Poussin's picture—an elegiac sentiment aroused by the contrast between friendship and love amid beautiful scenery and the tomb of one who has left these joys for ever—seems fairly clear." Then he adds (and here is where the problems that his study will address are formulated): "But when we come to think of it, we are puzzled by two problems, one bearing upon the Arcadia conception as a whole, the other—seemingly a mere philological one, but in reality connected with what I should like to call the 'History of Types'—bearing upon the wording of the inscription, which, as it stands, is not at all in harmony with the above analysis."[15]

Let us begin with Panofsky's text and construct its theoretical and methodological problematics. We note first of all that in a few short lines Panofsky brings about a precise correspondence between the (summary) description of the painting, its immediate affective impact on the viewer, and the formulation of the inner meaning of the work. Although perfectly distinct, the three stages are unified by a common trajectory that binds them together. It is here that the two questions—What does Arcadia signify? Just what does the wording of the inscription *Et in Arcadia ego* mean?—open up a problematic gap between the first two moments—the description of the painting and its effect—and the third—the intrinsic meaning of the work. Which amounts to asking: Was *the voice from that grave* (which the Arcadian shepherds seem to hear, and whose words the viewer "hears" in turn through his gaze, and which the art historian reformulates finally as "elegiac sentiment") an exact paraphrase-translation of the *inscription legible on the tomb?* For the voice of which Panofsky, along with the shepherds in Poussin's painting and along with ourselves as viewers of the painting, has been the spokesperson and the interpreter is a fictional voice that expresses itself in the mode of "as though . . . ," whereas the half-effaced inscription that it is supposed to be translating from the Latin is really written as an archaeological and documentary fragment—in the painting. This fragment, which makes the figures of the work "speak," which makes the viewer's gaze "hear," which causes "meaning" to become "fairly clear," according to the art historian, has the massive, unimpeachable self-evidence of the (represented) real. But by the same token, owing to its very self-evidence, it interrogates the too-easily acquired certainty about the meaning of the representation immediately conquered in the fiction of the voice of the figures, the spectator, and the historian.

We understand, then, why Poussin's painting, through the inscription it bears on an object that it represents, fascinates Panofsky: it is, as it were, the reduced model of a theory and a method of the "science" of art: it is at once the proposition and the experimentation of which the great 1939 essay, "Iconography and Iconology," will register and systematize the results.

We also understand how iconographical analysis, a form of expression whose documentary and writerly values must be emphasized, turns out to be required, so that it can fill—through its discourse, in which the theory-history of art is ultimately engulfed—the gap between the description of the painting (pre-iconographical level) and the interpretation of its inner meaning, of its intrinsic content (iconological level), for iconographical analysis alone can establish, justify, and legitimate, through its critical questioning, in the Kantian sense of the term, the immediate correspondence between description and interpretation, between the concrete experience of objects and events that allow their identification and expression in the pre-iconographical description and the synthetic intuition of its symbolic values.[16] Iconographical analysis, through the critical problematization it introduces and the responses it elicits, occupies, between the a priori assumptions of sensibility and the regulating ideas of reason, the field that is occupied in Kant's critiques by the schematism of the transcendental imagination, as it will be reinterpreted culturally and historically by Ernst Cassirer with the notion of symbolic form.[17] This explains Panofsky's somewhat mysterious allusion to a history of types, with reference to the philosophical problem posed by the expression *Et in Arcadia ego*. In the 1939 essay, the history of types constitutes what Panofsky calls the corrective principle of iconographical analysis: the analysis of images, narratives, allegories, the secondary or conventional subject matter of the work, in terms of themes and concepts.[18]

Iconographical analysis is the cognitive moment of the theory-history of art, and that is why this theory-history tends to be reduced to such analysis. It is the moment of understanding (in the Kantian sense of the term), the moment of knowledge ("knowledge of literary sources"), just as the history of types, which is the corrective, is the mediating moment of the episteme in a three-stage history of the tradition, where the first stage is a history of style and the last a history of symbols as cultural "symptoms." This analysis introduces the immediately acquired harmony between the experience of the gaze and the synthetic intuition of meaning, between sensibility and reason in the sphere of thought, of understanding, that is, of knowledge and familiarity, and it discovers or discloses the legitimation of that harmony. The gaze listens to the voice of meaning (icono-logy), but what is the signification of the graphy in the icon whose meaning the gaze seems immediately to understand in the fiction of a voice? What does Arcadia mean? What is that *ego* saying, the *ego* inscribed within the epitaph on the tomb, *Et in Arcadia ego?*

Now, it is the very position of this problematic, which we have just illuminated obliquely on the basis of Panofsky's theoretical and methodological text from 1939, that turns out to be displaced, twenty years later, when the author revisits his 1936 essay. Its point of departure is no longer the visual exemplification of "I, too, lived in Arcadia" by Poussin's painting in the Louvre, but the opposition between two translations of the Latin formula *Et in Arcadia ego*—"Death is even in Arcadia" and "I, too, was born, or lived, in Arcady"—two translations of which Panofsky, from the beginning, finds occurrences in literary texts or in documents relative to works of plastic art.[19] By the same token, not only has the "philological" problem been foregrounded in the essay, but it is specifically focused on the referential assignation of the *ego* in the formula: "I, Death," or "I, the dead person." This difference in translation or interpretation—in the philological, not the philosophical, sense of the term—is then "historicized": it is a matter of a change of interpretation—in the philosophical, not the philological sense this time—a change "of paramount importance for modern literature,"[20] about which it will be a matter of trying "to fix the ultimate responsibility for this change," in this instance "not on a man of letters but on a great painter."[21] I should add that Panofsky does not mention the painter's name, thus reinforcing the "suspense" of his inquiry.

It is remarkable that all direct contact with a particular painting is excluded from this introduction, which poses the questions and constructs the problematic of the essay. The reference to Sir Joshua Reynolds's double portrait of Mrs. Bouverie and Mrs. Crewe with which the text begins is only a pretext for quoting a conversation between Reynolds and Dr. Johnson. What is more, the essential material from the description of Poussin's *Arcadian Shepherds* reappears here, but as a paraphrase of what "Mrs. Felicia Hemans expressed in the immortal words: *I, too, shepherds, in Arcadia dwelt.* They conjure up the retrospective vision of an unsurpassable happiness, enjoyed in the past, unattainable ever after, yet enduringly alive in the memory: a bygone happiness ended by death."[22] After this, it is not surprising that philological analysis of the formula "Et in Arcadia ego" constitutes the theme of Panofsky's text:

> I shall try to show that this . . . rendering—"Death is even in Arcadia"—represents a grammatically correct, in fact the only grammatically correct, interpretation of the Latin phrase *Et in Arcadia ego*, and that our modern reading of its message—"I, too, was born, or lived, in Arcady"—is in reality a mistranslation . . . [that] did not come about by "pure ignorance," but, on the contrary, expressed and sanctioned, at the expense of grammar but in the interest of truth, a basic change in the interpretation.[23]

Not only has the iconographical analysis, in 1955, outstripped the description of the painting and its iconological interpretation, but it is also reduced to a philological effort of which the long study that follows on the theme of Arcadia throughout first Greek and Latin, then medieval and Renaissance bucolic literature supplies the historical base that finds its framework in the thesis on primitivism presented by Lovejoy and Boas.[24] The description of Poussin's painting and the synthetic intuition of its intrinsic meaning have disappeared from the text. Iconographical analysis, transformed into a study of historical philology, is paramount: it is the point of departure for the study, and this beginning is assimilated, in 1955, to what in 1936 constituted a foundation, the legitimation—in the Kantian critical sense—of an immediate correspondence between the description of a painting, its expressive effect, and the formulation of its intrinsic meaning. After this, iconographical analysis (and ultimately philology as a historical science) is what supplies the framework and the presuppositions not only for iconological interpretation but also for pre-iconographical description. Table 3, modeled on the one in Panofsky's 1939 essay, summarizes the foregoing remarks.

As we have known at least since Descartes, the order in which material is presented is not a matter simply of rhetoric or style. It has crucial theoretical and methodological effects on the definition of a problematic, on the position of the hypotheses, and perhaps even more on the content of the answers offered. We can observe this in reading the 1936 essay and the rewritten version dating from 1955. In the first instance, the perspective that informed the entire discussion of the theme of Arcadia, from Pausanias and Polybus to Theocritus, from Ovid and Virgil to Boccaccio and Tasso via Sannazzaro, was simply a return to an interpretation-description of Poussin's painting in the Louvre, but an interpretation-description now based on and legitimized by a movement of analytic regression characteristic of the Kantian critical approach (from a given to its transcendental possibility conditions) that all of Cassirer's work aimed to specify historically and culturally.[25] The 1939 essay, "Iconography and Iconology," had systematized this movement through direct reference to the philosopher of symbolic forms. In the 1955 study, however, the inquiry into the Arcadia theme, while it goes

TABLE 3. *Iconographical analysis and iconological interpretation*

Anticipation of the model (1936)	Theoretical and methodological model (1939)	Application of the model (1955)	
1. Pre-iconographical description	1. Pre-iconographical description	1. Iconographical analysis	
2. Iconological interpretation	2. Iconographical analysis	2. Pre-iconographical description	3. Iconological interpretation
3. Iconographical analysis	3. Iconological interpretation		

through the same stages in its evolution as those we saw in the 1936 text, ends up with the appearance of the formula *Et in Arcadia ego* in a painting by Guercino (1621– 1623). Since no reference has yet been made to Poussin's Louvre painting, and since in fact Poussin's name has not yet even been mentioned at this point in the revised text, Guercino's painting is of interest only in that it offers the formula for reading and thus for translation: it is a philological document, just as any passage by Sannazzaro or Virgil would be.[26] And this is indeed how Panofsky uses it: without any reference to the painting except for the expression *Et in Arcadia ego* that is inscribed in it, on the basis of its first attested occurrence, he raises the fundamental question of the entire essay: "What is the literal meaning of this expression?" And once the only grammatically correct translation, according to him, has been produced, Panofsky proceeds to offer a five-line description that confirms his translation. He appeared to be doing the same thing in the 1936 essay: "This interpretation is confirmed by a painting in which the canonical—although certainly non-classical—formula *Et in Arcadia ego* seems to appear for the first time," he wrote then.[27] But there Guercino's painting was not primarily a record confirming an occurrence. It was invoked to corroborate the translation proposed for the formula that appears in it and as a pendant contrasting with Poussin's *Arcadian Shepherds* in the Louvre,[28] whose (iconological) interpretation is taken up again, but this time in the name of a cultural history of symbolic forms:

> This brings us back to Poussin's picture in the Louvre. In it the sombre pathos of Tasso and the lingering melancholy of Sannazzaro have given way to an earnest though uncomplaining pensiveness, and this calm attitude is much in harmony both with the spirit of the new era that had overcome the struggles of the Counter-Reformation, and with the new style that had replaced the constraints and entanglements of Mannerism either with baroque richness and freedom or with classicistic dignity and equilibrium.[29]

Thus the essential displacement from 1936 to 1955 is the following: not only does the iconographical analysis change *function* in Panofsky's theoretical and historical work, while at the same time modifying the philosophical conception of the description and interpretation of the work of art in general, but also Panofsky's study itself comes to adopt a historical mode of exposition, if it does not take on a resolutely narrative turn. The philosophy of history and the aesthetic philosophy of symbolic forms that came from Cassirer—essentially the "historicizing and acculturating" of the schematicism of the transcendental imagination and the aesthetic judgment of taste in Kant's third *Critique*—have become an ordered narrative following the chronological axis of "before" and "after," a narrative that retraces an empirical history in terms of influences and contacts.

In the 1955 essay, let me stress the fact that Poussin's name has still not been mentioned on page sixteen of the twenty-four-page text. Poussin appears only in the last act of the study, coming on stage as an actor in the plot. "Poussin had come to Rome in 1624 or 1625, one or two years after Guercino had left."[30] The Louvre painting still has not been referred to, much less described, and the first Poussin painting that Panofsky intends to consider, a *chronologically* anterior work, will not be the Louvre's *Arcadian Shepherds* but rather the Chatsworth painting. At the beginning of part two of the 1936 essay, Panofsky argues, "the evolution which led from Guercino's Corsini picture to Poussin's Louvre painting gives us an insight into the mental processes of a great genius who . . . subconsciously conceives an entirely new idea while consciously keeping to a traditional formula."[31] In the 1955 study, in contrast, Poussin's invention—that is, the decisive turning point marked by the Louvre painting in the *philological* history of *Et in Arcadia ego*—is *explained* by the historical context, the spirit of the moment, and the principles of "Arcadian" literature. The description of the painting produced in some ten lines (a weaker version of the one that opened the 1936 study) has the sole *function* of showing that one of the two possible translations ("I, too, lived in Arcadia") is a philological misconstruction, but that it accurately reflects the meaning of the composition. Whereas in 1936 the seventeenth-century translation offered in Félibien's *Entretiens* is said to expose the intrinsic meaning of the work—the meaning that the viewer had grasped at the outset through synthetic intuition while contemplating the painting in the Louvre, which meant that the entire iconographical analysis had founded and legitimated the immediate iconological interpretation—in the 1955 essay the very expression of the work's intrinsic meaning gives way to the expression of its "new meaning." Thus we have arrived at a paradox: the 1955 essay concludes precisely where the 1936 essay defined its starting point for a crucial development, both for the study of Poussin's work and for Poussin's philosophical and aesthetic posterity in Watteau.

What the 1955 essay aims to do, with the help of a philological argument related to the attested and contrasting translations of the expression *Et in Arcadio ego*, is to write the narrative of a history of a genre in literature and in painting, precisely the legend (*legendum*) of the elegiac tradition, and the iconological interpretation of a given work is reduced to this history of a genre. What the 1936 study sought to grasp was entirely different: it aimed to construct the transcendental conditions of historical possibility for apprehending the immanent meaning of a work of art. Or, to borrow the terms of the 1939 "Iconography and Iconology," in 1936 Panofksy was seeking to show how an essential tendency of the human spirit (in Kantian language, the play in the imagination of an a priori sensibility and of an idea of reason, in this instance the sense of time and the idea of happy immortality) came to be historically expressed in variable historical conditions by specific themes and concepts recognized by a history of symbolic forms. That is why, in 1936, the study of the theme *Et in Arcadia ego* on the basis of Poussin's *Arcadian Shepherds* (Louvre) was undertaken as part of Panofsky's inquiry into the metaphysical principle that had allowed Poussin to reconcile the transitory character of life with the happiness of its indestructible beauty. That is why that inquiry was carried out at the time, all too briefly on the formal level ("the formal qualities of Poussin's style")[32] and, on the iconographical level, by the study of the notions of metamorphosis and rhythm, of which the *Kingdom of Flora* (1631, Dresden) was the most remarkable example.

This accounts, too, for part three of the text, the part devoted to Watteau. In 1936, Panofsky viewed the latter's *Fêtes champêtres* as the historically and aesthetically accomplished expression of the Poussinian "metamorphosis." One has only to compare the concluding paragraph of the 1955 essay, which is programmatic, to be sure, but of exceptional quality. Fragonard has replaced Watteau, in an eight-line evocation of an admirable bistre wash drawing by Albertina:[33] "Two cupids, probably spirits of departed lovers, clasped in an embrace within a broken sarcophagus while other, smaller cupids flutter about and a friendly genius illuminates the scene with the light of a nuptial torch." Panofsky adds: "Here the development has run full cycle. To Guercino's 'Even in Arcady there is death,' Fragonard's drawing replies: 'Even in death, there may be Arcady.'"[34] This is an elegant, brilliant conclusion in which I cannot help hearing the attenuated echo, twenty years later, of the voice from beyond the grave of which Panofsky had been the spokesperson in 1936, with respect to the Louvre's *Arcadian Shepherds*, at the beginning of his essay on the transitory in Poussin and Watteau. However, that essay concludes with *Gilles*, "a lonely figure emerging abruptly from the emotions and fluctuations of common life which he denies and leaves behind, facing the only non-transient reality that he can accept, namely the void."[35] And

Panofsky ends with a personal revelation that, to paraphrase his own earlier reference to Poussin, allows us to glimpse the subconscious mental processes of a mind of exceptional penetration beneath the conscious formulae of traditional knowledge. In its way, this revelation completes the cycle of inquiry initiated with Poussin's shepherds meditating on the inscription *Et in Arcadia ego* engraved on a tomb: "I cannot help feeling that the very face of Gilles shows a strange resemblance to Watteau's own features as interpreted by himself in an earlier drawing; but even if 'Gilles' need not be called a self-portrait, he is certainly a self-revelation."[36]

Here is an unconscious intuition on the part of the meditative gaze; the text that is coming to a conclusion bears its implicit trace in the blank space where it dies away, where the philological inquiry has twice run aground, in 1936 as in 1955, because the instruments of philology do not allow it to reply to the impertinent question: Who is *ego*, inscribing its name on a tomb? Gilles is not facing the void, he is facing the painter who is painting him, just as Watteau's self-portrait is looking at him: *ego*, I, functioning like the three letters, EGO, that Poussin paints on the wall of the sarcophagus, assigning him to the place of painting himself when he paints them, and they assign me, a viewer, as well, when I read them thus iconographized on the canvas. Yes, to be sure, even in Death, Arcadia can be, as Fragonard's wash drawing "says," I, the dead painter in the painted tomb; I, in the utopian happiness of painting, Arcadia.[37]

§ 5 The Classical Sublime

"Tempests" in Some Landscapes by Poussin

The classical sublime, or tempests in some landscapes by Poussin: here is a theme that invites tendentious observations. I shall first focus on the notion of the sublime, which has most often been approached in the historical, cultural, and aesthetic context of Romanticism, especially when landscapes are at issue; by the same token, this notion has often been called into question in relation to classicism, and to Poussin in particular. Then I shall turn to the notion of landscape generally and of landscape in painting, where the rich ambiguities of the semantics of the term are prolonged and projected but also refracted through the historical, social, cultural, and aesthetic milieus and fields that they traverse.[1]

In keeping with the time-honored philosophical and rhetorical tradition, I shall posit the sublime as the unrepresentable of representation, an unrepresentable aspect that defines neither the outside of representation nor even a blind spot that would hollow out its center; rather, it results from the very operation of representation, from its panic or its exuberance. Understood in this way, the sublime is representation at its apogee: that is, in one of the precise senses of the term, "that which stands above the edges of an already-full measure." This sublime is the "almost too much" (the expression is Kantian) of representation, its internal excess.[2]

To say that the sublime is unrepresentable is to signify that it will be representable, or more precisely, assignable (put into signs or summoned up in signs), only through its effects. The approach to the sublime can only be pragmatic, and the pragmatics of the sublime will be primarily and essentially a pathetics. The sublime effect is affect; some would call it the encounter with the "real." The pathetics of the sublime does not derive, then, from a treatise on the passions; it does not take its place, its space, from a typology of the passions; rather, the pathetics of the sublime provides the foundation or the generative structure for a theory of the passions. The sublime effect is the pathos of two "ideas" in the Kantian sense, the idea of death and the idea of violence. Every mechanism of representation ensures mastery of these two ideas by *delimiting* and circumscribing the shapeless indeterminacy of the former and the absolute totalization of the latter, through the return of the absent and through the power without alterity that is lodged in the imaginary. In representation itself, the affect-effect of the sublime is the pathetic presentation of death and violence under two aspects (which are elaborated in the texts of the Second Sophistic and of middle Stoicism):[3] stupefaction through astonishment and the ostentatious display evoked by two fabulous figures. The Medusa and the Monster: each names a space of figuration in texts and images, a schematism productive of schemas, that is, of tropes and figures.

The tempest is one of the elementary figures of the sublime: lightning and thunder, blinding flash and deafening roar, cataract, flood, endless falling, but also whirlwind, cyclone, or tornado, in which primitive elements, classes of beings, fundamental categories reach the height of their senseless churning through the exacerbation of their difference. The tempest: a Medusa, a meteor as fascinating as it is ostentatious, as stupefying as it is monstrous.

Tempests, cosmic meteors, lead us naturally, as it were, to landscapes, to representations of landscapes in painting, to representations of tempests in representations of landscapes, in particular in Poussin's landscapes.

Hence three further observations:

The landscape in painting was constituted as an established and recognized genre during the Renaissance. I shall be concerned here only with this genre, with landscape as an aesthetic and artistic institution. The emergence of the genre and the institution is not merely a historical event, not simply the dated and situated avatar of backgrounds in paintings. It is also rooted in theoretical configurations—themselves historically dated and geographically situated—involving the arts in general, the painting, sculpture, and architecture in particular, that were developing at the same moment in time.[4] Others have commented on the growing importance of representations of natural and cultural space in the background of fifteenth-century paintings; such representations came to absorb even mythological, historical, and religious "subjects"; Lott and Altdorfer point to the appearance of landscape paintings without even the pretext of a designatable "subject."[5] But landscape really became a genre around the middle of the sixteenth century, and the painter became a specialist producing for an open market of clients, serious collectors or amateurs, especially in northern Europe.[6] Still, it was in Venice that the term "landscape" (*paesaggio*) came into use, as early as 1521, to designate a painting by Marc-Antoine Michiel and also—and doubtless not by accident—to refer to Giorgione's *Tempesta*: "a little landscape [*paesetto*] on canvas with a storm, a gypsy, and a soldier."[7] The birth of landscape as a genre seems to be bound up with a more general autonomization of art as a free and disinterested sphere of creative activity.

Thus the landscape *genre* finds its aesthetic conditions of possibility in *general* artistic theories, even as it responds historically and culturally to a widely shared taste for painting that does not illustrate religious, historical, or mythological narratives or rituals of devotional piety. Still, and by that very token, the advent of an institutional and instituted landscape genre ensures that this genre will take its place within a hierarchy of genres in painting. The landscape, a form of art pleasing to the sensitive eye, cannot help but contrast with the "great art" that speaks to understanding and leads to contemplation, to religious or philosophical "theory"; it cannot help but occupy an inferior position in the hierarchy corresponding to the specific requirements of the social groups concerned with art.[8]

I have no intention of rewriting the history of the development of the genre, even schematically. The basic landmarks of this history can be found in Gombrich. Let me simply note that in the interpretation of Barbaro's Vitruvius and in Perrault's interpretation of other sixteenth- and seventeenth-century landscapes, the genre itself is subdivided into categories corresponding to the three hierarchically ranked stage decors: the tragic, the comic, and the satyric.[9] This schema might serve as a guiding thread for reading chapter 66 of book 6 of Lomazzo's *Trattato dell'arte* (1585), for example—a work that Poussin knew well. It offers at least six new subdivisions of the genre that Poussin, Claude, Salvator Rosa, Magnasco, the great Dutch landscapists, the Flemish genre painters, and others will exploit (or in which, at any rate, the discourse of art history and criticism will situate them).[10] From this perspective, Poussin, the paradigm, the model painter and the model theorist of painting, finds himself at the problematic intersection of a "sublation" of landscape painting and its genre with the major genre of "historical" representation, on the one hand, and of what brings representation in painting to its apogee, on the other hand: the effect of sublimity, that is, the presentation of something unrepresentable. Poussin found the notion of the unrepresentable in Leonardo's *Treatise on Painting* and, beyond the Italian masters, in Pliny's *Natural History.*[11] Pliny declared that Apelles, the mythical master of all painting, knew how to represent the unrepresentable—for example, thunder and lightning: in a word, *tempests.*[12]

I do not propose to write the history of this sublation of the landscape in Poussin's work, or the history of the effect of sublimity *within* the history of this sublation. The first calls into question all history and sociology of genres, publics, markets for painting, and the ideologies that subtend them; but it may also be the case that the second makes it possible, if not to respond to the first, at least to open up the field of a potential response.[13] Thus I propose to speak of the representation of tempests in Poussin's landscapes. A study of Giorgione's *Tempesta* was the starting point for my investigation; in another study focusing on Poussin's great *Landscape with Pyramus and Thisbe* (Frankfurt; see Figure 10), I have pursued the topic in somewhat greater depth (see chapter 3 in this volume).[14] The latter study enabled me to observe how the figure of the tempest, in its pathetic effect, presents the sublime, but at the same time I could also see how the sublime, pulling back from the figure that represents it, opens up a difference or a variation that is the very condition of its presentation. Poussin's landscape in the Frankfurt museum presents the pathetic—human and animal—of the cosmic tempest, but it is also the mirror of still water at the center of the landscape, the symbolic eye of the painter-subject who, figuratively showing us his contemplative apathy, is, as it were, the mysterious wellspring productive of pathos that overwhelms the rest of the painting. The sublime is played out in the place of the figure that represents it and by the space of its difference from that figure itself within which it withdraws.

To introduce the next phase of my study of Poussin's tempests, here is a text by the pseudo-Longinus: the "definition" of the sublime that inaugurates his treatise is a "definition" in which one can look beyond the image and perceive the play or schematism of figurative variation:

> What is beyond nature drives the audience not to persuasion, but to ecstasy. What is wonderful, with its stunning power, prevails everywhere over that which aims merely at persuasion and at gracefulness. The ability to be persuaded lies in us, but what is wonderful has a capability and force which, unable to be fought, take a position high over every member of the audience [*or viewer of a painting*]. Experience in originality, and arrangement and "economy" are not things we see from one or two passages, but we see them appearing gradually from the whole web of speeches and writings; and sublimity, brought out at just the right moment, makes everything different [traces difference in everything], like lightning, and directly shows the "all-at-once" capacity of the speaker [*or the painter*].[15]

We shall also look at a descriptive text by Félibien and at some paintings by Poussin that confront the question of the sublime and its pathetic effects in the classical landscape.

We read in Félibien's eighth *entretien*: "The following year [1651],

Poussin painted . . . two landscapes for M. Pointel, one representing a storm and the other calm and peaceful weather: they are in Lyon, at the home of M. Bay Marchand."[16] Thus the two paintings constitute a pair and an opposition: on the one hand, one of the paintings represents a tempest, the figure of the sublime; on the other hand, in the schematism of variation, *the two together*, as a pair, *present* the *unrepresentable* of representation, the sublime.[17] Thus the single tempest of the *Landscape with Pyramus and Thisbe* has become the *subjectless pair* of *Landscape—A Storm* and *Landscape—A Calm (see Figures* 8 and 9).[18]

In the same way, whereas the painting and its description, its *ekphrasis*,[19] had been exchanged between Poussin's brush and his pen, between the painting and a letter he had written to J. Stella,[20] the two paintings that he did as a pair a year later are given a double description by the theorist and critic Félibien, in his fifth *entretien*.[21] We accompany Félibien and his interlocutor Pymandre on a walk in Meudon, onto the terrace of the castle at Saint-Cloud and into the castle itself, as we read the account of a storm that arose suddenly during fine weather. Here is the description of two landscapes that are moments in "real" nature, subjects of two paintings by Poussin:

> Several days had passed since our last conversation in the Tuileries, when we left Paris to go walking in Saint-Cloud. When we arrived at the magnificent palace, where Monsieur, the King's brother, has allied the riches of Art with the beauties of Nature, we went down into the gardens whose beds, enameled with a delightful variety of all sorts of flowers, were still embellished and perfumed with Myrtle, Jasmine, and Orange trees, which by the beauty of their leaves, flowers, and fruits surpassed the richest compositions of emeralds, gold, and silver.[22]

The art of the landscape-garden is allied with the beauty of the Nature-landscape, but the latter surpasses the former.

Once the ground of the scene and its place—whose "reality" in the descriptive text is precisely measured by this excess—have been established, the writer proceeds to set up the point of view:

> We chose to sit down in a convenient place, from where we could see at the same time both the Seine, which snakes between the prairies, and the hills bordering the river. There were a few light clouds in the air; their shadow, spreading unevenly over the mountains and in the plain, created a situation where our sight found darker places to rest from time to time after a period of true delight in which silence reigned with so much sweetness that it was interrupted only by the sound of the fountains, whose waters we saw sparkling through the shade of the trees.[23]

The viewer's vantage point, situated high up,[24] is chosen so that the natural landscape is composed into a panorama in the complex unity of its variety: river, prairies, hills. A single time frame, that of simultaneous presence, governs the contemplation of the things that coexist in the space whose depth is ensured by the "snake" of the Seine,[25] an aerial space of play for the light and shadow that punctuate the trajectory of vision with tension and repose, in the unified presentation of a single gaze posed in a place that is all the more convenient for offering an overview. And the silence, scarcely interrupted by the sound of the fountains, is noted by the descriptive eye only as the sonorous echo of the water's luminous flashes in the shade of the wooded groves and thickets.

The viewer takes the place, occupies the place, of the painter,[26] and the writing he produces in that place to express the place in words has no function except to construct the "subject" of the painting that he *could* paint there. But it is a painting that would be contemplated before it is painted, unless through his description, in which the "reality" of the natural spectacle is constituted textually, the writer, as a professional viewer, art critic, and theorist of painting, can identify himself as a writer only by identifying himself with the painter, and unless the descriptive text, embedded in the account of a walk in Saint-Cloud, can be read as a "description" only if it is identified with a possible painted picture that it presupposes. Here, on the spot, we grasp a feature that Gombrich rightly emphasized: perceived nature becomes a "natural landscape" only because art has constituted a visual symbol that singularizes and expresses it.[27]

Ekphrasis, the painter-writer's "experimental" mechanism, aims to show the picture in the text, the picture as text, and to formulate the theoretical propositions on which the painter bases his painting; thus it is not surprising that the dialogue between the two friends is initiated, *within* the written spectacle, by an interrogation of the pictural *Mimesis*: "Are you not admitting to me," says Pymandre, "that in seeing Nature in her beauty as she is today, it would be difficult not to prefer her to the most beautiful things painting can do; and that paintings, however excellent they may be, appear as nothing next to as delightful a landscape as the one we see before us? . . . Painting, however excellent it may be (through its work) must yield to Nature as the disciple to his Master, and the copy to the original."[28] What is the reason for this limitation, then? To answer the question, Félibien goes on to list the problems the painter encounters: the use of black and white to represent light and shadow and to depict something like the roundness seen in Nature; the perception of the painting and its figures represented on a flat surface; the nature and use of colors, a topic that takes up most of the rest of the conversation, which is punctuated with drawings and schemas destined to illuminate the painter's demonstrations and theorems.

> "And that is why painters must not be ignorant of optics, which lets them see according to definite rules why and how objects change upon sight or appear in different ways. M. Poussin was not unaware of this. . . . There is a painting at the home of M. Stella in which, in a landscape, Poussin has painted Moses exposed upon the waters. Here is where you can recognize in how learned a manner he treated the reflections." [Pymandre interrupts:] "It is true that nothing is more delightful than such paintings, where one sees waters that represent the objects that surround them, as in a mirror, because these are charming images of what Nature herself makes, when she paints the sky and the earth on clear and tranquil waters."[29]

Starting with the initial description of a peaceful landscape (but also with an indication of how the theory was constructed), the demonstration is completed here with theorems about reflections and mirrors. For by representing the reflection of the object in calm water, a painted object in a painted mirror, the painting represents pictorial representation itself, just as Nature itself becomes the natural Art of painting by offering to the gaze the same play of appearance in the "reality" of its spectacle. By representing the representation of natural things, Nature reflexively attains a sort of natural self-consciousness, a natural art that the painter attains in turn as artist-nature by representing the process of representation in the mirror of his painting. With the equivalency of the processes of reflection thus established, the excess of Nature over Art theoretically absorbs the deficiency of Art with respect to Nature in a double parallelism. For the lack to be represented, the lack that characterizes the pictorial mimesis with respect to the representation of the natural object, is *in* Nature itself: Art and Nature *are* equal here. "It is further necessary," observes Félibien, "to note that the things one sees in water by reflection never appear as marked as they are in the natural state, because the light and colors are weakened by the reflection; this is still more true for the parts most distant from the true things than for the ones that are near them."[30] Thus it is perhaps not by chance that Pymandre can evoke the lake of Bolsena, whose calm surface is assumed to be depicted in the center of most of Poussin's great landscapes with figures: "I have seen nothing that has attracted my eyes with more pleasure on the roads of Italy than the lake of Bolsena: it appeared to me as an ice crystal of marvelous size, through which I thought I saw another sky, mountains and hills opposing those which were there around the lake."[31]

And the storm arises precisely in the middle of these observations devoted to reflection and the mirror by the describer-writer and theorist. A second *ekphrasis* reverses the one that had opened the conversation; in a matter of moments, a second description compromises the first and its conclusions, through the irruption of an unrepresentable element. Can there be a representation of Nature's sublime that is itself a sublime painting? "We were occupied with these observations when we heard a loud noise from the direction of the château." The second description begins where the first left off, with a violent noise instead of silence: the commotion takes the interlocutors by surprise.[32] It is hard to suppose that the rumbling could be produced by the air, "since the sky was very calm and there was no appearance of bad weather."[33] The *quiete* is pregnant with the *tempesta* that threatens it, but invisibly: the interlocutors hear only the repeated rumbling whose cause must be sought. On the one hand, then, we have the stable and convenient place of the overall vantage point, chosen so that Nature can deploy in depth the space in which things arrange themselves in the punctuating play of sunshine and shadow; on the other hand, we have the uneasy move to discover the cause of an inexplicable sonic effect in a calm sky: "Having approached the broad terrace, . . . we noticed a very thick cloud, spread out like a black sail, that was approaching us from the direction of Meudon."[34] From the vanishing point on the horizon, a nocturnal sail was approaching to double the luminous canvas of the painting on the scale of the approach of the gaze to the viewing point: the black of the shadows was invading the white of universal daylight, bringing the threat of "a storm that was not very far off."

And this is how the sublime of the tempest erupts amid the beauty of the gentle, colorful arrangement of the painting, in the modulations and harmonies of its nuances, sowing disorder throughout. And this is how M. Poussin got the idea of pairing *Landscape—A Calm* with its pendant, *Landscape—A Storm.* How can the beauty of the order of Nature, unsurpassable by the Art of painting, in one mysterious instance become the sublimity of its unrepresentable disorder? The tempest is at once a natural challenge and a provocation to paint—but to paint a Janus-picture, two paintings, front and back, beauty and sublimity, a sudden metamorphosis. The artist will take up the challenge of painting this "antithesis." But from what place?

The tempest is a sudden instant and it is a process, an "all at once" and the duration of a change. The painter-writer's precise description organizes the syntax of its discourse so as to open the pathways of the gesture of painting—unless, in so doing, he simply describes the syntax of a possible painting.[35]

The shock of a commotion, and the uneasiness of the search for its cause: a movement of approach, begun twice over, toward the point of view on the basis of the multiplicity of a gaze:

> Having approached the broad terrace that is almost at the river's edge, we noticed a very thick cloud, spread out like a black sail, that was approaching us from the direction of Meudon; and its form and blackness brought the threat of a storm that was not far off. Indeed, having moved forward so we could tell what side it was on, we saw that lightning flashes were already coming from the large cloud, and rain was beginning to fall in some distant spots; the air was so dark that it was impossible to see anything else. While we were watching the cloud burst open on one side, we admired the various effects that the lightning brought into view in the part of the earth that was covered in darkness, and the way bodies are illuminated in such moments.[36]

The second phase begins here. Having come too close, so he will be in a better position to see, to understand, and to admire, the painter-writer is caught by the storm. "*During that time . . . all at once* the sky changed and . . . clouds gathered from all sides; the sky was overcast *in an instant.* A furious wind blew *at the same time,* stirring up whirlwinds of dust and so disturbing the air that one could scarcely see either the sky or the earth."[37] During the time spent in contemplation, the simultaneous and immediate instant of cloud, wind, and dust storms bursts forth at the place of the gaze. It is a pure and sudden moment of the unrepresentable, since the eye that had been admiring *from afar* is in an instant the eye of the hurricane. The only thing perceived in this blackness, in the light of the darkness that immobilizes and blinds, is the dazzling flash of lightning.

Now for the *third phase* of the storm and its gaze: the describing eye retreats to the château, not so as to hide there but so as to take up a position at a window: once more it finds a convenient place for the theoretical view and a frame for its contemplation. Resting there, it considers the storm's violence and its disorder—*suave mari magno.*[38] From its order of reason, the eye contemplates, (de)scribes, writes. The painting of the storm is complete, and it is "almost" that of M. Poussin. Thus Pymandre evokes the painter by approaching the place of the scriptor eye, by coming as close as possible to the eye of the painter: "Do you not believe," he inquires of Félibien, "that it was in such an encounter that M. Poussin made the plan for the painting that you showed me, some time ago, in which he represented a storm almost comparable to this one? and gave reason for admiring him no less than people admired Apelles once upon a time; since both of them, having so well painted these sorts of subjects, can be said to have imitated perfectly things that are not imitable?"[39] Through the evocation of Apelles, which I have already mentioned, we encounter the design of the painter's picture, and we find that it is virtually identified with the design of the writer's description. The former equals the latter because the latter was already the former and because the natural "reality" of the tempest is equally shared between the written text and the painted picture. And this is how things that are not imitable come to be perfectly imitated and how a common admiration grips the reader of the description of the tempest and the viewer of the painting of *Landscape—A Storm.*

Thus the theorist can experiment with formulating the theorems of the sublime in landscape painting, although these theorems will never articulate anything but the breakdown of theory. *The first theorem* has to do with an equivalent parallelism. The discourse comprehends the cause, and the image imitates the effect; however, the equivalence in question is that of a double defect. To provide a rational explanation for these prodigious effects of Nature by exposing their cause is at least as difficult as to imitate the visible effects of Nature's efforts on the canvas. If painting is defined as "an imitation on some surface with lines and colors of everything that one sees under the sun," if "its end is to please," and if "nothing is visible without light, . . . without a transparent medium, . . . without boundaries, . . . without color, . . . without distance . . . [and] without instruments," how can the visible effects of a tempest be represented?[40]

The second theorem is a simple empirical observation: if the painter succeeds in imitating these effects, that is, these prompt and transitory actions, the "suddenness" of the irruption of the sublime, then he accomplishes a miracle of art as aleatory and isolated as the sublime itself. In other words, one may only observe that a painted picture corresponds feature for feature to Nature's sublime, the one and the other being incommensurable in their double incommensurability! "Thus the cleverest ones do not often risk themselves upon such enterprises. Those who are particularly attached to copying Nature well have sought some favorable accidents, by means of which, while representing only a part of what appears most beautiful and most extraordinary, they could proceed in such a way that one would judge the rest to advantage, guessing at what is not seen there."[41]

The third theorem contradicts the very definition of painting, in a way: painting of the sublime is painting that shows the invisible, presenting it to be seen *by divination*. This accounts for certain paintings by the Master, Poussin.

Let us return to the two paintings whose pairings constitute a picture of difference itself, *Landscape—A Calm* and *Landscape—A Storm*, to (de)scribe and read the second as the antithetical transformation of the first: How does the beautiful suddenly turn into the sublime?

Still, to do this, it is not enough to expose the paintings one part at a time, whether the parts in question belong to the picture or to the painting process; whether we are considering figures, levels of represented space, architecture, or inventions, compositions, distributions of light and shadow, manners of painting and modes of expression, there still has to be, between the two paintings, beyond the identical format of the two canvases, an element that permits the transformation and operates the displacement of the one into the other, its metaphor, up to the overturning that initiates and authorizes this process to which the movement of the reader-spectator's gaze responds.[42]

Landscape—A Calm might appear as an illustration of the theory of reflections expounded in Félibien's fifth *entretien*. The deep blue of the lake that occupies the entire second level of the painting reflects, according to the rigorous laws of catoptrics and according to the subtler laws of light in painting, not only the vast edifice that occupies the central position in the upper half of the canvas, but also the farm on the left and the herd of cattle, not to mention the pale, faded blue of the sky, which finds in the depth of crystal-smooth water the occasion for the colored density that is so intense on its surface.

Landscape—A Calm might also illustrate the problems raised by the ordered distribution of shadow and light, especially with the figures that invest the rectangular geometry of the composition, and notably in the second frame constituted by the powerful tree on the left and the slender trunks of the two trees on the right. The horizontal lines of the lake's edges and the wall of the castle keep are articulated with the pathways and the incidental features of the terrain; these slice the whole space into parallel bands, from foreground to background. Far from disturbing the equilibrium, the zigzag of the pathway on the "forestage" of the canvas leads the gaze even more imperiously toward the mirror of still water in which the world pensively reflects itself on the scale of a smooth and, as it were, unified execution, "in such a way that if all these colors are combined to form a single nuance, gently united with one another, a harmony is formed as in music . . . it being true that there is so great a resemblance between musical tones and degrees of color that the fine arrangement that can be made of the latter creates as sweet a concert for the eye as a harmony of voices can be agreeable to the ear."[43]

Nevertheless, in this general harmoniousness, in this painting that reflects itself in itself, here and there a few dissonant elements emerge, a few figures stand out, if only to make the peaceful calm of the harmony perceptible to the ear. Where is the rider going on his brown horse, galloping off toward the left at the edge of the lake? What *impetus* is pushing him to abandon so abruptly the covered watering place where his companion on a white horse has stopped? What violence is carrying him away amid all this serenity?

Where does that dark cloud come from, rising toward the sky near the top of the painting, spreading out to the edge of the painted canvas? It is as if the steep mountain that occupies the background of the right-hand section is smoking like a volcano, smoking like the Sant'Angelo castle in the background of the *Landscape with Orpheus and Eurydice*, so similar in composition and "mood" to *Landscape—A Calm*.[44] What fire smolders in the depths of the mountain that irresistibly evokes the great rock on which the flute-playing shepherd giant, Polyphemus, is perched, or the steep rocks where Hercules flushed out Cacus, that other giant, from his cavern open to the gaze?[45] Where does that uneasy smoke-cloud come from, signaling the imminence of death in the immobile place of happiness, announcing the snake that Eurydice is already fleeing, the irreparable act of Eve seduced by the snake in the spring of the earthly Paradise, or at the very least a danger in the giant Orion's blindness to light as he heads toward the sun?[46] Could it be the fire from the mountain, and the cloud that is its sign, which the horseman *divines* and flees at a gallop? For anyone with the intuition to detect its early warning sign, the storm is announced and initiated in calm weather.

Let us displace our point of view from the convenient place from which we were contemplating the measured beauty of Nature reflected in the water of a lake. Let us move closer so we can see better: the *tempesta* is there, on the other side, already in its full violence, and the open fire we saw a moment ago is nothing now but the black veil of a storm, spread over the upper right-hand fourth of the painting. Here is what operates the painting's transformation into its double, its other. In the same place in the represented space, fire, smoke, and cloud have become cloud formations gathering from all over: a violent wind, a whirlwind of dust roiling the air so that now sky and earth can scarcely be seen. What was beginning over there finds the instant of its acme here: there, here, a single place on the canvas.

Here is where the narrative of the instantaneous metamorphosis, its description, can begin. In one painting, the peace of horizontal lines rhythmically punctuated by verticals reigned: the order of Nature in the landscape, the order of Art that reproduced the truth of the order of Nature with its architectures, volumes, and surfaces: order and measure, the repetition of a single standard for grandeur, the beauty of a cosmos in which each thing is in its place.

But there is an instantaneous change of viewpoint, an acceleration of lines toward the vanishing point in response to the spectator's approach to things: it seems as though the viewer is suddenly transported to the other side of the lake, placed in the lower right-hand corner of the canvas right up against the wall surrounding the garden of the noble dwelling; walls, buildings, and towers flee toward the rear of the painting up to the mountain perceived momentarily in the background of the landscape. And yet everything is suddenly *too* close to the eye, as if the architectural construct suddenly came into contact with it, along the same oblique line: the viewer is dazzled, in an effect of the lightning's light, which, unlike the light of the sun, does not offer things to contemplation but reveals them while reducing them to nothingness, the things and the gaze directed toward them as well, in the instantaneousness of its flash. The dwelling suddenly comes into view at the punctual limit of its disappearance, and all along the oblique line of the castle wall, bent over against the violent wind, the silhouettes of Félibien and his friend Pymandre are running toward shelter.[47]

The lake has disappeared. We are on its other shore; and at the lower edge of the painting, instead of the path where the herdsman was tending his goats, a crevice has opened up onto the depths of the earth: the rim is stable, to be sure, but it tilts toward the left; and below, there is the abyss, a nocturnal orchestra pit in which the strident sounds of the Phrygian mode resound.[48] On the ground, instead of a herd of cattle making its way toward the prairie on the right, an oxcart is in transit toward the left, struck at the moment the lightning bolt splits the tree from top to bottom and tears off two large branches, "which a violent wind bends over toward the ground." The two oxen, their muzzles in the dust, their front quarters bent down to the ground, are beasts at a sacrifice, and their driver is prostrate under the force of the lightning bolt: such is God's epiphany, in the great tree that has advanced, between one painting and the other, from the edge, where it framed a harmonious spectacle, to the first quadrant of the painting, where it serves as support structure for the demonstration of omnipotence. At the right, a man halts in flight, immobilized in a gesture of fright and adoration; another runs along the rising path, heading into the wind and the dust, covering his eyes with his hand, and the two small silhouettes whose shadows have been pinned to the castle wall by the lightning flashes have already almost reached the castle gate.

Here let us bring to light three operations of the process through which the representation of Nature's beauty is varied in the display of its sublimity. The first has to do with space and its construction, the second with time and its specific aspectualization, the third with what, for want of a better term, I shall call meaning and its interpretation.

(1) From one painting to the other, the structure of the space represented, the syntax of its places, is pathetically affected by a radical transformation. The cosmos of *Landscape—A Calm* is an order of places rigorously governed by the order of perspective: the prospect that is the office of reason achieves ascendancy over the aspect, which is the simple perception of the things represented.[49] Three levels are stacked up in the depth of the space to which the organization of the surface of the space of representation corresponds exactly. The viewing point and the vanishing point occupy the geometric center of the canvas; the line of the horizon divides the painting into two equal halves. The figures invest this geometrically rigorous architecture not so much to conceal it as to stress the regularity of its directions. A skillful composition of cubes and parallelopipeds occupies the painting's center, closing off any escape into the remote aerial reaches of the landscape. The unified surface of a lake precisely reflects the highest building on the central vertical axis of the painting; these two features seem to me to signify a "formatting" of space according to a stable and immobile order guaranteed and legitimized by natural reason speaking the language of mathematics. The controlled structure of this space of totalization unfailingly ensures the measured copresence of the places that compose it. The descriptive discourse will express this with a calm succession of declarative statements, "there is . . . ," "there are . . . ," while the mirroring surface of the lake ensures for this order of copresences the reflective dimension in which the

theoretical gaze finds its figure as representation. No movement comes to disturb this theoretical order: *Midi le juste.* Hence the importance, in this configuration, of the smoke-cloud that comes from the mountain to *cross* the sky, and the rider who is *carried away* toward the left on his galloping horse.

In the other configuration, everything changes. The order of places in *Landscape—A Calm* is instantaneously transgressed: the statements of copresence, "there is . . . ," "there are . . . ," are replaced by a nucleus generative of the represented space, through divergent processes of spatialization. This nucleus is situated in the lower right-hand corner of the painting in the form of two governing forces: one, strongly oblique and rising, runs along the buildings in the right-hand section and is lost as it is subdivided in the upper left-hand section; the other, almost horizontal, traverses the entire painting from right to left and produces the ground of the stage for the figures. These two processes, generative of diversive and broken spaces, are themselves thwarted—violently: first by marks, spread among all the figures, of the effects of a furious wind blowing from left to right, and then by the vertical force of the tree, an essential figure in the left-hand section of the painting, directly below the two oxen that have been struck down and the prostrate man; the tree supports the zigzag of the two lightning bolts. In this exploding space, the gaze no sooner alights in one spot than it moves on; it is a space of rapid processes, with divergent dynamic foyers whose place of resolution is figured by the man on his knees, his forehead touching the ground, his eyes blinded, his hands over his ears.[50]

(2) The time of *Landscape—A Calm* is the very time spent in contemplation of the painting that presents it to view: the temporal marks of what the painting represents coincide with and are consonant with the specific time of the "theory" of representation, the time of beauty without past or future, the present of the copresence of the gaze and the copresences of the things painted in the order of their places. In aspectual terms, we find the same duration everywhere, at the moment of its accomplishment. These figurative marks are those of repose and stability: the architecture,

the lake and its reflections, the human and animal figures. There are no incidental events in which the contrasting times of a possible narrative might be reflected; a single present totalizes and stabilizes the temporal flow: the happiness of beauty, the happiness of contemplating the painting. This contemplation parallels, and is identified with, the picture of contemplation. The representation of representation as far as its reflection is pursued tends only to intensify a common presence. The supreme mark of this identification between theory and painting in the sovereign delight of the present is found in the even light of the sun in which beings and things bathe, each in its own stable place. There is no *accidental* illumination of things, but rather a common milieu of illumination in which the things painted take their proper place. The definition of painting is achieved here: an imitation on a surface with lines and colors of everything that one sees under the sun. The goal of painting is the pleasure of representation in the clarity of presence.

Here again, this is a way of stating the importance of the double dissonance. The figure of the galloping horse carrying its rider off toward the left—desire or fear, action, process—is in itself a mark of passion in which future and past are profiled beneath or beyond the present.[51] That figure and the accident of the open fire with its premonitory smoke rising across the sky constitute a double operator introducing variation into the calm weather through a break in the present and its representation.

The *storm* that results from the instantaneous metamorphosis of weather as well as of space shows an entirely different temporal regime. The space of dynamic and divergent *processes*, its temporal aspect is nevertheless still the present, but it is the punctual present of the instantaneous, which, far from totalizing the flow of duration, fragments it, divides it so as to *reduce* the present and *dissipate* it in the infinitesimal instant of the "sudden." The "now" of calm weather has become the "suddenly" of storm, an unthinkable, unrepresentable dimension, since it is the pure emergence of an accident-event with no beginning or end. The instant as instantaneousness is an incommensurable element of which only the *effects* can be grasped, with no possibility of representing their cause.

Writes Félibien: "Not all prompt and transitory actions are favorable to painters: and when someone succeeds with them, the things he does are so many miracles of his art."[52] Here again are two re-markings of the effects of the irruption of the sublime: the first, that of light as instantaneous fulguration of the lightning flash. Lightning's light does not in fact illuminate in the luminous diaphanous so as to *present* forms in their proper size and their exact distance *to view*, but it captures them simultaneously up close and far away; the processes are immobilized in "states of action," which exceed them by default, as it were. The second re-marking of the instant of the storm is the expression of the emotional affects that correspond to it in the figures: terror before the horror that nails the onlooker in place, immobilized flight, senseless blindness.

Nevertheless, in the painting, for the gaze that contemplates its representation and its effects, the lightning never stops striking. Such is the irrepresentable of the sublime of the tempest, in the final analysis. The sublime will always and necessarily exceed its contemplation. The equivalence of the time of the represented and the time of representation in the present of contemplation, through which the delight of beauty is accomplished, is broken forever by the representation of the effects of the sublime, because the instantaneous instant of its emergence—which, by a miracle of his art, the painter succeeds in grasping in its effects—is *incommensurable* with the present of the gaze that contemplates it in its inscription on the canvas. And it is this incommensurability that constitutes, paradoxically, the sublime in painting. The sublime is the impossibility of a theory of the sublime, the display or "monstration" of its impossibility.

(3) This is why the eye of the sage/painter can never be situated except in the interval between *Landscape—A Calm* and *Landscape—A Storm*, in the double margin of the two paintings, where the happiness of beauty under threat and the terror of the emerging sublime are exposed, between the dreaming, contemplative goatherd and the prostrate cowherd, forced to the ground by sacred terror. This would be the third operation that takes place between one painting and the other, the operation of meaning and

interpretation. But this one would require a third term for its accomplishment: the painter in the place where it is carried out, painting the two pictures as a pair—an antithesis. He would be situated in the place of differentiation *itself*, a place that cannot be occupied by a painter's eye. A failure of meaning, then, a lack of theory, but a failure that the antithetical pair, by filling in the contraries, reveals as such: the end of meaning and interpretation. The gaze of the sage/painter *does not alight* in the non-place of the interval: it *traverses* it, it is in transit there. The beauty of calm weather is not transformed into the sublimity of a tempest. We encounter neither transformation nor metaphor, but a schema of variation: *Landscape—A Storm*, in its sublimity, deviates from *Landscape—A Calm*, but the deviation can never be measured. What, indeed, would the measuring unit be?

To put it differently, the painter's eye (and with it the eye of the [de]scribe[r]) will never look at the storm except from the calm place of serene weather, and it will never capture the effects on the other canvas except to re-mark the trace of the instantaneous deviation through which the landscape of the storm is situated at an infinite distance from that of the calm landscape, even as that eye divines in the beauty of the landscape it is contemplating the premonitory signs, always present perhaps in happiness, of the horror of the sublime.

That is why in the *Landscape with Pyramus and Thisbe*, where the tempest breaks out in the heavens and on earth, in nature, animals, and men, the eye of the sage, the eye of the painter, will not hesitate to inscribe—at the price of a major inconsistency in which propriety, appropriateness, and verisimilitude collapse—the figure of theory: the figure of the theoretical apathy of its own gaze in the fiction of a lake whose waters reflect, unchanged, the disrupted things that surround it. In this inconsistency, representation is transgressed in its axiomatic principles, but in it, too, the flaw in all theory, in all contemplation, is *shown*, the flaw that is the sublime itself, its excess in the art of painting.[53]

PART II

"Great Theory and Practice Allied"

§ 6 Fragments of a Walk through Poussin's Ruins

We read in Vitruvius that one of the three modes of representation in architecture is ichnography: the design of the project, or the geometric rendering of the building. Design, plan (*dessin, dessein*): the graphic mark, the writing or inscription on the architect's sheet of paper, is the basis for his project, for the construction to come that will be erected on the ground thus marked out, at the origin. In his annotated translation of Vitruvius, Perrault explains the etymology of the term "ichnography": it comes from the Greek *ichnos*, print. The outline on the ground at the surface level is nothing but the trace that would be left by the building if it were to be destroyed by time, by the violence of meteors or men. The design, the preliminary drawing of the construction project, is *its* ruin. In this perfect structural equivalence, past and future are telescoped, origin and end are canceled out, though only if time, nature, or men push their frenzy to its peak and do not allow the slightest wall or column to poke above the surface, only if they do not leave the smallest stone standing on stone. The culmination is not negative but neutral: the trace of the wall, the print of the column, the mark of the stone as writing. The plan—the ichnography—is a proper ruin, proper to the ruin in which the rational design, the ordered structure, is revealed to the archaeologist's eye. Time in this structure of presence (or representation) hesitates between two directions: forward or backward flow, toward the origin or toward the end. Perhaps the same thing holds true for Poussin's painted ruins.

In "The Conception of Transience in Poussin and Watteau," a text published in 1936 in a festschrift for Ernst Cassirer, Erwin Panofsky evokes Poussin's representation of ruins; he compares them to certain Flemish works, noting that a ruin by Poussin is not really a ruin but a remainder, a present vestige of a past with all the "Romantic" or "picturesque" values of transience that the passage of time imports into the things it strikes. A ruin by Poussin is not a destroyed work of architecture whose remains are displayed in the painting. In the pride of its presence and not in the melancholy of duration, it is an idea of architecture, an essence presented in the form of a vestige. In order for the architectural object to assume this atemporal presence, it must at the same time show the marks through which it has ceased to be an object intended for use, show that it is no longer a building for worship, no longer a temple or a dwelling; it must display signs that it has shed its empirical and utilitarian character; it must show the negative marks of a temporal asceticism, signs that time, nature, men, and history have passed it by, have passed through it and in it, stripping it of its functional values in order to show its essential structure, its architectonic universality. A deconstructed architectural object, it reveals itself as a spiritual construction. The building is no longer a palace, the dwelling has been deserted by its inhabitants, the temple no longer shelters the divine statue, but the work shows itself in the power of its volumes and its lines of force, it reveals itself, because it is ruined, as an idea of pure beauty.

As one prepares to traverse this site, generalizing Panofsky's remark in a different language, one wonders whether Poussin's architectural ruins do not construct, do not "architecturize" the painted representations that present the ruins to the viewer's gaze, thus offering that gaze the pure pleasure of contemplation, giving it as a supplement of pleasure, sublimity, theory. One discovers in the "ruin" that the painting represents the metaphorical figure of the constructive power of a Poussinian representation. The same figure is at once a trace and a vestige of time's deconstruction of the human work and a constructive trace or outline, the matrix-structure of the work of the painter who assumes it. . . .

In the Dulwich Gallery, in London, one stops a moment, attentively, before *The Triumph of David.* At first sight, this is a magnificent historical painting. Having entered the scene of his triumph from the right, the young David advances toward the left, carrying Goliath's monstrous head impaled on a pole. Trumpets precede him, and soldiers with plumed helmets surround him; a soldier on a white horse follows him, between two rows of spectators who acclaim him as they discuss his exploit. These form garlands of women, men, and children in the foreground, at the bottom of the scene, and on the third level, on the temple's monumental base, between three colossal fluted columns, three groups of women and old folk are clustered. Here is a double scene of contemplation constructed by a powerful architectural mechanism and articulated in a plastic manner by the half-arch on the left, in the background, in the plan of the painting. Through this "construction" supported by the architecture it represents, the historical painting allows us to be present at the transformation of the narrative into discourse, the transformation of its story into praise of the event, or, to use the Greek terms, of *diagesis* into *epideixis.* The narrative of the confrontation between the enemy giant and the shepherd slips into collective memory through its remainder, the slingshot stone embedded in the severed head. The present parade creates the moment of memory, between the two registers of enthusiastic spectators—the lower register seen partially "from the back" and the higher, "frontal" one that the painter's skillful staging constructs in a specular face-to-face. But where, then, is the ruin? No doubt time is marked in the architecture of this scenography by the discreet fissures between the blocks of stone, by the accident that scores the marble with a splinter. Yet in the very foreground, in the lower left-hand corner of the canvas, we have a fragment-object whose implausible presence brings it to the attention of our gaze. The architect recognizes the detached cut stone as a piece from a toothed cornice that had fallen from an entablature hidden from view by the painting's frame. Standing in abstract, austere self-evidence, it has been overturned: a ruin-object, a figure of a figure that is in a way the matrix-sign of the construction of the painting by the "deconstruction" of an object that it represents. Through its position, with its six *modillons* lined up and pointing upward toward the six groups of spectators, three above, three below, emphasized by the constructed architecture of the double scene, the fragment, a metonymy for some ruined edifice, is a metaphor for the architectonics of representation and the instrument of its interpretation: the transformation of a historical narrative into a monument of memory. . . .

In *The Plague at Ashdod* (Louvre, 1630–1631; Figure 12), the architectural fragment seems to have an entirely different function, no longer architectonic but modal. It may be important to mention that, in two places in the painting, architecture becomes Music. Seventeen years later, on 24 November 1647, Poussin offered Chantelou a learned treatise on the various effects of the painting in the representation of "the subjects depicted. Our wise ancient Greeks, inventors of all beautiful things, found several Modes by means of which they produced marvellous effects. . . . " The variety of composition, Poussin continues, gave rise to "a certain difference of Mode," which in turn gave rise to the power to "arouse the soul of the spectator to various passions." Citing Giuseppe Zarlino's *Istituzione harmoniche* (1558), the master, addressing Chantelou, evokes various musical modes, including the Dorian and the Phrygian, the former "stable, grave, and severe," the latter "vehement, violent, . . . and capable of astonishing people." Architectonic orders of buildings, proportioned compositions of figures and colors, crafty modifications of voice in poetic speech, with modes and arts uniting to produce, each in its own specific field, an irresistible effect on anyone who is listening, reading, or contemplating—thus it is in *The Plague at Ashdod*, where the city struck by divine misfortune, with its buildings as decor, offers to the gaze its own monumental, religious, political, and civic history in which the history of ancient and modern architecture is summarized. But in this petrified history another history is staged, the event of punishment and death and its "marvellous effect," ex-

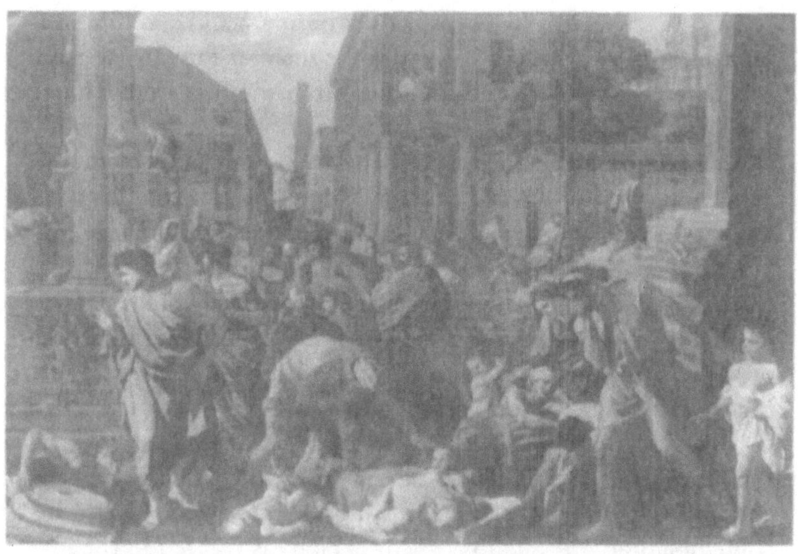

FIGURE 12. *The Plague at Ashdod.* Courtesy Photographie Giraudon.

treme, severe, violent terror: rotting corpses, dying bodies, terror and astonishment on the part of the living at the moment of death. The marble idol has collapsed, its head and one hand broken off, on the second level on the left. A rat makes its way under a bas-relief. In the foreground the dying are piled up, writhing, with the dead between the base of a Corinthian column that is on the ground and yet balanced unstably on the right and an overturned fluted shaft on which a figure of despair is leaning. Here is the music "of hard, rasping, harsh words." In the vehement fragmentation of a column, the ruin presents to the eye a singular tone; to the gaze, a specific mode; to the soul, the passion of the painting: the pathos of death and violence. . . .

Between Dresden and London, *The Adoration of the Magi* and *The Adoration of the Shepherds*: a single decor, a noble Roman ruin on which a wooden framework is articulated, reduced essentially to its laths, beams, and joists. We are in the time of Tiberius Caesar's reign, when the empire was at the height of its power, when

"Mary . . . gave birth to a son, her firstborn . . . and laid him in a manger because there was no room for them at the inn." Herod was tetrarch of Galilee and the Magi from the East were asking: "Where is the King of the Jews who has just been born?" In both stories, far from being the vestige of a past, the ruin anticipates the future of a present: the end of pagan Rome; and the wooden construction that is added on, "jerry-built," announces a different empire, that of the religion of the meek, that of the god of the disinherited, before whom all the powerful of the earth will kneel. The double decor of the ruin and the structure, respectively fashioned of stone and wood, expresses the exegetic figures of the subjects that the two paintings represent, Nativity and Epiphany; it is a figuration of their hermeneutic iconography under the aspect of time.

Through the present of a construction, the past as vestige of secular history is the future of sacred history. In the two works we are contemplating, the paradox of ichnography is realized in the image. Still, from one work to the other, Poussin modulates a variation that is not simply a feature of his stylistic evolution as a painter. In each case, the articulation between the ruin and the structure defines a layout that constructs the space of representation in the painting. In *The Adoration of the Magi*, this layout hollows out the plan toward a distance "figured" by three camels. The sign of this exotic flight is the shaft of an overturned column on the right, with its fluting aimed at that faraway place. We voyage into the space of the painting as the painter voyaged into the space of history. And all the agitation of the shift from the East to Galilee fades away with the movement of the figures in the foreground who are about to prostrate themselves before the child King, on the scale of the trajectory of the arrow of the gaze toward the temporal and spatial "beyond" of the horizon, launched by the pressing structure of the ruin. In *The Adoration of the Shepherds*, the layout of destroyed and constructed elements deploys the space in planes parallel to that of the painting. We see two right triangles upside down: the framework where *putti* are flitting around near the center, and the human figures on the right bending down toward the child-God. The far distances are framed by two Doric columns with cushion capitals and by a wooden beam, like a framed central canvas, from which two figures emerge facing the viewer's gaze, two shepherds who send the gaze back to itself at the same level, discreet pinnacles of a figurative pyramid that give the painting its solid vertical positioning.

. . . *St. Matthew and the Angel* (Berlin), *St. John the Evangelist on Patmos* (Chicago). A moment ago, in defiance of the history of art and styles, of the chronicle of moments and periods, I suggested pairing *The Adoration of the Magi* (Dresden) with *The Adoration of the Shepherds* (London), as paintings of ruin and architecture in a situation of variation, as much in the representation as in what is represented. *St. Matthew* and *St. John* constitute a legitimate pair. Both evangelists write: Matthew under the luminous dictation of the Angel, John filled with an inner vision, his back turned to the eagle moving away in the shadow. Both are surrounded by architectural fragments, as if the privileged place of sacred writing, the space of the poem of revelation, could be only a field of ruins. For Matthew, the vestiges of the temple or palace are posited in the immobile disorder of an earthquake on the side of a peaceful river, so calm that it does not seem to flow between its banks. John is seated in a wild desert with cork oaks and brambles; the earth is opened onto caverns, some of which have been made into walled tombs; a dark belt of vegetation hermetically closes off the place of meditation that is traversed by a little-trodden path. There are fragments of shafts of toppled columns, of overturned foundation-stones. The same turning-into-stone of the architectural bloc, the same palingenesis from art to nature, animates the foregrounds of the two paintings in counterpoint with the water that does not flow in the one case and with the earth of the material origin in the other. Cézanne used to talk about "doing Poussin on nature," about "treating nature by way of cylinders, spheres, cones . . . " Doing Cézanne on architecture is what Poussin seems to propose. Finding, through the ruins of art, shafts of columns, pedestals, paving stones, and shaped blocks, the architecture of the visible world: nature as architect. In *St. Matthew*, an erect pedestal is thrust into the earth; in *St. John*, another, with an upright cruciform section, is emerging from the earth. This double movement expresses the organic synthesis of the landscape's existence and the painted picture through the fragment. There is a final variation between the members of the pair formed by these two works: in the background of *St. Matthew*, the meandering river leads the eye to a ruined city; in *St. John*, temples and obelisks rise intact behind the curtain of trees up to the edge of an uncertain sea where the eye makes out the homes and palaces of men.

. . . *The Death of Sapphira* (Louvre). The subject Poussin puts on display is one of uncommon violence. Here I need to cite Acts 4:34–35 and 5:1–11. In the first Christian community, "all those who owned land or houses would sell them, and bring the money from them, to present to the apostles; it was then distributed to any members who might be in need." Ananias, in agreement with his wife, Sapphira, sold some property, but

> he kept back part of the proceeds, and brought the rest and presented it to the apostles. "Ananias," Peter said, "how can Satan have so possessed you that you should lie to the Holy Spirit and keep back part of the money from the land? . . . It is not to men that you have lied, but to God." When he heard this, Ananias fell down dead. . . . About three hours later his wife came in, not knowing what had taken place. Peter challenged her: . . . "So you and your husband have agreed to put the Spirit of the Lord to the test! What made you do it? You hear these footsteps? They have just been to bury your husband; they will carry you out, too." Instantly she dropped dead at his feet.

And the narrator adds: "This made a profound impression on the whole Church and on all who heard it."

Poussin chose to represent this ultimate moment: the pointing index finger, the outstretched arm of the chief apostle, "performs" the fall, accomplishes Sapphira's death. The woman is on the ground, dying, surrounded by men and women of the people; Peter stands on the platform two steps away from the portico of Solomon, where he is said to have stood with John and Barnabas. Thus we see two groups of figures, on the right and the left, separated by the thunderbolt of death. The unrepresentable violence of this gap is assumed by a powerful architectural mechanism: a double succession of solemn "constructions" accompanies—with the scansion of buildings deserted by living presence—an urban perspective punctuated by minuscule human silhouettes up to a monumental staircase rising toward the façade of a palace dominated by a rock wall crowned by the two towers of a fortress. Imagine a city of intact palaces that time and history have not even grazed; an entirely new city, the icy splendor of buildings that would be ruins without destruction, unmarked by time, unstamped by history; ideal architecture, a pure essence that ignores life and death, a neutral ascetics of a constructive hypostasis.

However, in the middle distance, at the center of the urban perspective, a scene interrupts the unbearable violence: a man is leaning over making a broad gesture of welcome toward a seated woman, at the edge of a body of water. An apostle, rather than causing someone's death, is curing a paralytic. Perhaps it is not by chance that some fragments of stone are aligned near the woman: the cylinder of a column shaft, a molded parallelopiped, a paving stone, and some blocks left over from a cutting—unused vestiges of the activity of the city's builders, debris of a completed, perfect edifice, presented there between the past of the construction site and the future of the field of ruins, at the very instant of a return to life, at the very instant when death strikes. Now, it is precisely in this place, in this interval, that the empty depth of the urban space, which the two rows of palaces had constructed, folds back up into the plane of the painting to create a strange ambiguity in the viewer's eye. In the narrative represented, Peter's outstretched finger had just been directing death toward Sapphira; on the plane of representation, that same index finger designates the seated woman, indicating the miracle of cure and of life in the forgotten debris of the constructive enterprise. It points up the paradox of the time of ruins. . . .

§ 7 Awakening Metamorphoses

Poussin, 1625–1635

Exploring the rooms of an imaginary museum where all of Poussin's works are on display, the viewer will discover the presence of a sleeping body in many paintings. In the first known canvas by Poussin, which the painter, who was not yet a master, copied from one of Josef Heintz's compositions, *Diana and Actaeon* (1614), the viewer will see a woman overtaken by sleep in the foreground; she is lying at the edge of a fountain where Diana is bathing. The sleeping woman is naked; her head rests in the crook of her elbow, in the almond-shaped opening of a drapery, inscribed in a gentle curve that is all the more inviting to the gaze because all the other figures are caught up in rather frenetic gesticulations in response to the arrival, in the background, of Actaeon and his dogs. The viewer will note with secret pleasure that, unlike the characters in the painting, he—and he alone—sees the lovely body, the grace of the neck bent under the blond hair arranged in slender braids, the supple and firm shape of the back, the loins, and the long, elegant legs. The left arm hangs down loosely as far as the hand, up to the tip of the index finger, which grazes the lower edge of the canvas, while a white foot stands out in the dim mirror of the fountain where the virgin goddess is taken by surprise. The viewer will suddenly understand that, in his own place and order, he is for the lovely sleeping creature what Actaeon is for the divine being at the water's edge, fully alert for her gaze. But, unlike the too-human hunter, the viewer will have nothing to fear from the woman sleeping at the edge of the painting. Her repose itself reserves her exclusively for the viewer's contemplative gaze, and protects the latter from any imminent and threatening metamorphosis.

How can one speak of a sleeping body? What power can we give language to express something that is apparently powerless? With what intention can we animate words and phrases in order to clothe them in consciousness of something that—it seems—no longer animates the sleeping body, the flesh that lacks force and that nevertheless contains hidden within itself the most powerful force of all, the force of inertia? How can we give this body language to express itself, since the body remains silent? Its very breathing, in which life signifies itself, is a different respiration, slower and more regular.

Language is always, more or less, an act of aggression against, or a negation of, what it speaks about. Things and beings are distanced by their arbitrary signs, which obey their own rules and laws and are mobilized by an intention to speak. In order to express the sleeping flesh of the world, and share it with others, that intention draws abundantly from the common treasure-house of language; it substitutes and exchanges, combines and articulates symbols while playing with an immense body of language that is itself, in some inner depth, a sleeping body. Or rather, just as I begin to speak, and even before, as soon as the intention to do so—or the intention to write—arises, at that very instant, the sleeping body awakens: the poem is about to be born. No, to tell the truth, speech is not in the first place aggression and negation, but the awakening of the body of language through an active intention: a poem.

Paradox: in the morning of an offering, as language emerges from its reserve—but by what grace?—to express things and beings, to duplicate the world and bring it to meaning, how will it ever be able to express the depth, the reserve, the secret of a sleeping body? How will it be able to express *my* sleeping body? For I have two bodies: one is always awake; but what will it say of the other, the body of the other, which is mine, which is the whole being, and which sleeps? How can the sleeping state of the one and the waking state of the other be made to coincide in speech in a single moment that will be the morning instant, the spring moment of a beginning, but that will always presuppose this silent reserve of words waiting for the speech that will arrange them into the sentences of discourse, and that other moment, that long duration which is an instant without measure, when the body is buried within its depth, its thickness, its fleshly weight?

My sleeping body, my body slipping in that slow, indefinitely slowed-down fall toward its own secret, descending through its own specific heaviness toward a mysterious center of gravity in the natural place of its origin and its presence absent to itself, my body, sleeping, will always—as if inexorably—be the body of another, the other body of the other which the awakened body of language in the first gestures of speech will never graze except from the outside to express it, write it, describe it? Words slipping, in their turn, over its surface, just above, without waking it.

Metamorphosis for metamorphosis, the viewer will stop for a moment before *Apollo and Daphne* (1627–1638?). In the right-hand part of the painting, the violent pursuit of love comes to completion: already the raised arms of the standing nymph have become laurels cradling her pained, exalted face. A branch grows from her belly, preserving her. His quiver and lyre thrown to the ground, the seated god attempts to embrace the body that is being transformed. The furor of his desire to possess is calmed in his uncertainty: his left arm still holds her around the waist, but his right hand can only pluck a branch growing out of a breast. A little cupid flies very close to the intertwined bodies. The band that had covered his eyes is raised to become a white headband around his forehead. He has just released the arrow of a desire that will not reach its goal. The river god Peneus is seated in the foreground. Water is pouring forth from an overturned urn under his left arm. His back is turned to the scene of divine abduction. He is sleeping, his bent head resting in the crook of his arm, his hand hiding his eyes. *He sleeps in order not to see* the rape of his daughter, which he believes must be accomplished, irresistibly. He falls asleep in mourning for the flesh of his flesh in order to forget the dramas of a desire against which he can do nothing. He withdraws into the blindness of sleep. But with a single glance, through the grace of a painted representation, the viewer will discover Apollo's powerless rage before the metaphor of a naked, inaccessible body, in an ongoing struggle with the plant that bears the virgin's name and whose crowning branches already adorn the head of the god. The viewer will discover that the great old man, asleep in his refusal to see what he cannot accept, is the negative double of his own gaze, which contemplates the scene and brings the fable to its bitter conclusion: the metamorphosis of a figurative sleep, in which mourning for the loved one leads to the acceptance of her loss, in the serene theory of the painting in which the passions find themselves, with their ordering on the scene of representation, unexpectedly calmed.

Yes, if there were not sometimes the memory of that buried discourse, a discourse that traverses the sleeping body, one night, by chance, a stammering discourse that my body does not hold, but will have held at the moment of its awakening, a discourse that, in truth, will have been the strange discourse of another who for a durationless moment seems to have elected that hidden place to express himself, without me, without intention: the language of dreams, the profound speech of a comical, pathetic oracle who, as we know, seems to muddle the rules and laws of the other as it pleases, with demonic pleasure. Its speech is that of images in which there may be words; figures may speak, but *in* the images of a story that will always surprise.

This memory of the sleeping body is a memory of images that, without having been taught, know how to make visible what is said but not seen; hence the "no" of negation that all language constitutes, in its system, that all speech constitutes, in its—symbolic—manifestation.

When, like Orpheus in the fleeting instant when he sees Eurydice fading, slipping away among the shadows, my speech turns back toward my body sleeping in the shredded scraps of the images that traverse it, it will always be foreign speech for the one slipping irresistibly away into the night. Impossible loves of my two bodies, which nevertheless coexist, the one within the other; their embrace is out of the question, or always after the fact, untruthful, or rather illusory, a fiction born of the morning of language, in the gray or sunlit dawns of thought. The one, the other, the one that is no more myself than the other, the one for the other; each always other to the other, except for the brief instant when the one fades away and the other awakens.

A call to dialogue, but in the language of the deaf; the one speaks, the other is silent because he does not hear; irremediably deaf, he does not reply. He will never reply, even in the brief instant of awakening that will never be anything but the suspended silence in which speech, and thought along with it, begins to soar amid the rustling of words and sounds. The other will always already have spoken, in the language of his images, or rather, he will have been the scene of their appearance, the scene whose speaking or mute figures will always already have traversed it while animating it and of which, in the morning, I shall be condemned to decipher the derisory meaning, the riddles of an ironic oracle.

Another river god appears in *Venus and Adonis* (Providence, Rhode Island, 1630?): but this one is keeping watch, and contemplating, stretched out on the rock where the river's headwaters flow from the urn. To this figure, placed at the extreme right of the composition, midway up the canvas, a garland of bodies is attached. First of all there are bodies of lovers who have fallen asleep after lovemaking: Venus is resting, abandoned, her eyes closed, her head lying on her bent arm; Adonis is slumbering on her breast, his body lying in a posture that retains the memory of a passionate embrace. But this scene of satisfied love under the attentive gaze of a fatherly god is juxtaposed with another scene that is noisy and animated, though not enough so to awaken the lovers. Two dogs are rushing forward toward the left, barking, and pulling with all their strength on the leashes that hold them back; four winged cupids on the left at the very edge of the painting are capturing a hare that is trying to leap out of the frame. Four other cupids, from their niche in the cloud that fills the upper left quadrant of the canvas, rush to the rescue of their companions, the joyous hunters. In the shade of the foliage, on top of the cloud, the viewer can make out the goddess's chariot with its two doves, while directly below the satisfied couple, the little god, blinded by a headband, lets fly the unerring arrow of desire. Thus the viewer's gaze closes the circle of its trajectory: it has returned to the god of water who is contemplating the two happy bodies in their sleep. Thus, likewise, with this gaze—which is also his own—the viewer surprises, but within the painting, at its edge, the agitated figures who are animating in secret the sleeping depths of the flesh of love. Like the attentive River, the viewer will be able, at will, to see the invisible: what the complexions of the bodies and the closed eyelids hold concealed, to be immediately forgotten upon awakening. In a dream of triumphant desire, the animal belonging to the insatiable Eros is captured by the joyous cupids; despite their momentum, the dogs are restrained, tied to the immobile tree. But the viewer will also be able to divine what the River no doubt already sees because it is god, in the love hunt, the other, fatal one, in which Adonis will die, his groin ripped open by the boar's tusk. The viewer will then hear what Venus had said to Adonis before she fell asleep: "Be brave with fleeing prey; against the beast who stands his ground, it is dangerous to stay and fight. Have pity! O, my young love . . . "

Then I shall watch for the signs of that sleeping body, that of the other: solar plenitude of an attentive gaze covering with its rays the thick night where the other is buried. Signs? Are they even signs, the clenching of a hand, the ripples that course over the skin like a brief burst of wind on the surface of calm water, the great turnings, waves from the depths, that momentarily lift up the fleshly weight, only to lapse quickly into an immobility that has the rhythm of the even, toneless sound of breathing, a mere index of a living being asleep? Are these signs, the brief iridescences, the intentionless movements, the fleeting catastrophes? Or are they only mysterious elaborations of the humors, agitations of flesh in repose, with no meaning other than the muffled values of life recreating itself? Surface effects of a dream: this is how the awakened body in the poem's discourse goes about dreaming that other dream that it will never know, like the images deployed on the stage of a theater whose curtain always stays closed; in its contemplation of the sleeping body, my language dream is caught up in the nets of the movements that traverse it. There, it believes it is reading signs of that body, signs that are perhaps uncertain but whose images can never be expressed, whose story can never be told. A language dream takes the place of a dream of which I am not the stage, as if in this empty theater, with the curtain lowered, I were magically crossing the footlights in order to see the play being performed from the other side, yet without being able either to say it or see it. My speech thus slips into the fiction of an unthought thought, a voiceless word, a mute poem: in a word, the other as mirror of self.

Yes, but there is desire—not a body's desire to embrace in shared possession, but a desire to know the secret hidden and offered, a desire already to experience that silent contemplation, at rest, and which nevertheless searches out signs that grasp it as so many insinuations of that secret, signs that show, in their brevity—or seem to show—that there is a secret to be reached and that create, perhaps, its intuited presence: the other, in a word, a mirror of self that allows me to imagine a strange powerless power; yes, a power without representation, a power that is incapacity, an illusion of mastery, a power whose illusion I know, a thought that does not forbid me to contemplate, a power that, on the contrary, calls me to contemplation even though it will never grasp anything, except its own power. Imagine a caress that does not arouse: the gaze.

The irreparable has occurred at the Musée des Beaux-Arts in Caen, where Venus, shrouded in her grief, accompanied by two cupids, religiously pours the funereal nectar onto the prostrate body of her lover—so handsome in death, so fully abandoned to his definitive rest that he seems to be sleeping. One of the cupids is crying; his hands cover his eyes. The other is already tossing anemones onto the hero's hair, the anemones of the metamorphosis of his blood through the divine libation. The right-hand portion of this long painting is cut off by the diagonal line of the goddess's chariot, on which two doves have alighted. But at left, in the middle distance, a man—is it a man? is it a god?—is sleeping soundly, heavily, without memory. A double of Adonis (?), revealing the mysterious equivalence of sleep and death, the apprenticeship of the one by the repetition of the other, its happy daily announcement and thereby the most persuasive of consolations. A double body of sleep and death; in the interval between the two, the viewer will draw from memory the dead Christ mourned at his graveside by John, his mother, and Mary Magdalene (Munich, 1629). There the cupids have become weeping angels. The time of pagan metamorphoses of the most fatal misfortunes has passed into the tranquil life of Nature's things and beings: drops of Adonis's blood changed into fragile anemones; violent death transformed into sleep forgetful of past grief. The paving stone of the grave points its diagonal toward the obscure crypt of the rock; God is death; all that remains is the message announcing his death elsewhere, "there in Galilee, as he had said," outside the painting, outside the representation, the message to the Holy Women that Poussin will never paint. The dead Christ; Adonis and his double in death and in sleep, and the awakening of life as metamorphosis. Between the two prostrate bodies, in the center of the composition, the spectator will not fail to note the wheel of Venus's chariot, its hub and spokes finely chiseled. He will be able to dream of the cycle of transformations and exchanges, life, death, sleep, awakening, the rhythm in the circle of Nature and the ever-repeated alternation of night and day, light and shadow. But he will also be able to see the serene eye of the theory of the painting figuratively reflected in the wheel's immobile hub and spokes, the apathetic wisdom of its gazes that awakened the painted representation of its thingly repose, that brought it to the attention of its contemplation.

The painted picture is a sleeping body: a mute poem. For centuries, the oxymoron has been the most precise figure of speech for expressing that body, but we have to acknowledge that more has been said about the term "poem" than about the feature that cancels it out in silence; the word "poem" has elicited more words to repeat it than the overly modest prefatory term enclosed in its own mutism. Discourse, in speaking, forgets that it speaks and forgets the silence that it has been called to express—its power—as if it had the power to speak that silence. Such a forgetting is the mark of the mastery that can only be accomplished in rigorous possession, legitimate propriety, perfect appropriation: the desire to know the secret.

But what about the gaze that is a double for speech, the caress from afar that grazes without touching, that does not awaken the sleeping body of the painting but that exhausts itself in its total offering without ever being able to get into its reserve? How, really, can we make the gaze a double for language without saying, simply, "poem" and letting the silence of that sleeping body escape where the gaze finds the space of its wanderings and the places of its journeying? The sleeping body of the painted picture is not an "image," but the most precise of its definitions, mute poetry, in which is signified—on condition that it is heard—the secret of its muteness in its perfect exposition. I shall always imagine that, like the closed lids on the eyes of a sleeping face, the lips of a mouth half opened by a voiceless breath, this painted surface seals up a mysterious secret, as if it were the crypt where the secret is buried, whereas the secret weaves its insinuations only because it is that surface, exposed to the gaze. I may sharpen the gaze and traverse the surface with all the tools and prostheses of science and technology, but this will not uncover the secret for me—no doubt because it does not exist; I will merely reveal the painter's regrets, or the figures he has erased, or the monotonous splendors of his fillers and varnishes, or the lumps of paste, the successive and simultaneous thicknesses of the brush strokes, the colored transparencies of the glazes. . . . Before this sleeping body that I contemplate and where my gaze is gripped by what it believes to be the signs and perhaps the images of the story I imagine that body is telling itself, images of its dream, the body whose skin I imagined I might traverse in order to enter into it, as into a theater, to be present as a spectator, at the ephemeral representation in which its secret is told and shown (whereas in truth, if I were given that power, like a surgeon before the anesthetized body that he is opening up, or even, less aggressively, like a radiologist before the body he is exploring in the invisible flow of particles), I should never see anything but the black and white expanses of the humors, the translucent or opaque surfaces of the tissues in the architecture of a skeleton at bottom similar to all the others. Hence the painting, the thin film of an image.

Still, it can happen that the painting puts on stage and into figures its inexhaustible and calm offering to the gaze. The painting can replay the game of its reserve and its exposition without memory: things nestled in their being, resting in themselves in their flesh of colored paint, surprised in their full silence; and their names, which tell their ordering on the surface of presentation, hesitate between a tranquil life assumed by the painter's eye and exalted by the viewer's admiration, and a peaceful death given them by the painting, unspotted by any threat of corruption: *nature morte*, still life, sleeping bodies of things in the great slumber of painting.

On a table, a glass full of water, two carnations in full bloom, stems crossed, a wicker basket piled high with wild strawberries, two cherries, a peach. Chardin contemplates the flesh of these sleeping things. The secret he captures, their secret, is of pure painting; it neither falls short of nor exceeds the perceptible appearance of the objects on the canvas. There is no hidden enigma; everything is an offering, but no palate will savor the strawberries, no mouth will slake its thirst with the water in the glass, no nose will breathe in the perfume of the two flowers. There is only the eye: it caresses and smells the flavors and odors, the texture of the

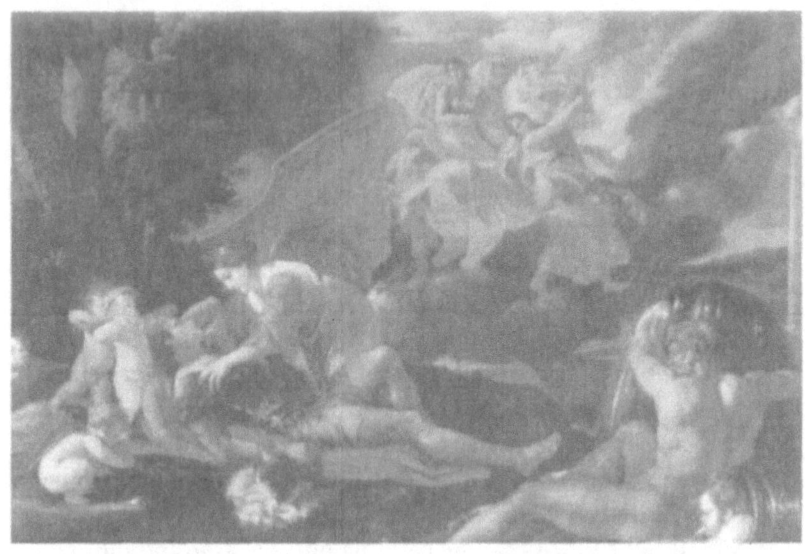

FIGURE 13. *Rinaldo and Armida.* Courtesy Photographie Giraudon.

skins and the envelopes, the matter of the objects. Only paint: grainy, wrinkled whites, reds as smooth and polished as mirrors, downy vermilions and yellows, fresh crystalline transparencies where all the colors meet—nameless. And because, in all this, it is just a matter of painting, brush strokes and impasto, values and modulations, suddenly, yet without haste or surprise, enclose the things depicted in themselves, unattainable, impenetrable in their depth because they are only colors on a surface, assembled in a certain order. Thus the exposed sleeping body that I am contemplating reserves itself infinitely because it is exhausted by showing itself; it withdraws into itself in precise proportion to its oblation. I catch myself thinking that the flashes of light on the edges of the glass, on the surface of the water it contains, and on its flutings, those that settle as grains on some of the strawberries, that traverse with their accents the twists of the willow or dot the skin of the cherries—I catch myself thinking that those flashes are like the quickly interrupted moments, the ephemeral agitations, the instantaneous twitchings that animate for a moment the hand or the face of the sleeping body that I was contemplating: but far from grasping my gaze, as before, through the illusion of their significance—what mysterious tale is being recounted under that skin?—because it is a matter of painting, their very self-evidence renders them in some way painfully opaque to all knowledge, their ostentation leaves my knowledge, poignantly, to its desire.

In the Dulwich College Picture Gallery in London, or in the Pushkin Museum in Moscow, the viewer will rediscover the pagan hero asleep in death in the figure of the Christian hero, lulled to sleep by the charms of the nymphs: Adonis according to Ovid portrayed as Rinaldo according to Tasso (1630–1635). The viewer will be able to read the story and the two paintings according to two successive moments in the same sequence. In the first one, Armida the enchantress, dagger in hand, is preparing to kill the warrior, taking advantage of his sleeping state. But already the gaze on this valiant body that is yielding, defenseless, the gaze on the face resting in the plenitude of peace, is changing hatred into its opposite: an instant of pathetic metamorphosis of the soul through the inertia of a sleeping body contemplated for a moment in a suspension of the murderous act. In the second painting, the metamorphosis has been accomplished (Figure 13): Armida is already leaning over Rinaldo for the embrace of love, the *putti* are bustling around her weapons, and the magician's chariot harnessed to leaping horses has moved forward to transport him to the enchanted isle. But in both paintings, different as they are in circumstance and composition, the viewer will unfailingly see the same movement through which Armida bends down and leans over the sleeping body, the same ample movement of her outstretched arms reaching toward embrace, each body taking charge of the other through the complementarity of their oppositions: sleep and wakefulness, a figuration of the sudden change of hatred into love. Between the one and the other, there is only the brief variation of a gap that is reduced or an attraction that has grown stronger. What radiating power could emanate from this unarmed body whose waves could fill the adverse soul and incline it to love? The charm diffused by Rinaldo's slumbering flesh holds out the invisible mirror of capture by the magic power of the infidel Armida and submits it to the bonds of Eros. The Moscow painting, even more than the one in London, offers the spectator the precise confrontation between two profiles, one of which, with closed eyes, is the masculine counterpart of the other's fascinated gaze: a mysterious mirror traced invisibly by the diameter of the ellipse drawn by the two figures. The sleeping body is, on the other side of the barrier of gender, belief, and race, the perfect image of the waking body, its other, which puts it outside of or beyond itself in the secret affect where its soul changes and where it recognizes its truth. Here, already, is Narcissus, as sung by Tasso:

> Esce d'aguato allor la falsa maga,
> e gli va sopra, di vendetta vaga.
>
> Ma quando in lui fissò lo sguardo, e vide
> come placido in vista egli respira,
> e ne' begli occhi un dolce atto che ride,
> benché sian chiusi (or che fia s'ei li gira?)
> pria s'arresta sospesa, e gli s'asside
> poscia vicina, e placar sente ogn'ira
> mentre il risguarda; e'n su la vaga fronte
> pende omai si, che par Narciso al fonte. . . .
>
> E, di nemica, elle divenne amante.
>
> Then the false sorceress comes forth from her ambush and stands over him, eager for revenge.
>
> But when she fixed her gaze upon him and saw how calm of countenance he breathes, and how charming a manner laughs about his lovely eyes, though they be closed (now what will it be if he opens them?), first she stands still in suspense, and then sits down beside him, and feels her every wrath becalmed while she gazes

> upon him; and now she bends so above his handsome face that she seems Narcissus at the spring. . . .
> And from his enemy she became his lover.[1]

And by leaning over the mirror of the surface, the viewer will understand that the lyric play of death and love in which Rinaldo's sleeping body is engaged under Armida's emotion-filled gaze repeats on the stage of the fable what the viewer's own gaze is playing out on the sleeping body of the work.

It is not so far as we might suppose from the tranquil state of Chardin's still life, provided that one lets oneself go, outside genres, outside those official institutions of art, outside the periodizations of history that punctuate acts and manners of painting with their chronological limits, toward a vagabondage of thought and imagination on the motif of the sleeping body. Poussin's *Echo and Narcissus* (1627–1630; Figure 14), which I go to see in the Louvre, strikes me as not so different from the sleep of the still life, dead nature in its body of paint, if only for the very simple and profound reason that the death that catches up with the two separated lovers is nothing but their metamorphosis into flower and rock, and imagination, guided in its divagations by the wisdom of myth, will pass by imperceptible transitions from these beautiful bodies abandoned to the sleep of agony to the tranquil life of narcissi at the edge of a pool and to the block of stone awaiting the resonance of a sound. By the grace of the gods, death here becomes nature sleeping sweetly in the peaceful life of things. But what unfortunate lover, what unhappy hero, is slumbering in the two carnations, in Chardin's peach, in his cherries and berries? Can the gift of my gaze substituting for celestial mercy operate the inverse metamorphosis and awaken their sleeping bodies from their envelope of fruit and flower? Because it had contemplated the image of his body in the mirror of the fountain and had tried to embrace with its gaze the handsome adolescent it saw there, the eye of Narcissus drowns slowly under its lid. It is no longer look-

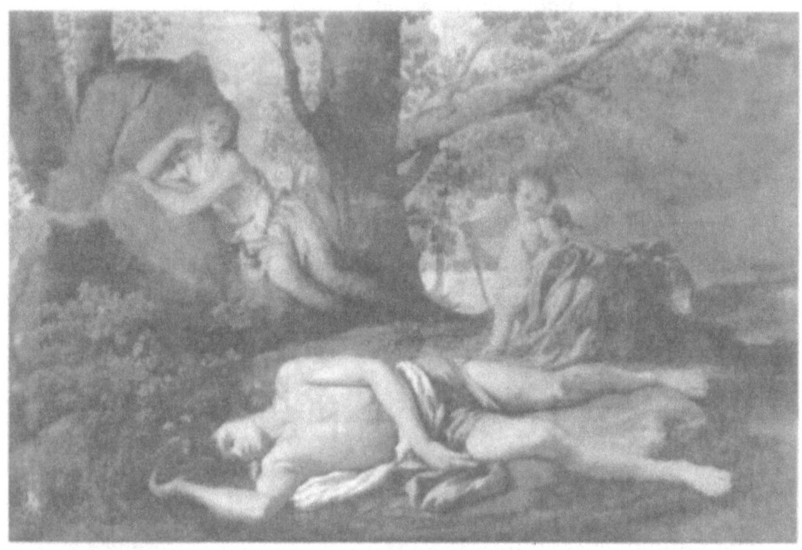

FIGURE 14. *Echo and Narcissus.* Courtesy Photographie Giraudon.

ing at itself; death is creeping up like the weight of sleepiness, a vertigo toward a bottomless bottom, an *I* that absents itself from self, through a density of the entire body, the density that extends it at full length along the base of the canvas.

By leaning over the mirror of the painting, like him, toward the mirror of the smooth water that constitutes its edge, I believe I am deciphering in the mouth with lips half open upon a final breath, in the rings under the eyes, in the clenching of the hand as it relaxes, the surface quiverings of the unhappy passion of self-love, which deadly sleep fixes in an ultimate mask. The hair mingles indistinctly with the grass, and already some flowers are appearing, discreet and fragile, into which the great prostrate body will pass forever. Behind it, the chattering and yet mute nymph, forbidden by the jealous queen of the gods ever to say anything of her own but condemned to repeat the last sounds of whatever speech has been addressed to her, is caught up in the rock against which she is leaning: one hand is indistinguishable from the stone, and in the dark earth her legs push against the veins of the block that welcomes her. Echo slips toward the left in the stone where her face is melting, her mouth is opening in a crack to breathe out a null voice; her eyes no longer see—not that the lids are lowered onto the gaze of the uneasy soul; rather, two holes hollow them out toward the full repose of a thing, the inexhaustible and immediate heaviness of her sleep.

Between the prostrate body sleeping and the bent-over, seated body fusing with its support, there is, standing, a painted being, the child Cupid, awake, holding the funereal torch, the strap of his quiver invisible over his shoulder. He is smiling, it seems to me, with an enigmatic smile, an instrument of the two lovers' punishment and a messenger of divine grace; an allegory of what is no longer and what is not yet, he participates in the two dimensions of time that the lovers who are sleeping in the presence of their metamorphoses into flower and rock will no longer experience. A poetic allegory, a creature of painting, the child Cupid smiles in a reverie from which he absents himself in his turn. Three gazes flee from the space of the painting: that of Narcissus, fading, falls heavily toward the lower depths of the still water; that of Echo, flowing back into the density of the rock, opens its holes toward a sky that is not the sky of painting; that of Cupid loses itself in its thoughts toward the right, where it grasps nothing at all. Three gazes without origin or end, without subject or object, since they are passing simultaneously into the sleep of things or into the reverie of the imaginary and yet are absenting themselves from the canvas according to the three dimensions of its space as painting. I catch myself thinking that the child Cupid, in its painted allegory, is the waking dream of the lovers who are sleeping in their metamorphoses, the waking dream of the inexhaustible depth of the sleeping body of the painted picture awaiting the gaze that will awaken it to contemplation. For the unhappy story of Narcissus—that strange love of self as another which is realized, in its impossibility, in the discovery that the other is oneself—and whose lesson recounts the fate of the desire for knowledge—the story of Narcissus is also the story of the origin of representation, and perhaps, too, of its end.

"I am in the habit of telling my friends," Alberti writes, "that Narcissus, changed into a flower according to the poets, was the inventor of painting. Since painting is already the flower of all art, the story of Narcissus fits it perfectly. What do we call painting if not the embrace by art of what is presented on the surface of the water in the fountain?" In citing this well-known remark, I believe that we must not forget the evocation of metamorphosis and wordplay for which, it seems to me, it is the pretext. What change does painting accomplish, and all art through painting, if not the transmutation of the flesh of things into the fragile surface of colors and the fiction of their presence, there, like narcissi at the water's edge: an awakening of the thing from the sleep of being where it burrows down in the morning light, where it is no longer anything but the tremor, the quivering of its artifice. But what a strange awakening, the embrace which—as the story of Narcissus shows—has never embraced anything that appeared in the mirror of the fountain, on the surface of the canvas, unless that embracing, far from being erotic possession, a realization of desire, should be the caress that neither touches nor grazes, the caress from afar of the gaze, which, in its turn, awakens to its (unrealized) desire to understand the fiction of the metamorphosis of art in which, once again, the painting has fallen asleep. Waiting for the eye that will gather the flower of painting at the edge of the surface, waiting for the voice that will cause the mute wall of the canvas to resonate. The figure of the little god Cupid, awake but dreaming his awakening, reveals in Poussin's painting that other dream that animates not the lovers separated in life by a cruel fate and fallen asleep in the death of their double metamorphosis, but the work of painting, painting itself, withdrawn from the surface of its artifice. Painting, the narcissus-flower of all art, metamorphosis again, to the rhythm of sleep and waking: Echo's beautiful body falls asleep in the rock where it is being transformed, but the stone will henceforth and forever conceal a statue awaiting the chisel of the sculptor who will come, one day, to release it from its sheathing and awaken it to contemplation. And painting, in turn, metamorphoses the sculpture into its flower while showing through its own art the model retreating into the block of marble in order, one day, to be withdrawn from it as a work.

The painting, a mute poem: how can the poem be awakened to its own mutism? If the story of Echo is, in painting, the story of the metamorphosis of the art of sculpture, it is also the story of the burial, in stone and in its wall, of articulated speech, words, phrases, and discourses, or rather of the possibility of its re-presentation, of the power of its re-production. Every rock, because it conceals in its indolent immobility, in the dense somnolence of its matter, the possible statue of a beautiful mute body, is also the chance of its awakening as the listening of my own voice returned outside itself, of my mouth still open to the sonorous breath that traverses it to my surprised ear, my voice, that is, the voice of my double, the voice of echo. I catch myself then imagining to the point of vertigo that the painting I am contemplating with an attentive gaze, through the rock that it represents and in which the body of the nymph and its face are changing, through the flowers that are growing, already woven into the hair of the prostrate adolescent—just as he is dreaming the waking dream of his sleeping body through the figure of the little god with the funeral torch—I catch myself imagining that the painting is dreaming the body of mute, waiting language that I bear within myself, right up to the tip, the *acumen* of my gaze, that it awakens a voice of that language and, by a strange reversal, that the voice it animates in me, at my surface, articulates words only to repeat—like an echo—what it is already saying silently. And in this way, through a grace that is beauty in its perceptible effects, it sometimes happens, between sleep and wakefulness, silence and speech, that the gaze finds its end in a voice, this voice, in its turn, in something visible, through an incessant metamorphosis in which the space of the subject is opened and from which the *I* emerges from its sleeping reserve. Metamorphosis in painting proposes through its mute poem the scene of this opening and the figures of this emergence. It proposes its play at the beginning of the end of a story always already known that whispers its episodes at the edge of a memory more ancient than that of my story, since it gives my story its chance to be, the fate of its constitution. The sleep of things awakened to their metamorphoses in art, the lulling to sleep of painted figures awakened to their metaphors in language, the secret ecstasy of the nascent *I*, through words and gazes, of a body at rest . . .

§ 8 A Gaze Rewarded, or Moses Saved from the Water

> Kant, like all philosophers, instead of envisaging the aesthetic problem from the point of view of the artist (the creator), considered art and the beautiful purely from that of the "spectator," and unconsciously introduced the "spectator" into the concept "beautiful." It would not have been so bad if this "spectator" had at least been sufficiently familiar to the philosophers of beauty—namely, as a great *personal* fact and experience, as an abundance of vivid authentic experiences, desires, surprises, and delights in the realm of the beautiful! . . . "That is beautiful," said Kant, "which gives us pleasure *without interest.*" Without interest! Compare with this definition one framed by a genuine "spectator" and artist—Stendhal, who once called the beautiful *une promesse de bonheur.* At any rate he *rejected* and repudiated the one point about the aesthetic condition which Kant had stressed: *le désintéressement.* Who is right, Kant or Stendhal?
>
> —Friedrich Nietzsche, *Genealogy of Morals,* 3d diss., sec. 6

I have often had the feeling while going through the rooms of a museum that the paintings were awaiting the visit of a gaze that might be mine. A visit: I should like to say a "visitation," to give the possible encounter the solemnity of a ritual, a ceremonial aura. The feeling is not as strange as it might appear, or rather its strangeness is in proportion to that of the entities we call paintings. Populating places reserved for them with the images they bear, they would end up going unnoticed owing to their very familiarity if the stroller did not occasionally feel, in the gallery where he wanders for an hour or two, a vague uneasiness of the sort he might feel in the street in response to a beggar's overly insistent plea. The paintings, hanging from the picture rail, have no other being, no other purpose, no other reason except to show themselves. They exhaust their reality in this ceremonial display;

they spend themselves in this osten(ta)tion, an expense consisting of pure loss unless a gaze intervenes to stop the infinite ostentatory consummation, if an eye does not come to gather in the mad prodigality of colors and forms. Let an eye suddenly alight on the painted surface: then to the painting is offered the grace of a return to its place of origin, and the sweetness of a return to peace in a site of which it retained the secret memory, since it was just as much in the dress circle of an orbit, in the obscure concavity of an eye, that the crystalline waters of vision were trembling, as it was in the basin of a fountain that a body had exalted itself to the point of rivaling the world, its light, its colors, its forms, making them appear on that painted surface and offering them there in return, to be seen. It is thus indeed a mysterious ceremonial of exchange whose ultimate gesture comes, when, seemingly without reason, the stroller stops before a painting and looks at it.

One might think that a painting is in some sense the final document concluding the pact by which the visible is accomplished, since a painting is the trace, the index, and the sign both of a fold in the world that has become a seeing body and of a body changed into a world seen. A painting implies a contract, one might say: "I show only myself, I offer only myself, I am an offering of colors and forms only if you see me, only if in a prolonged gaze you give me back what I give you to see." Such is, in this view the essential reciprocity on which the visible is based and of which the painting is the trace, the index, the sign. How can a painting stop a gaze for a moment? Invocation, convocation, provocation: some paintings fix the eye by addressing to it a humble prayer, thereby putting it in the place of a sovereign god, that of the dominating vision, from which nothing is hidden. But this is perhaps a ruse to trap the gaze with its own power and then to grip it through its own image, in endless fascination. Thus in one of the myths of the origin of painting, Narcissus died by virtue of his own gaze, at the invocation of Echo. There are paintings that convoke the viewer through their own authority and with confidence, imposing upon him his place and the site of his vision; they guide his gaze in the coherent traversal of their space, from place to place, where even the hesitations, the reversals of direction, the changes of itinerary are mysteriously programmed to offer the eye the delicious deception of complete freedom, even including the lags and delays in reaching the horizon that it seems to allow itself. This is sometimes the case with Cézanne or Poussin in their great landscapes. There are also paintings that provoke the gaze through a bursting palette of colors, the attraction of a form, paintings that stake their all in an instant, that satisfy the eye all at once as if by suffocation, irresistibly winning, even if their victory is ephemeral. With this observation one can recognize the time-honored discourse about perversions of color that runs through the history of painting since Plato. Let me add that when the stroller stops before a painting, the painting has very probably deployed the triple appeal of prayer, order, and charm to fix his gaze.

I imagine, too, between the painting and the contemplative eye something like a circle of Graces, one of those that Edgar Wind has skillfully described in his fine book, *Pagan Mysteries in the Renaissance* (1958), between Seneca and Spenser, Servius, Boccaccio, and Goethe, a circle that accentuates the generosity of the gifts. To the simple exchange in which the first Grace gives and the two others give back doubly, I prefer for the work of painting the triplet rhythm in which, between the gift and its counterpart, the gift given in return, the Stoic philosopher arranges for an intermediate moment: that of acceptance, greeting, and hospitality. That moment, if we may slip from time to space here, is the very place of the painting that has given itself up to the offering of a gaze only because it has been made to take in the gaze and in so doing to render it measureless. The painting offers itself to view, and in that offering it inexhaustibly exhausts its own being, in the expectation of a gaze as a counterpart to its ostentatious expense. Should a gaze come to (re)compensate that expense, should an eye grant a gaze of recognition to the painting because originally the painting is harmonized with the gaze and because its recognition by the gaze is also the recognition of the gaze by the painting, then a double recompense is exchanged, a double compensation, that of a gaze and a painting. This double compensation is not egalitarian, however, never coldly equivalent, for the place where giving and giving back are exchanged in greeting is the place of excess. To the gift of the gaze, the painting responds by giving again and as a bonus, for not only does it show itself, but it shows that it represents, and what it represents will give pleasure as a supplement. What the painting represents is what it shows by showing itself, what it shows as a recompense for the countergift of the gaze. The painting is that very strange place in which a representation is exchanged for a gaze with the benefit of pleasure.

But one can also describe the inverse movement, and this is why the dance of the Three Graces is never interrupted, whatever the direction of their circle. The painting shows itself gracefully, free of charge. Such is its nature—and without spirit or hope of counterpart. The eye receives this grace: it consents to see, to look, to contemplate; it accepts the representation that the painting shows, if only because the place of the painting is a place of hospitality for the eye that is willing to recognize it. But to consent to see is to give in return; it is to return a gaze. By consenting to see, the eye returns a gaze, and the painting gives back a hundredfold with a pleasure as strange as itself, that of beauty, in which the promise of happiness is irresistibly announced, even if, as a promise, it cannot be kept. The dance of graces in the painting and the gaze is a circle dance that repeats itself endlessly: it never begins or ends, since there is no single starting or stopping point but an indefinite recommencing of a pact of seduction between a painting and an eye through the untenable promise of the happiness of the contemplating gaze, through the beauty of the work of painting. Who then has begun to dance: the eye halted and fixed without being fascinated, the eye that traverses the surface along paths that have been arranged for it in the work (Paul Klee), or the painting that offers itself, immobile, enclosed in its frame but open to all explorations? Who then will stop the circle of the graces: the gaze that contemplates and admires, or the work that promises, even as it defers the keeping of its promise?

It also happens—and perhaps more often than we think—that paintings stage the rewards offered to the gaze. This is not surpris-

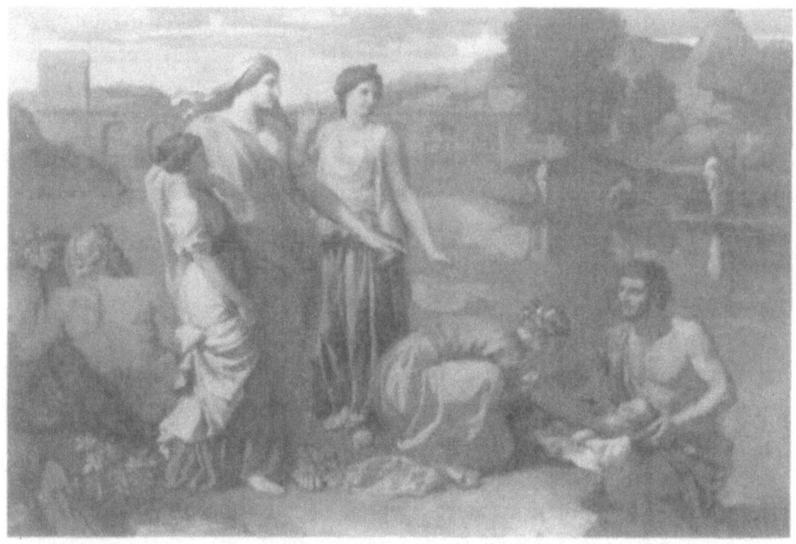

FIGURE 15. *The Finding of Moses.* Courtesy Photographie Giraudon.

ing, for a painting shows itself and represents, it shows that it represents, and by that very token, what it represents is the fact that it is showing itself. It turns out then to figure the osten(ta)tion that constitutes its being as an artifact of painting; it happens that the painting constitutes the story that it presents to be seen and read, that of a hidden and published history of beauty, forgotten, unrecognized and recognized, of the exchange of gazes and beings, through which, therefore, a loss is compensated to the point of excess by a recompense about which no one knew, when it was granted, what promise of happiness it announced. This is the story I have often had occasion to read and see, here particularly in a painting by Poussin, *The Finding of Moses* (1647; Figure 15), known as the Pointel Moses, currently in the Louvre. Why this painting? Poussin will answer for me, in seemingly anecdotal fashion, in his well-known letter of 24 November 1647 addressed to Chantelou, the letter on fashions (see Appendix 3). At the starting point of the great theoretical and practical problem of judgment in painting—

what Cézanne will call, two and a half centuries later, for Emile Bernard, truth in painting—is the pact of seduction between a painting and an eye: "If you feel affection for the picture of *Moses Found in the Waters of the Nile*, which belongs to M. Pointel, is that a proof that I made it more lovingly than I did yours? Do you not see that, along with your own disposition, *in the nature of the subject lies the cause of this effect?*" (emphasis added). So we must first of all hear, one more time, the curious story of Moses' birth: the only things at stake, we note with surprise, are gazes and their rewards.

We know about Pharaoh's order: "Take all the boys born to the Hebrews and throw them into the river, but let all the girls live." We also know that a child was born to a man and a woman of the tribe of Levi, a firstborn son. But we often forget the reason that determined his salvation, a reason that both the writer of the Acts of the Apostles (7:20) and Paul, in Hebrews (11:23), were at pains to record: "Moses, when he was born, was hidden by his parents for three months . . . [because] they saw he was such a fine child." A first look upon beauty, a gaze threatened with death, a gaze whose consequence is the descent of beauty to the secret of burial and death before its exposure and its publication on the river.

We are familiar with the basket made of papyrus coated with asphalt and pitch and the child who found in it a second cradle amid the reeds of the river bank. But we sometimes forget that there was again, in the secret of this exposure, a second gaze, not enamored of beauty this time like that of the mother, but the gaze of an attentive viewer who desires to know. "His [Moses'] sister stood some distance away to see what would happen to him." Her gaze had everything required for defining the conditions of good visibility: the position at the viewing point and the proper distance of the eye. It is under this gaze—and if one may say so, as the reward for its waiting—that a painting is going to arise in the text, a narrative sequence that is immobilized in a perfect image: young garlanded followers of the princess Thermutis, Pharaoh's daughter, who comes down to the river to bathe, stroll and cavort along the bank. Then the event occurs. We have to reread the account in

Exodus: we recognize the three moments of the gaze and the dance of the eye and the image. First of all the glimpse: the provocation of detail in a scene that brings the procession to a halt, fixes the movement and briefly immobilizes it: "Among the reeds she [Pharaoh's daughter] noticed the basket, and she sent her maid to fetch it." Then the gaze itself, which responds diligently to what it constitutes as an object by bringing to light what up to then had been hidden in shadow, by exposing and publishing what, up to then, had been hiding in secret. "She opened it and looked, and saw a baby boy, crying." Then the gaze of re-cognition (which must be understood in the double sense, objective and subjective, of this genitive and which, for this reason, oscillates between knowledge and gratification) is invested in its object as affect. *Touched with compassion* for the child, she says: "This is a child of one of the Hebrews." The invocation of a prayer that tacitly formulates its object for the benefit of the gaze: to this prayer, the eye responds by its passion. The latter delivers the access of language to simple knowledge with an initial name, that of the group and the lineage.

The long royal gaze on the accident, having become compassion in the object, is internal to the painting and to the story, to the historical painting that a gaze contemplates, positioned at the proper viewing point and placed at the proper distance, the baby's sister who in an instant is going to intervene. In a sense—and perhaps it is all the more true in that we are only, for yet another moment, readers of this story—the gaze of the princess is the passionate reflection, the affect-investment in the painting of that other distanced gaze that aims only to see what is going to happen, the reward for its waiting: the event occurs, the happy occasion arrives, and beauty is published in the passion for seeing that is a promise of happiness. We have indirect proof of this, in a sense, with the entrance of the viewer into the painting in the form of a ruse of language, a trap of discourse: "Then the child's sister said to Pharaoh's daughter, 'Shall I go and find you a nurse among the Hebrew women to suckle the child for you?' 'Yes, go,' Pharaoh's daughter said to her; and the girl went off to find the baby's own mother." The rest of the story does not need to be told, except to note first of all that, in the narrative, the witness-viewer, the baby's sister, enacts the passion of the princess. She causes the affect to pass into action; then she causes the child to be given back to its real mother, who passes for a mere paid wet-nurse, and to Pharaoh's daughter, who becomes "like" his real mother ("Pharaoh's daughter . . . treated him like a son"). Finally, she causes the child to be given a name by the princess: receiving him as a son, the latter gives him, in exchange, his proper name, a name that summarizes the whole story, "Moses," or "the-one-I-pulled-out-of-the-water." The dance of the graces is uninterrupted, from one exchange to another, giving, receiving, returning, giving again, receiving anew, rendering to excess, and the beautiful hidden infant, exposed in his basket, at risk of death, becomes the "son" of the daughter of Pharaoh, as Paul will say to the Hebrews, in receiving the name of his story, a name that names the passion of a gaze, the passion for seeing and its object; its recompense, a name.

This is the painting that Poussin did for Pointel in 1647, the one that seduced Chantelou to the point of provoking his amorous jealousy. Whence, likewise, the haste in his judgment of the Master's works, a haste for which the Master reproaches him. "Do you not see that the nature of the subject is the cause of this effect?" What effect if not love, the seduction exercised by the painting and the subject that it represents on those who look at it; a certain subject, Moses or the-one-pulled-out-of-the-water, whose story in Exodus we have just reread after our fashion. Do you not see that the nature of the subject is the cause of this amorous passion, the recompense of your gaze; is not the nature of the subject the exchange of gazes at the edge of the river at dusk, is it not the circle dance of gestures of offering, of welcoming and gathering right up to the return of the viewer's eye from what was given in the narrative, that the painter recounts after so many others, the beauty of a nameless child in the form of a painting known as *The Finding of Moses* by Nicolas Poussin, the reward for our gaze in the Louvre, after that of Pointel, "who is one of those heretics who believe that Poussin has some uncommon talent in painting," that of Chantelou, the jealous lover, that of the duc de Richelieu and of Louis XIV, the future owners of the painting?

Here one ought to express the dance of the Graces in the painting by setting the words in the traces of their steps and gestures: the beautiful child taken out of the open basket like ripe fruit, the child who is presented by a kneeling servant-girl and who appeals with his imploring gaze to the princess Thermutis, who is standing, monumental, robed in pale orange, with open arms, already gathering him in; the servants on the left, three in number, like the Graces, are looking at the one being offered, looking at each other and holding out their arms in an embrace; the two royal companions standing on the right, in white, yellow, and blue, wait for the mistress to make a decision, a decision that has, however, already been made. The dance of the figures is an immobile circle dance around the child and the princess: the child, object of the gaze and subject of the exchange; the princess, thanks to whom the promise is fulfilled.

To this mystery of figures who belong as much to painting and narrative as to sacred history and exegesis, there are two witnesses who displace the entire economy of the painting: its composition, by decentering it toward the left; its narrative, by giving the simple anecdote the dimension of an allegory; its meaning, by diverting the offering of the viewer's gaze outside the frame. On the right, in the foreground, the scene is being contemplated by a very different gaze. The River, leaning on the overturned urn from which water is flowing and holding in his hand a cornucopia of flowers and fruits, turns his head toward his right; apathetic, almost severe, he sees the discovery occurring on his bank. He appears passionless, serene: his is a simple theoretical gaze. At his side, immobile, crouched down, turned toward the edge of the canvas, ignorant of what is happening behind it, the Egyptian sphinx contemplates, walled up in stone, what no one will ever see. Another scene then develops in the depth of the canvas on the right. In the middle distance, imported from ancient mosaics, a long fishing boat is engaging in a hippopotamus hunt; still further back there is a city with its temples and its pyramid at the foot of mountains under a blue sky in which a few gray and pink clouds are floating: another painting which only the gaze of the River God between history and allegory (since he sees from the vantage point of the same life as the other figures—though he may be slower and more solemn) connects with the central scene. But the gaze of contemplation that distracts the River God briefly from his apathy as symbol for the history of men and their anecdotal agitation, this gaze that belongs, in the last analysis, by delegation, to Pointel, Chantelou, Richelieu, Louis XIV, or to us, is brought back by the sphinx to his own blind immobility; he takes it back and returns it to an atemporal and memoryless externality because that is where the secret of the future is kept, the rest of the marvelous story of which a scene from the first act, on the left, is being recounted in the foreground.

If the river is the calm delegate of our gaze in the painting, if we have momentarily lent it our sight so that our sight may thereby gain access to the theory of history and painting, then the sphinx in the shadow sends our gaze back outside the frame, outside the painting, back to our own eye, though not to its site of vision, to the place from which it sees, but to a place, a space, where there is nothing to see because everything is to come; to a place, too, where, unlike the figures belonging to the narrative, we already know what comes next, we already know the end of the story, when the promise borne by the infant in the basket is kept; a place, finally, where, in spite of this knowledge of times and of meaning that the sphinx gives us to recover, I cannot prevent myself from feeling, in the recompense of the theoretical vision itself, a secret frustration, a tragic breakdown, as if what the sphinx might see if it were not walled up in the stony immobility of its knowledge had been denied me forever.

It is this feeling or intuition that I believe I read in the eyes of the princess Thermutis, whose gaze I am unable to reconcile with the gesture she is making with her arm. The arm is expressing the decision to welcome dictated by compassion; the gaze is slipping into reverie beyond the beauty of the child condemned to die, beyond the servant-girl who is begging, yet it still does not rejoin my own gaze. Behind the princess, however, the sister posted at a distance from the beginning, the second spectator who knows the workings of the trap, is emerging from the shadow to insinuate the cunning counsel. But the princess is not listening to her; she is not looking at anything or anyone. Could it be that, after noticing the basket in the reeds, after seeing the child of beauty that it contained, after being touched by compassion at that sight, she glimpsed in the mists of time what the sphinx would have seen had he not known them already, the misfortunes gathering over the land of Egypt, the plague, the locusts . . . like the dark cloud that lurks in the sky over the imperial capital, the palace and the temples, the cloud that she would see if she turned around, but that I see invading the sky?

"Read the story and the painting," Poussin could have written to Chantelou in 1647 as he did in 1639, concerning, once again, a story about Moses, "in order to see whether each thing is appropriate to the subject." A story of gazes given, taken in and returned, where beauty passes from one to another, expressing itself as a promise of happiness, no sooner formulated than disappointed—no doubt because the promise of that recompense cannot be kept. A firstborn son saved from death . . . a beautiful child, crying, found in the reeds of the river . . . the mother becoming wet-nurse to her own son who is lent to her as the son of another, Pharaoh's daughter . . . the latter becoming the mother, without conceiving or giving birth, of a prince who is secretly Hebrew . . . the prince murdering the Egyptian and fleeing into the Midian desert . . . and so forth. Read the story of the gazes recompensed and disappointed and the painting that shows them while leaving to be guessed at, in their very representation, the breakdown that strikes them in succession, while protecting the past and reserving the future in the present—the only time the painting knows. The Egyptian sistrum negligently tossed into the left-hand corner of the scene gives the eye the sign of musical tonality, the mode or the tone of the dominant passion that envelops the figures and the landscape, "a certain suavity and sweetness," Poussin writes to Chantelou, "which fills the souls of the spectators with joy; it lends itself to subjects of divine glory, and paradise." A glory, a paradise, that can be felt by the figures of the narrative in that scene of a history of gazes exchanged only as the present-absent recompense for happiness, only as the promise which beauty presents to view: joy traversed by a mysterious bitterness. If then you feel affection for the picture that M. Pointel owns, do you not see that the nature of the subject is the cause of this effect, an amorous jealousy, a passion for an object of the gaze rendered inappropriable by the gaze that delights in it by that very token, the same passion, but in a temperate mode, which I see in the eyes of Thermutis, whose allegory I read in the couple formed by the River God who is contemplating with complete serenity the scene of the offering and the sphinx who is paying no attention to it because he knows the secret of its consequences?

In these open and repeated breakdowns of the reading of the narrative, in these recompenses given and taken back to be given again by the representation in painting, I have long found the peace of the gaze in one point of the painted surface, the ultimate gift, the final grace, the grace beyond which the painting cannot give or accomplish anything more—in a word, the promise. This point is a burst of dazzling, inexplicable, unbearable light, untenable like the promise of happiness, flashing at the tip of a promontory, directly underneath God, at the foot of a tomb, as if the water of the river from which Beauty has just been drawn had retained, for a very brief instant, the light that had disappeared from the coming dusk; a very brief instant, the dazzling solar gaze, but which endures in the work to soften and perhaps to erase the loss of things that it consecrates.

§ 9 Variations on an Absent Portrait

Poussin's Self-Portraits, 1649–1650

The story of Poussin painting his own portrait, as presented in his correspondence with Chantelou, is a strange one. Like a classical tragedy, it has five acts, but there is a difference: the story takes more than three years to come to a conclusion.

Act One: At the end of a letter written to Chantelou on 7 April 1647 we find a reference to a portrait of Poussin that Chantelou had requested from the artist and for the fabrication of which Poussin has sought a painter in vain: "There is now no one in Rome who does good portraits, which is the reason I will not send you what you want right away."

Act Two: The search for a portraitist lasts nearly a year and a half. On 2 August 1648 Poussin decides, as if he has no choice, to do his portrait himself: "I would already have had my portrait done to send you, as you wish. But it annoys me to spend some ten *pistoles* for a head in the manner of M. Mignard, who is the one I know who does them best, although they are cold and pinched-looking, with complexions that look like makeup, done without any skill or energy."

Act Three: Less than a year later, a little theatrical surprise: we learn in a letter dated 20 June 1649 that there will be two self-portraits. One is already painted, the other is about to be done, and Poussin adds for Chantelou: "I shall send you the one that comes out best, but you must say nothing about it, please, to avoid causing any jealousy." Who, then, is in question in this jealousy, or rather who is really the jealous one?

Act Four: 19 September 1649. The second self-portrait is begun.

Act Five: 19 May 1650: "I have finished the portrait you wanted of me . . . M. Pointel will have the one I promised him at the same time; you won't be at all jealous of it, for I kept the promise I made you, choosing the better one and the best likeness for you: you will see the difference yourself." Poussin then adds solemnly: "I maintain that you must take this portrait as a sign of the obedience I have promised you, all the more in that for no other living person would I do what I have done for you in this matter." Has Poussin forgotten the first self-portrait he sent to M. Pointel? Not really, because what distinguishes the second from the first, it seems, is the difficulty he encountered in painting it, which the Master underlines through paralipsis: "I do not want to tell you how much trouble I have had in doing this portrait for fear that you should believe I want to call attention to its worth." We may be tempted to take him at his word, when we discover, in the correspondence, the muffled echoes of the argument that the painter is having at the time with his "client and friend" Chantelou.

In any event, what produced the "story," or "history"—in every sense of the terms—in this matter is the passage from the self-portrait done by another (painter), the biographical subject in painting, to the portrait of "myself" done by "myself-the-painter," in which the pictorial equivalent of the biographical gesture is deployed. But what poses a problem in this "(hi)story" is the surprising incident of duplication of the self-portrait in 1649, the decision made to paint another one when the first was not yet even dry and Poussin's reticences about painting himself were as strong as ever. The painting is doubled, but there is no question of a copy. The painter repeats himself, not in his identity but in his difference, which, because it is grasped at the same moment of his life, could not transcribe any change in his existence or in its apprehension, any biographical nuance, any anecdotal humor, not even some situation related to the demands of his clients, admirers, and friends. "I shall send you the one that comes out best."

The Master tries out a difference; he experiments with his own difference in *painting*; he risks a variation; he risks *his* painting.

The fact remains that this whole "(hi)story" is subtended, no doubt right up to the incident of the *two* self-portraits, by the jealous rivalry of the two intended recipients. That rivalry had broken out more than two years earlier, in a letter dated 24 November 1647 (see Appendix 3): "If you feel affection for the picture of *Moses Found in the Waters of the Nile*, which belongs to M. Pointel, is that a proof that I made it more lovingly than I did yours [that is, *The Sacraments*]?" Chantelou's jealousy of Pointel, his sensitivity to the more or less well-informed criticisms on the part of the public, criticisms that he does not hesitate to take up on his own account in his letters to Poussin, had already provoked, on the part of his correspondent, a solemn reckoning with respect to M. Pointel six months before. "He is one of those heretics who believes that your servant Poussin has some uncommon talent in painting." This characterization reveals the sharpness and the vivacity of the Parisian debate over Poussin's work, moreover. An earlier letter gives Chantelou a stern warning: "But I am afraid that he may be stoned if he does not keep silent," the Master adds with reference to him, "for it is no longer the moment to enlighten the blind; even Christ would have been resented for it."[1]

But the competition between Chantelou and Pointel is developed also on a theoretical basis of exceptional importance: in that same letter (24 November 1647), Poussin puts forward the theory of musical modes in painting, that is, precisely the principle of variation. An application of this principle that approaches a "tour de force"—and this doubtless explains the extreme difficulty Poussin experiences in painting himself, a matter to which he returns several times—will consist in displacing it from the historical painting to the self-portrait. Now, this is to say a great deal, for it will be a matter of bringing into play the principle of variation not only in the relation between the painter and his "subject-to-be-painted," the epico-tragic narrative, the imitation of human passions and actions, but in the relation between the painter and the painting, in the field of representation, as well. What is thus in question at this point is not "myself," Nicolas Poussin, in Rome, at midcentury, when "my" life was beginning to decline; what is in question is the painter whose name is "Nicolas Poussin," the painter who is in the process of completing the second series of *The Seven Sacraments*, the one that he painted for Chantelou, starting from scratch, instead of *copying* the first one he had done some years earlier, for Pozzo, a series that is in itself an extraordinary field of experimentation on the principle of variation. What is in question is the painter who asks himself the question of the relation between the "painter-subject" and painting, a relation that stems less from Tasso's definition (shared by the entire tradition) of the heroic poem—"an imitation of those human actions that are properly imitable"—than from the one Poussin will propose later on as death is approaching—"an imitation made on a surface with lines and colors of everything that one sees under the sun," and whose goal is "to please."[2]

To attempt, to risk the principle of variation on the relation between the "subject-painter" and painting, is to attempt, to risk, painting at least two self-portraits, more or less at the same time; it is to test oneself, to risk oneself as a painter in painting itself, and to ask oneself, without being able to reply in advance, whether one will succeed better than the other.

The principle of variation: with reference to the *The Baptism of Christ*, in comparison with *Extreme Unction*, Poussin had already written to Chantelou in March 1647: "I am not among those who always sing on the same note, and . . . I know how to vary when I wish."[3] On 7 April he had confirmed:

> I am not unaware that the average painter pretends that he changes his style as soon as he forsakes, however little, his usual manner; for [today] poor painting is reduced to cliché [i.e., *to the repetitive copying of the same model*]. It would be even more appropriate to speak of burying painting (which nobody has ever seen come alive except at the hands of the ancient Greeks). I could tell you things on the subject that are quite true and known by no one. . . . I only entreat you to receive with a favorable eye . . . the paintings that I shall send you, even though all are *differently* painted and colored, assuring you

> that I shall do my utmost to give satisfaction to art, to you, and to myself.[4]

The letter on modes (24 November 1647) will reveal true things known by no one, the modes that "our wise ancient Greeks, inventors of all beautiful things, found [and] by means of which they produced marvelous effects."

This is not the place to go into a detailed analysis of Poussin's letter; I shall focus here on just two points. A mode is a complex totality of parts: it is defined as a system of differences, one that has only differential value (in relation to other modes). By that very token, a mode offers a principle or, perhaps more precisely, a schema of variation whose effect, differential once again, is "to arouse the soul of the spectator to various passions." At bottom, Poussin, commenting on Giuseppe Zarlino's *Istituzione harmoniche* (1558), brings together in a single notion of mode, an *ontological law*, "a certain determined manner or order . . . by which the object is preserved in its essence," a *poetic or rhetorical principle*, "a combination of several things put together," a *schema of variation*, "when all the things which entered into combination were put together" proportionally, and finally a *pragmatic affect mechanism*.[5] It is of little importance that Poussin slips first from a Platonic and Aristotelian topology of modes to a different one by displacing the definition of the Phrygian mode (from smaller and sharper-appearing modulations to vehemence and severity), from the severe, modest Dorian mode to the Lydian mode that suits lamentable things, from the suave and sweet Hypolydian mode to the "festive" Ionian mode to represent bacchanalian dances and feasts. What matters is that the musical modes—the "sound of speech" and its diverse variations—constitute the theoretical context that makes it possible to understand the "history" of the two self-portraits: two modal variations of the expression of self, of the painter-subject, in which what is at stake is nothing less than "the artifice of painting," as Poussin says, that is, painting itself.

The problem posed by Poussin's self-portraits, I repeat, has to do less with a displacement of the theory of musical modes to painting in general or the displacement of the "sound of speech" to historical painting than with the displacement, internal to the field of painting and pictorial representation, of what is essential: the principle of variation, when the "subject-to-be-painted," the epic narrative, the tragic fable, the heroic romance, is identified, as if by substitution, with the "subject-of-the-painting-process," when the "subject-of-painting," the heroic poem—to borrow the title of a speech by Tasso that Poussin had used—is covered over by the "painter-subject," the lyric poet—to fall back on the one given by a painting that Poussin had produced a few years before. This evocation is significant in itself: on that occasion Poussin had painted the allegorical "portrait" of two poets, the epic poet who wrote the words of the narrative under dictation from Apollo and the lyric poet intoxicated by inspired fury, whose mouth drinking at the cup of the divine liqueur is a simple metonymy for the one from which the sound of words sung will breathe forth. Epic fables, like historical narratives, are written to be read; lyric poems are written to be sung and heard, and how can one allow the singing and the hearing to be seen in another manner? Thus Poussin would oppose two poetic genres by presenting to view the contrasting representations of their figures, whose attributes, at least as much as the setting in the composition, translated into painting the great debates within literary theory during the Cinquecento and the beginning of the Seicento.

The experiment with the two self-portraits of 1649–1650 is all the more hazardous in that with the transfer of the principle of modal variation to the "painter-subject" in his relation to painting, the problem of the redistribution of the epic and the tragic in the field of the lyric is posed directly in painting through the painting of the painter himself. Hence the questions that articulate this painterly quest: Can a variation, even a rule-governed one (but how are such rules to be formulated?) initiate the imitation of self by self? What meaning does the very notion of imitation maintain if the representation that puts it to work is taken from the play of lyric variation? If the self-portrait is subjected to a principle of variation, what value is to be given to its emotional effects? How can the painting of its painter and the painter of his painting aiming at recovery and coincidence induce the passion characteristic of the mode in which the painting has been treated? How can the painter, in representing himself, convert himself into an actor of passion in the one who is looking at him, who is no one but himself and who remains himself throughout all the phases of the painting of the picture?

First we must see.

Place the two portraits side by side, and the differences they manifest seem to form a system, a system that may be governed by the principle (or perhaps we should say, out of a certain faithfulness to Kant, the schema) of the variation that they put into play, as if both portraits were conceived and constructed according to a dominant mode and a specific variation that is bound up with it. In any event, one will note that the discourse of this gaze oscillates between the overall impression and the collection of descriptive features without being able to state the formula of the productive schema, without being able to articulate the generative principle of variation.

On the one hand, then, softness, gentleness, sadness; on the other, gravity, severity, modesty. With the first one (Pointel, *A*; Figure 16), we have a Hypolydian variation of the Lydian mode; with the second (Chantelou, *B*; Figure 17), a Phrygian variation (second manner) of the Dorian style. Still, these labels do not mean very much. It is much more appropriate to try—in our turn—to measure the variation and to show, if not to demonstrate, the *difference*.

The formal and plastic construction of space, the manner in which the space of the painting is articulated, the manner in which *painting*, as "theory and practice allied," shows itself in the painted word, constitutes the first field of our assay. Mode—one understands this now—is a *concept of the theory of painting* that is constructed only in a determined practice of "the painting process," just as this "process," this "painting" on the part of the painter, carries with it its own theory. What Poussin is proposing

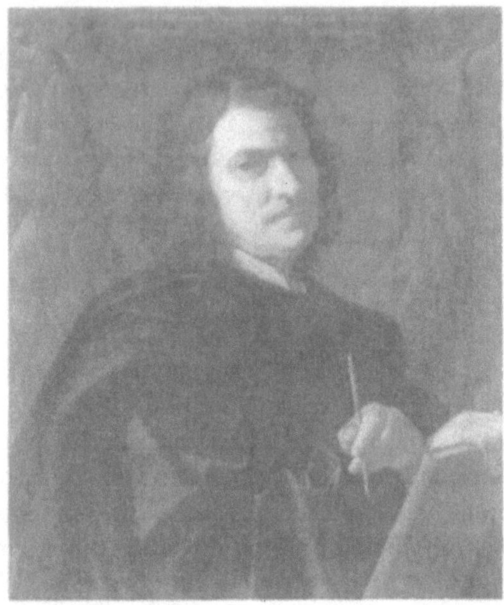

FIGURE 16. *Self-Portrait*, 1649. Courtesy Photographie Giraudon.

with the two self-portraits finally amounts to two "manners," two variations of two modes of painting, that are presented by the figure of the painter himself.

The figure we call Poussin's self-portrait masks, or to put it better, perhaps, is a mask for, Poussin's theoretical propositions concerning manners of painting.

If, in the two self-portraits, the principal figure finds itself confined within a narrow open space between the back of the painting and the picture plane, the spatial and plastic structure of *A* is that of a related curve and countercurve, isomorphic and dominant, that play with obliques (the fold of the coat, the edge of the book, the pencil, and the axis of the face) and that are modulated, in a sharper manner, by the broken folds of the garment and the two hands crossed like birds' wings.

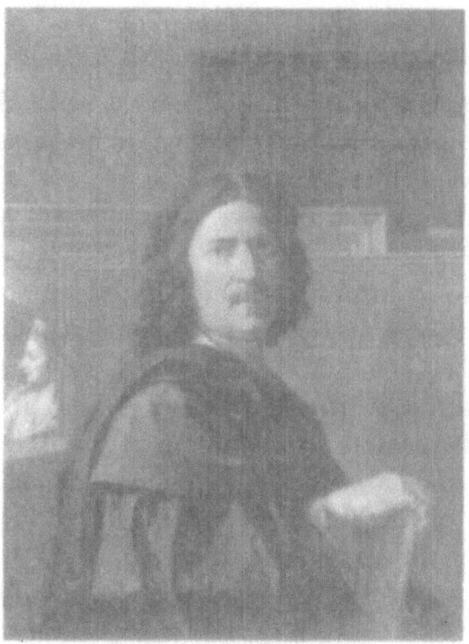

FIGURE 17. *Self-Portrait,* 1650.
Courtesy Photographie Giraudon.

In *B*, the "cupola" of the central figure's cloak or toga, resting on regular and almost vertical columnlike folds, confronts the orthogonality of the level rectangular cuts in the background. There is a single spatial and colored variation: a flat rectangle opens out, in the left-hand portion, onto a depth in which the tonal unity of the painting between gray and brown is broken by dull dark blues and muted golds. In comparison with *A*, the obliques have straightened up—the face, the book, the folds.

In *A*, the model's head is framed and inscribed in a rectangle that is itself inscribed between the two curves of a festoon-wreath: the difference between the figure and the background is in supple conformity with a regular harmony. In *B*, the model's head is detached against five or six overlapping rectangular planes. The upper edge of the frame of the principal canvas of the background and the inner edge of the second painting, which the first one partially hides, inscribe behind the face, at the level of the eyes, something like the narrow slit in a visor through which the figure's gaze seems to pass. The horizontal moldings of the frame of the second painting "traverse" the temples and the forehead, while the vertical edges of the frames of the other canvases are planted on the top of the skull, as if to fix the figure in its verticality, setting up an immobile, "grave" confrontation between the figure and the background planes, a tense asymmetrical equilibrium, in a Phrygian variation of the Dorian mode. Thus, in *A*, the rectangle inscribed in the curve and in which the head of the figure is inscribed symbolically makes visible the structure of the mirror where the painter is looking at *himself* in order to paint himself. In *B*, the narrow band of the cut of the rectangular planes in the background, by defining a network of coordinates for the eyes of the figure alone, constitutes, as it were, a site of visibility for the figure of the painter *from the starting point of the painting* (and the paintings that are represented in it).

The directions and orientations of space also supply interesting reference points for differences and variations. In *A*, the profiled figures of two *putti*, in the background, open the painting up at right and at left: their arms raised, the *putti* are carrying the wreath, which is cut off by the edges of the painting. The painter looks out of the painting, toward the exterior, pointing his pencil downward, a little askew in relation to its summit, as if it constituted the axis of an arrow aimed toward the bottom and formed by the edge of a book and the great oblique fold of the coat. His pencil points precisely to the book's title, which is legible on its spine, *De lumine et colore*, and more precisely still to the word *et*.[6] The painting is open on its sides, but not toward the rear, which is closed off by a wall of simulated architecture and sculpture, *nor* is it open toward the top, where an inscription—two continuous lines and two half-lines at right and at left—close off the space.

In *B*, on both sides, all the rectangular planes composing the "background" are interrupted by their overlapping: the painting appears to be made up of surfaces sliding over one another toward the edges. The figure planted vertically by the frames in the rear, fixed onto the base of the painting, is looking toward the outside. The lateral openings are dominated on the left by the figure of a woman in profile looking toward the left and wearing a diadem-mask in which is embedded, like a precious stone, a "living" eye. This movement is emphasized by the two hands that surround her and seem to be drawing her outside the frame; on the right, the movement is accentuated by the shadow of the "painter's" figure, which covers a part of the interrupted canvas where the shadow is interrupted as such.

On one side, on the left, there is a painted figure in a "represented" narrative; on the other, on the right, there is a shadow, the shadow of the central figure slipping over an equally slippery plane. In contrast, the powerful central and vertical immobility of the painter's figure asserts itself strongly.

In opposition to *A*, where the rear is rigorously closed, despite the *putti*, by simulated architecture and sculptures and where, on the other hand, the central figure is playing in the curves, counter-curves, and obliques, *B* is animated at the rear by a vanishing point, by a slippage of planes that nothing, it seems, can avert: the diadem-adorned woman painted there takes flight outside the painting, as does the "painter's" shadow; hence the telling contrast of the figure placed in a pyramidal structure on the "cupola" of the toga.

In *A*, the background with its monumental architecture is what immobilizes the central figure; in *B*, the central figure remains immobile as the background flees toward the vanishing point: two lyrical tonalities of the self.

We must also try to "read."

We must look first of all—in what is seen, and not in a dictionary or a code of symbols—for meanings that are not immediately of the iconographic order: those that are presented by the figures themselves in their *collocatio*, in a given painting and between one painting and another; the semantic mechanism of the figure of the painter and its meaning effects; variations.

In *A*, the central figure of the painter, presented from the waist up, holds in his right hand a book whose title is legible, *De lumine et colore*, and in the left hand a *draftsman's pencil*, a propelling instrument. In *B*, the central figure of the painter, also presented from the waist up (though in *B* the torso appears in profile, whereas in *A* the painter is rotating in a forward direction), has lost one of its hands, and with it, one of the painter's attributes, the draftsman's pencil. Then too, the book has become a portfolio of drawings or engravings, tied up with a red ribbon held in the figure's left hand, a hand whose little finger wears, with brilliance, a ring set with a diamond.

In *A*, the figure of the painter holds in its left hand the instrument that defines him as a painter and master draftsman, which is the structure of intelligibility and the soul of the painting, the leading part of the painting; still, what the figure is holding in his right hand is neither a sheet of drawing paper nor a painting, but a book entitled *De lumine et colore*. An inconsistency of decorum? One would expect to see either a quill pen and a book, or else a pencil (a brush) and a painting. If there is an inconsistency, it nevertheless induces a deeper analogy: the pencil, the draftsman's tool, is *like* a quill for writing, and the book is *like* a painting or a sheet of drawing paper. "Read the story and the painting," Poussin had written to Chantelou some ten years earlier when he sent him *The Israelites Gathering the Manna* (1639). The rest, if one may put it thus, the light and the shadow, the harmonies of colors, what gives a painting body, its flesh, and its seductiveness, are found in the *book* that the painter is designating in his great learning. Are we not told that around 1650 Poussin was planning to write a book on painting, *De lumine e umbre, colori e mesure*? Chantelou says that Cerisier had seen a manuscript with this title to which the frontispiece of Bellori's life of Poussin alludes: a seated woman pointing to geometrical drawings and to the inscription *lumen et umbra*. And Félibien reports that "in speaking of painting, Poussin says that just as the twenty-four letters of the alphabet serve to form our words and to express our thoughts, in the same way the lineaments [i.e., *the lines of a drawing*] of the human body [serve] to express the various passions of the human soul, to bring to light outside what one has in the spirit."

We must ask ourselves whether, in *A*, the crossing of the hands, the sort of chiasmus that may be the graphic and plastic translation of the rhetorical trope, does not bring into play the *reversal of right and left, of front and back*, achieved by a mirror, a reflecting mechanism necessary to the portrait that the painter is making of himself, light on the figure's left hand, the hand with the pencil, and shadow on his right hand, the hand with the book.

We must likewise ask whether the crossing of the hands with the crossing of the drafting pencil and the book does not designate the crossing with reciprocal effects of the two semiotic universes, the iconic and the scriptural, and also the time of biography and the time of autobiography, past and future, in and beyond the present of the painting. For this book of art theory that Poussin perhaps intends to write in 1649, the viewer—Pointel—now sees its image, as he will see the volume in his library when it *comes to be* written. The viewer even reads its title now: the wonder of painting, which not only brings the dead back to life, as Alberti used to say, but shows as realized what does not yet exist.

We must ask, further, whether the crux of the chiasmus that is presented to view by the two hands, the painter's pencil and his book, would not be the lofty assertion, in painting, that his book of art theory must be written only with *his* practice of art; that *his* practice of art exhibits the theory of art; that *his painting is the theory of painting*. Had he not written to Chantelou on 24 November 1647, and precisely with regard to the meaning effects of his paintings: "To judge well is very difficult, if one does not possess both the theory and the practice" of painting.[7] "Such is the whole artifice of painting," he will write later on, and, in 1665, before he dies, he will call that widespread judgment "the Golden Bough of Virgil, which no one can find or pluck unless he be led to it by Fate."[8]

With *B*, the chiasmus of the hands has disappeared: the figure now displays only the left hand. The "painter" in his image no longer bears any attribute of his art but the portfolio of drawings. The book, in particular, is no longer there with its title allowing the viewer to read what the book would be about, what it would offer to be known, the theory of painting, *De lumine et colore*, a painter's discourse on the artifice of painting, its theory, addressed to the viewer of the painting (Pointel). But in its place, on the little finger, we find a diamond. Now, a diamond, the hardest, the most brilliant of all stones, distinguished by its brilliance, its weight, and its hardness, has, when it is perfect, no other color but white—but with "this peculiarity[:] that when the sun shines on it, it gives off as many rays as it has different faces and colors, red, green, yellow, blue." A diamond engenders colors starting with white, the universal color of sunlight. Through white, *light* is reflected in *lumen*, and *lumen* is fragmented by producing *colores*. The book *De lumine et colore* of *A* has become the diamond in *B*, an emblematic diamond that not only miniaturizes, through *metonymy*, in the pyramid of its beveled cut, but also *metaphorizes* the whole theoretical and practical work of painting, the *friendship* between the light (*lumen*) of painting, "an imitation on a surface with lines and colors of everything that one sees under the sun [*lux*]," and the *color* that painting generates in its diversity.

The diamond is, in *B*, at the crux of the chiasmus that *A* presented to view, between theory *and* practice, between the viewer's *and* the painter's "judging well," between the iconic *and* the scriptural, the pencil *and* the book, light *and* color. It occupies the position of the word "and" in the title of the book, which, in *A*, is designated by the tip of the pencil. It is, emblematically, the "and" of all these oppositions.

We must thus try to see *and* to read.

We must situate the gaze, place the discourse at the geometric locus of the crossings and exchanges, and first gain access, beyond the figure who too easily captures the gaze and the discourse, to what secretly animates the background; penetrate into that crypt where other more secret figures show themselves and signify.

In *A*, the background is a sculpture, or rather a mock bas-relief decorating a monumental architectural construction: a stone slab bearing three lines of engraved inscription framed by a festoon of laurels in a garland, carried by two *putti* shown in profile turning their backs to each other; the one at left, with his head bent and his arm raised up, seems to be asleep. The figure of the writer-painter is inscribed against the background of a sculpture-architecture (simulated and painted): it is framed there; that pretense of painting is its frame. A work of painting, the picture represents, *in the figure of the painter*, the cross between a drawn icon and a written sign and, *in the relation between figure and background*, the tension and the hierarchy of painting and the architecture of sculpture.

The stone slab bears an inscription that reads as follows:

> Nicolaus Poussinus Andelyensis Academicus Romanus Primus
> Pictor ordinarius Ludovici justi regis Galliae. Anno domini
> 1649 Romae Aetatis suae 55

First name: Nicolas; surname: Poussin; place of origin: Les Andelys; profession, title, and distinction (painter, Roman Academician [member of the Saint-Luke Academy]), first among academicians. But on the second line, an earlier title is inscribed in the simulated stone, a title that Poussin had once had, since in 1649 Louis XIII (Louis the Just) had been dead for six years (1643). Finally, the first half of the third line bears the date and place of the painted picture, on the left: "1649 Rome"; and in the second half, on the right, the age of the model that year, fifty-five, his age when he was put into a painting.

The two fragments of the same line of writing present for reading and seeing simultaneously a coincidence and an interval, those of two figures separated by an empty space that is to be occupied, below, by the head of the figure: the date of the "birth" of the painted figure of the painter that begins its life as a painting in Rome, starting in 1649, and the date of the "death" of the model for the figure, the painter, who in 1649 had reached his fifty-fifth year of age, and who will be that age *forever* in the place of the painting. Death and birth in the same place and the same moment, the painting: 1649/55; the autobiography of the painter in his origin, beginning, and foundation, in his beginning, destination, and end, at once *autography* (book of writing) and *zoography* (drawing pencil), his autobiography is an "autobiothanatography," or rather an "autoptic," a painting that folds in on itself, that is reflected in itself, death and life.

Now, as it happens, this inscription, this stone slab, this sculpted monumental architecture is indeed a *tomb*, the monument to the *renown* of the painter for whom the *putti* of death and birth are bearing the laurels of glory.

And, as it happens, this tomb, simulated and painted, of the figure of the painter Poussin is constructed according to the model of a tomb built by his friend, the sculptor François Duquesnoy, who had died, like Louis the Just, in 1643, six years earlier, the tomb of Ferdinand Van den Eynde at Santa Maria dell'Anima, in Rome. Might Poussin be painting Duquesnoy's tomb, giving a painted interpretation of a tomb conceived and sculpted by him, Duquesnoy, who was not only a close friend but one to whom Poussin was linked by a great number of theoretical and aesthetic affinities and, in particular, a common admiration for "our wise ancient Greeks," inventors of the modes?

But is not this tomb, simulated and painted, also the tomb of painting itself, that poor painting about which the letter of 7 April 1647 announced to Chantelou that it was reduced to engraving: "It would be even more appropriate to speak of burying painting (which nobody has ever seen come alive except at the hands of the ancient Greeks)";[9] the same letter that announced again "that there is now no one in Rome who does good portraits" and that, in responding to the criticisms addressed to *The Baptism of Christ*, announced the theory of musical modes in painting and the theory of the principle of variation that presides over their enactment?

The tomb of Duquesnoy and by Duquesnoy is also the tomb of painting, of painting in its "painter-subject," in the figure of the painter.

From the monument to dead painting *to the name* and *under the name of the painter*, the painter is *reborn* to the name and under the name of painting; thus the identification occurs *on the level of the subject*, and the gap between the "subject to be painted," the "subject-of-painting," and the "painter-subject" opens up in the

Hypolydian variation of sweetness and softness, a variation of the Lydian mode adapted to the lamentable things of death. But if to paint oneself is to do the portrait of the image of oneself in the mirror, it is then to cause oneself to die and to be born; it is *on the level of the I*, to cause oneself to die to the body and to the living face of the reality of the individual in its natural sign and to cause oneself to be born to the I, to the singular essence of self, in the artificial icon of self constituted by the painting.

In the place of François Duquesnoy or of painting as subject, the friend Nicolas Poussin or the "painter-subject," the painter inscribes himself then in the painting: he is *written* as a *name* and in the form of an *epitaph on* the tomb; he is *painted* as the *figure* of the *model before* the tomb. *In the place of* the reflecting mirror, the stone slab of the epitaph is erected, in its pretense, as frame and opaque background which is its symbolic structure, even while it serves as the painting's background. *In place of* the image and the living body, the natural sign of the one who is in front of the mirror, according to the paradigm of the Port-Royal *Logic*, the painted icon of the I that eternalizes it in its reflection of a particular essence, its figure in the form of a figure in the artifice of painting.

This motif, which the expression "in place of . . . " designates, is the key motif of the *autoptic*; in the double sense of "what is in the place of . . . , in the place in space occupied by . . . " and "what is being substituted for . . . , what replaces as its delegate, stands in the stead of . . . ," the "in place of . . . " defines, in its ambiguity, the deep structure of representation and, more generally, of the sign as reflexive-transitive. But it is also the mainspring of a strategic mechanism, since, in the same place and owing to this substitution, the "same" dies and is born at the same moment, a form of the divine dream of being the author of one's self.

We must, once again, first try to see.

We must allow the gaze to traverse surfaces, stop dragging it down into the depths; give it the chance to pass over to the other side, the opposite side, the back side, though without ever leaving this side.

"Paroptic" paradoxes.

B introduces into the autoptic a first and obvious variation: the relation between the painted and simulated sculpture-architecture and the writing-drawing gives way to a tension internal to the field of painting itself—the tension between two overturned frames and a canvas that has been prepared but not painted. However, among the frames and canvases, a painting of which only part is perceptible glides toward the left. In the background, in the farthest reaches of the background, there are paintings that show what is not (usually) shown, their opposite side, their back side. In the background, on the surface of the background, serving as background for the figure of the "painter," is a *canvas that exhibits what is not seen of the painting*, the *underside* of the simulated appearances, the simulations in painting. Painting is no longer celebrated in its tomb, in the glory of its death, under the name and in the name of the painter; it is shown and presented to view in the painter's workshop, unshowable and invisible. Or rather it is celebrated as that which is shown and presented to view between something unshowable, the back of the painting, the chassis supporting the canvas and an invisible element, the *underside*, the *underplay*, of the painted and feigned space. But all this still takes place within the field of the painting itself; the back of the painting, like the underside of painting, is still painting, a pretense of painting. Now, since the background of this painting consists only of rectangular panels, of painted supports, these pretenses, these misleading appearances, produce the background of the painting as surface effects or surface spaces: the background space is so narrow, it tends so insistently to be surface or plane, that the Master introduced a red volume on the left (kneeling stool, armchair, pedestal . . .) to give himself the necessary place for his figure.

We must notice that all the rectangular panels constituting the background serve as background for the central figure of the painter, and more particularly for his face: the back wall (of the workshop), the two "unshowable" chassis, the painting presented as a representation of painting and represented as that presentation, the invisible dimension of a canvas prepared for painting and not painted. The "painter" in his painted figure (he is represented not painting or drawing or about to paint or draw, but wearing on his little finger the emblem of painting as light and colors: a diamond), the "painter" has his back turned to that background, he sees nothing of the background that shows the unshowable, offers the invisible to view, or presents the representation of painting. The painting chassis plant the central figure in its verticality; the prepared, unpainted canvas draws its frame precisely *under* the figure's painting, the painting presented inscribes its painted sky on the level of those eyes. But this mechanism for viewing—the slit of a visor or the groove of the sliding of a lateral gaze toward the left—remains entirely unseen by the figure of the "painter," *unless he sees it outside the painting, outside the frame* (in the mirror where he is painting himself?).

Nor does the figure of the painter see the sliding play of the rectangular surfaces behind his back. He does not see their drama. For the canvas that shows its back, its "invisible" aspect, partially hides the painting behind it, against which it is leaning. The *canvas* prevents the *painting* from showing and offering to view what is showing itself and the visible that it represents. Or at the very least, the *painting* manages, in the sliding of backgrounds between right and left, to show a part of what it represents: a figure of a painted woman in the painted picture within the painting at which Chantelou, of course, but first of all "Poussin," is looking. It is an allegorical figure of Painting, Bellori tells us in his "life of Poussin." But even if it is not an allegory of painting, it is still painting, a figure in paint.

The canvas that reveals its invisible back hides a painting that reveals, in spite of that, what it represents through one of its figures: painting. Painting is what is hidden by the unpainted canvas; it is nevertheless what is seen of the painting on the basis of the frame of the blank canvas.

The viewer, Poussin (or Chantelou), notices two hands that surround the figure in paint, two hands belonging to a figure that we do not see. The rest of this painting-within-a-painting on the left is hidden, but it is no longer hidden by the unpainted canvas. The remainder of the painting, the remainder of the figure from the painting that we do not see, is hidden by the painting at which we are looking along with Poussin and Chantelou, hidden by the edge of its frame. Thus painting (a figure of Painting and a figure in paint) turns out to be twice hidden, by a canvas that presents to view its invisible back and by the painting that presents to view what it represents, through *the one* who presents himself to view in what is presented: the painter, the "painter-subject."

More precisely, what, of painting, presents itself to view (both of Painting and of painting), presents itself "between," in a gap, an interval between the invisible of painting of the canvas, its back? And what, of painting, presents itself representing? What makes a painting: the painting in its subject, the one who makes the painting, the "painter-subject," the painter?

The identification between the "subject of painting" and the "painter-subject" opens here on an interval of edges. Painting is what presents itself to view between edges: the edge of a canvas (the unpainted canvas and the edge of its frame) and the edge of a "presentation" of representation (the edge of the painting that we, along with Poussin or Chantelou, are looking at). The re-presentation of painting is what presents itself to view between a canvas and a presentation. In this case—and this is perhaps the most important thing—the presentation of the representation is the "painter-subject" (the "I" that Poussin is painting), and what the "painter-subject" is looking at is perhaps not so much the viewer—Chantelou, you, or me—it is perhaps, by a sliding of his gaze a bit to the side of his image in the mirror, in that very mirror (of) painting, I mean that representation on the edge, between the edge of the canvas and the edge of the mirror (or of the painting that we are looking at) where the "painter-subject" is looking at himself.

But then what the "painter-subject" is looking at in the presentation of the self-representation constituted by the painting (which we are looking at) is not only what we see of the painting between the edge of the unpainted canvas and the edge of the painting in the Louvre; it is also all the rest of that painting, which the representation of itself both represents and hides. Thus, to cite Pascal, "a picture includes absence and presence, pleasant and unpleasant."[10] The figure of the painter sees in particular (or might well see) someone, a figure that we do not see because the "proper" presentation of the represented painter hides it from us: the owner of the two hands that appear in the painting surrounding the effigy of the woman in paint who is perhaps Painting.

We must read.

A bore two inscriptions, one on the upper edge of the background, the epitaph of the tomb, the other, obliquely, in the lower right section, the title of the book. Hence the relation between the volume of the book and the wall of the tomb, since the *name* of the author of the future book on art theory is transposed to the wall of the tomb as the name of the one who has been deposited there, the *name of the dead man* in paint, in the place of another, Duquesnoy, in the place of another, Painting.

In *B*, there remains only one inscription, which results from the displacement, "literally and figuratively," of the two inscriptions in *A*, the name of the book and the name of the author, *into* the right section, *onto* the unpainted canvas; displacement too in the "form" of the inscription and in its meaning:

Effigies Nicolai Poussini Andel:
Yensis Pictoris. Anno aetatis 56
Romae Anno Jubilei
1650.

Whereas in *A* the funerary inscription closes off the background of the painting, crowning the figure of the painter, that of *B* is written as a sort of negative, in its form, of the figure to which it is juxtaposed. This is what brings to light the date of the jubilee year, the half-century mark, 1650. Nevertheless, a cut affects the name of the painter's place of origin: the edge of the painting, which "we" are looking at, makes it impossible, on the right, to write from a single venue and consequently to read, likewise, the word *Andelyensis*; similarly, the other edge of this painting, on the left, makes it impossible to see a figure of which we perceive only two hands, two hands thus brought to light as the letter Y is at the beginning of the second line of the inscription, the Y whose powerful emblematic value we recognize: the Pythagorean letter of choice between good and evil, virtue and pleasure, soon to become a symbol of virtue itself.

The displacement of meaning is even more noteworthy: it is no longer the "painter" whom the inscription names in his ultimate biographical reality, but the "subject-of-painting" or the "painter-subject." The inscription names both the painting, by the painter's name, and the name of the painting representing the painter:

> Portrait of Nicolas Poussin of Andel-
> Ys, painter. In the year of his age 56
> in Rome, the jubilee year
> 1650.

In the title-name of the painting (as, for example, on a museum label where one would read "Nicolas Poussin: Self-Portrait"), what is named above, but in the form of a genitive, "nominative complement" (*Nicolai Poussini Andel / Yensis pictoris*), is at once the name of the painter of the picture (*Nicolaus Poussinus qui faciebat, qui pinxit*) and the name of the model for the figure, the name of the person whom the painting represents (*Nicolaus Poussinus Andel / Yensis*): a single name, or rather three names in one just like the three strokes of the Y, a letter that is both triple and unitary, appearing owing to the interruption of the toponym of origin, returning like the bevel of light and color of the diamond, an emblem of painting in its theory and practice.

Effigies Nicolai Poussini . . . the name of the painting: but what painting? The painting we are looking at? The painting that presents the representation of the "painter-subject" and whose title offers the simultaneous declension of his name, origin, age, profession, and so on? Not only does the painting present the representation of the "painter," but by including its title, its name, as one of its parts, it presents itself not only by offering its "name," the name of the figure represented and the name of the one it represents, to be read, but also by offering to view, in these four lines of writing, the rhetorical figure, the trope by means of which it designates itself, a synecdoche, since the part (the writing) stands semantically for the whole (the painting). The inscription, a part of the painting as a whole, is actually in excess in relation to that totality: it is, as it were, greater than the whole, since nowhere does the whole make it possible to see either the temporal marks of the represented figure (*anno aetatis* 56) or those of its own presentation (*anno jubilei* 1650), still less those of its location, neither that of the figure (*Romae*) nor that of the model's origin (*Andel / Yensis*). In exchange, the painting as a whole "says" more than the part that is inscribed within it to name it: no word states the feminine figure painted in profile that is slipping toward the edge drawn by two mysterious hands.

Perhaps *effigies* does not designate the painting that we are looking at, but only the figure represented that it is presenting to the gaze: Nicolas Poussin of Andelys, painter; perhaps it refers to this portrait, this *effigies*, an image, a copy, a pretense. The true Nicolas Poussin, the real one, is outside the painting, outside the frame . . . "The portrait of Nicolas Poussin is Poussin." A few years later, the logicians of Port-Royal will explain that that very statement is said with signification and as a figure, through metaphor, metonymy, synecdoche, antonomasia, and ellipsis. One part of the painting on the right, four lines of writing, "makes" the reader "say" what another, adjacent part "makes" the viewer "see," and all the rest of the painting is swallowed up in silence as it shows the slippage of its rectangular panels and the diamond on the little finger and the portfolio of drawings and the great painting that a woman of paint is preparing to leave, dragged off by her companion.

But where, then, is the inscription written? Without hesitation the eye responds: on the canvas that has been prepared but not yet painted, a gray surface tinged with brown, hardly more sustained than the gray surface of the wall at the rear of the painter's studio (in the background of his painting). Is the shadow cast by the represented figure not projected onto the unpainted canvas in order to cover part of the inscription and to allow light to fall only on certain words or fragments of words?

Effigies Nicola
Yensis Pictor
Rom

Effigies is also a shadow, a phantom, a ghost. Why, then, might the illuminated inscription not designate the shadow of the figure of the "painter"—that second figure slipping toward the right on the surface that has been prepared and not painted—both by naming it "shadow," and with fragments of names, where only two complete names would emerge from it: *effigies*, the name by which it is designated, and *pictor*, the name that it designates. Thus in this light the prepared canvas is not entirely unpainted, since a "painter's" shadow slips over its surface and since an inscription names it: a dream of a painting to be done, a painting that is in the process of coming into being, that we do not yet see and that passes at the limit between the visible and the invisible, on the underside of the canvas (something invisible is offered to view here), a dream of the painting to be done, which is also the dream of the origin of painting, a shadow on a surface that is at once prepared and virgin. The portrait of Nicolas Poussin of Andelys, painter, is thus played out *between* this pyramiding and frontal image of the painting we are looking at and the shadow that slips and passes by on the canvas and its underside, *effigies . . . pictor*, between the two, where *effigies* means "portrait" and "shadow" and of which *pictor* is at once the author and the product.

Then again, and to conclude, we must come back to the gaze and the eye.

The gaze of the figure of the "painter-subject" slips into the dark blue slit of the visor that the canvas and the represented painting set up behind his back; it is directed obliquely outside the frame, somewhere on the left, and it settles with extreme tension on a point of that space from which we are looking at it, a place that is not the one occupied by the viewer but a little bit beside him. As viewer, I accompany that gaze from my own vantage point. As reader, I follow the first line of the inscription from right to left, and, reading the story *and* the painting, instead of the "and," I find an eye, in a beautiful female face seen in profile, an eye that, under a smooth forehead and golden hair, is gazing, between surprise and joy, at someone whose arms are held out to her, someone of whom I perceive only the simulated hands that are drawing that painted figure toward himself, someone whom the figure of the painter is looking at with his two tense eyes. What story is being told there, between the two edges of the canvas that has been prepared and not painted and those of the painting that we are looking at, on the represented painting? It is a story in which we shall never see more than one of the protagonists, a painted woman; of the other, we shall see only his hands. The two eyes of the figure of the painter have slipped into the crack: the woman's figure, in profile, nevertheless has two eyes, since it is crowned with a mask in which a second eye, as alert as that of her face, is open. Even in profile, the figure has two eyes, the eye of nature and the eye of artifice, equally alert; a painted figure, she is also the figure of Painting, and the one whom the figure of the painter discovers from the place within the painting where he is planted, from the space represented in the painting, the represented space of painting, the workshop of the painter—it is *the lover of Painting* who draws her outside the frame, it is the *painter*. The figure of the painter uncovers itself, but it is then no longer a figure. The painter, lover of painting, is unrepresentable or at the limit of representation, of all representation, whether presented or represented. It is this *true* self-portrait of the painter that the figure of the painter is looking at outside the painting, a self-portrait, *invisible because true*, that only the painter in his representation of painting can see, but beyond all representation, and which he leaves to the viewer to guess at, through his hands which are drawing Painting to himself, hands that draw and paint, on the canvas, the appearances, the shadows, of things and beings.

But the "true" painter, the "real" painter, the lover of Painting, is still only a character, a figure in a story that is painted and represented, at least partially, in the painting which the painter's self-portrait represents in its own order. It is a figure—but an invisible one—of a story, of a story painting, but one that allows us to understand (or to anticipate) that the story told there is the story of painting and of its painter. For the story to take *place* (in all senses of the expression: for it to come about and for it to find a space), the identification of the "subject-of-painting" and of the "painter-subject" must be forever deferred, the identification of Painting and of its painter, the amorous attraction of the one by the other, must not be offered to view in the painting itself—the self-portrait of Nicolas Poussin in 1650, in Rome—where that attraction seems to operate.

This gap that the *Pointel self-portrait* of 1649–1650 allowed us to understand, in a Hypolydian variation of the Lydian mode, like that of the funerary monument of painting offering to the painter the mirror of death so he could grasp in it the singular and essential icon of his *I*, the *Chantelou self-portrait* of 1650, is offered to view in the Phrygian variation of the Dorian mode, as the gap between the *invisible* figure of the "painter-subject," the unrepresentable lover of painting in its story and the *visible* figure of the painter whose "I" is summed up in the contemplation of his double outside of representation, outside of figuration, outside of painting. If lyricism is the love song and the swan song of the self, then Poussin's self-portrait is indeed a double pictorial variation of that song, addressed to Pointel and to Chantelou, in which are read and seen the epic poem of the (hi)story of painting and the heroic poem of the (hi)story of the painter.

§ 10 The Sublime in the 1670s

Something Indefinable, a "Je Ne Sais Quoi"?

The following text presents elements of an inquiry into the emergence of the notion of the sublime in seventeenth-century France and some of its avatars in the rhetorical and poetic theories of that historical moment, as well as their impact, their long-term importance for a philosophy of art and an aesthetics in general.

Boileau published his translation of the treatise by the pseudo-Longinus, the *Peri Upsous, du Sublime*, in 1674, the same year his own *Art poétique* came out. However, we know that he had begun his translation, like the *Art poétique*, toward the end of the 1660s. The year 1674 can thus serve, for France, as the chronological emblem of the 1670s, a decade that has been considered—rightly, in my view—as a major turning point, as much for literature and the arts and the aesthetic theorizations of both as for the political and ideological realms.

One of the elements of this inquiry into the seventeenth-century sublime appears in my subtitle in the form of a question: the "je ne sais quoi." Here, too, my historical justification is the appearance, in 1671, of a text that I consider very important for the critical decade in question: Dominique Bouhours's *Entretiens d'Ariste et d'Eugène*, six conversations, the last one of which deals specifically with the "je ne sais quoi."

I should like to begin by articulating the notion of the "je ne sais quoi." Like the notion of the sublime itself, it antedates the critical period, the period of the sublime. The articulation can be formulated schematically in the following way: the sublime stems from the "je ne sais quoi," but the "je ne sais quoi" cannot be reduced to the sublime.

Let us consider the articulation of the "je ne sais quoi" to the sublime, first of all. The sublime is a "je ne sais quoi" to the very extent that it appears difficult, if not impossible, to produce or construct a "concept" of the sublime, to the very extent that the definition of the sublime raises a question, poses a problem, that is an integral part of the notion of the sublime itself. Hence the question of how to define the "sublime." In his preface to Longinus's treatise, in what will constitute one of the guiding threads of his *Réflexions* at the end of the century, Boileau posits the crucial distinction between the sublime and the sublime style. In other words, in both the preface and the *Réflexions* proper, X and XII in particular, the sublime is not a determining adjectival qualifier, characteristic of the third, or elevated, style of discourse; rather, it is a full-fledged substantive that names "something specific" which can appear in simple and mediocre styles as well as in the high or sublime style. According to the examples Boileau chooses (and this has often been taken as one of the marks of Boileau's "classicism"), it is actually in the simple style that the sublime is encountered in privileged fashion.

In order to locate the sublime, moreover, one must not look simply at what is being said (the topic, the subject matter), but at the way in which it is said and the occasion on which it is said (and I shall stress for my part the term *occasion*, which is also found in Longinus with the notion of *kairos*)—in short, one must look *non quid sit sed quo loco sit.* By stressing this fact, Boileau brings to light the indetermination of its marker. The place in question is not a logical or rhetorical *topos*; instead, it characterizes the context of a discourse, the circumstances that "surround" a singular relation of enunciation (that of a sender to a receiver). In other words, the sublime, unlike the sublime style, does not characterize a style, a genre, or a sort of discourse or poem. It can be borne by all styles, all genres: it belongs to none. It does not belong to a rubric or a class in a rhetorical taxonomy, it does not stem from a lexicon or a vocabulary; it is not the distinguishing feature of a figure or a trope, even though in his treatise Longinus attempts to recognize how figures and images contribute to the sublime. On the contrary, it stems from what today we would call pragmatics, from an art of circumstances, singularities, and meaning effects. It is easy to re-cognize the sublime in discourse, in a poem or a painting, but this re-cognition is in exact proportion to its theoretical indefinability, the impossibility of producing rules for the construction of its concept. As Boileau writes, it is not properly "something that is proved and demonstrated but something that makes itself felt." The sublime feature *shows itself* in a speech or a poem. It does not belong to the order of representation; it belongs to the order of presentation, to a *deixis* in interlocution—but to a particular type of *deixis*, to a particular form of presentation.

Hence a second articulation of the "je ne sais quoi" with the sublime: here it is no longer a question of definition, of the taxonomic, rhetorical, conceptual, generic delimitation of the sublime, but of the pragmatic search for the reason for its effects, as Pascal would say (and Pascal knew a good deal about the sublime). To remain in the year 1674, in his preface to the translation of Longinus, in the subtitle he gives his translation, Boileau is already proposing a term that substitutes for the sublime: the marvelous or its parasynonyms, the extraordinary or the surprising.

Still, in Boileau's preface or in the tenth *réflexion*, what distinguishes the marvelous, the extraordinary, or the surprising is the fact that they are defined by their effects alone, but these effects are of a certain type or category; they are in turn definable only with reference to the *definiendum*. What is the marvelous, after all? It is what delights, transports, carries away; what strikes, seizes, surprises, enchants; what arouses emotion. The movement is circular and tautological, but it posits the pragmatics of the sublime as a pathetics. This pathetics is itself quite singular, however, for in its turn it does not stem from a taxonomy of the particular passions and their expressive signs. What is involved is rather a pathetics of pathos itself. Hence the remarkable sublime presentation of representation (discursive, poetic, iconic, etc.): remarkable in that the presentation is unrepresentable according to the tabular, taxonomic, classificatory mechanism of representation, according to the order of representation of ideas, images, affects of which it is nevertheless a distinctive feature. The sublime presentation is itself sublime in this sense. It is an affect-effect without any articulable difference; it is not *a* passion but the *pathos* of all the passions; it is not *an* emotion but the *motion* of all the emotions. In short, it is an indefinable, an unrepresentable, an unclassifiable, both on the part of the enunciator (Boileau speaking of Longinus writes, after all: "His sentiments have something indefinable [*ses sentiments ont je ne sais quoi*] that marks a sublime spirit, a powerful soul well above the ordinary"; or, in the tenth *réflexion*, in connection with a passage Longinus cites from Herodotus: "One feels here a certain energetic force which, marking the horror of the thing that is uttered, has something indefinably sublime about it [*a je ne sais quoi de sublime*]") and on the part of the statement, since the sublime affect-effect is always marked by an alteration, a breakdown in the identity of the subject, a disappropriation of the subject by himself (whether it is a question of being ravished, transported, carried away, or stupefied, astonished, staggered) which every individual passion no doubt modulates or modalizes, but which would be exercised here in the state of pure *pathos*, pure motion.

The sublime or the "je ne sais quoi" not only of the rhetorics and poetics of genres and styles, rules and tropes and figures, but also of all aesthetic theory, that is, evaluative judgment, judgment of taste, any theory of art—in this sense, with the "je ne sais quoi" a gap within the theory, the sublime names an internal gap, a gap with respect to the "je ne sais quoi," an end of art itself designating both its destination and its cessation. Boileau puts it this way: "The sublime is that indefinable element [*ce je ne sais quoi*] that charms and delights us, without which beauty would have neither grace nor beauty"; this "je ne sais quoi" or sublime in Boileau one can readily translate into contemporary critical language with the notion of peak (*comble*) and supplement. The sublime *is added* to beauty as a supplement, a surplus, a plenitude enriching a plenitude, but it *compensates* (*supplée*), it names that without which beauty would not be beautiful. The position of this "je ne sais quoi" (its place) is at the limit of beautiful form, on the limit of beautiful form, which renders it limitless, which is its lack of limit, its lack of definition, but which is at the same time the space, the place, the line where form finds the limit, the finishing touch that forms it, the line that makes it a form, that makes it beautiful. Just as in the semantic tension that animates the verb "to fill to the brim" (*combler*), which means both to fill up a hole, a void, a lack, but also to fill something that is *already* full, to overfill. The "je ne sais quoi" of the sublime, then, is what is between the brim and the brimming over of measure, of form.

This is what is indicated, it seems to me, in the introduction of the term "marvelous" in Boileau's preface as a "supplement" for the sublime je ne sais quoi, in connection with which we might repeat the movement we have just accomplished: the marvelous is not the distinguishing characteristic of the epic genre, still less of the Christian epic genre that Boileau evokes in Chant II of the *Art poétique*, even if it is incumbent upon the epic genre to bear its features even more than tragedy does. In the preface to the treatise, as I see it, the marvelous is much more inclined to mark the confrontation between the *mimetic representation* governed by the imitation of nature or at least its ideal order (a mechanism of the reproductive imagination, to use Kantian language), on the one hand, and *phantasia*, on the other hand, a notion developed by middle Stoicism (Panaetius of Rhodes, Posidonius of Apamea) and the Second Sophistic, all the theoretical elements of which are found in Longinus's *Treatise on the Sublime* and which are viewed as the mark of the productive imagination. A frequently cited text of Philostratus the Elder in his *Life of Apollonios of Tyana* could serve as the emblem for this confrontation, as could a whole series of Italian, Spanish, or German treatises on poetics and rhetoric; I shall mention here only Francesco Patrizi's *Della poetica* (1586), which is in its entirety an attack on mimesis as source or origin of poetry. It is not imitation through resemblance that makes the poet and the poem, for this would mean limiting poetry to human actions, passions, and characteristics alone. Unlike the other discursive arts, poetry derives its power from enthusiasm, a natural movement of the spirit driven by the *phantasiai*, which are presented to it by the light of a god, a genius, or a demon. "This infusion into the subject who receives the light operates in him without his knowing, thus illuminated, what he is saying or doing." The *mirabile* is the quality common to all true poems and true poets, and the *mirabile* is the specific effect of the poem on the public constituting the *maraviglia*.

Here we recognize the motifs of Longinus's *Treatise on the Sublime*, published in 1554, and the culmination in the High Renaissance of a whole trajectory of Platonic notions by way of Plotinus, Aristotle, Stoicism, the Seneca of the *Letters to Lucilius*, the poetics of the *Idea*, of *phantasia*, of the *concetto* that had been ripening for a long time in the unfathomable depths of divine thought, other elaborations of which are found in Philo of Alexandria and in Plutarch, with the distinction made by the Church Fathers between the *logos endiathetos*, internal speech linked to divine speech, and the *logos prophorikos*, speech actually produced, the image of the other, projected into the perceptible world. (Was it not in 1674 that Malebranche published his *Recherche de la vérité*, in which this motif is taken up again, between Augustine and Descartes?) And when Patrizi seeks to shore up the theoretical foundations of this poetics of the marvelous, is he not led to introduce between the cognitive faculty and the sensitive or affective faculty a *potenza ammirativa*, which, between understanding and sensitivity, communicates with both and ensures the dynamic passage from one to the other, the creative power of figurative fictionalizing (*finzione, formatura, trasfigurazione*) where we cannot fail to recognize Longinus's *skhematizein*, that is, precisely the schematism of the productive imagination which Kant will position in the same way "in the depths of the soul," "art hidden from Nature," at the abyssal center of the *Critique of Judgment*? The poetic theory of the marvelous and the marvel would function then in relation to the governance of genres and species of poetics like the philosophic theory of *phantasia* in relation to mimetic representation: by marking the internal rupture of the relation of language to things and essences, the internal rupture of the ontological power of language. It introduces into the very workings of the mechanism of representation, that is, at the outer limits of this mechanism, the questioning of the sublime in order to try to find the truth of poetic discourse in a free functioning of language, productive of new associations, and not a restitution of an ideal order of being: a truth that would be the mysterious one of the singular variations of subjective judgment and of the infinite variety or diversity of the circumstances of things.

But here I should like to present my central hypothesis, which is at once theoretical and historical. According to this thesis, in the pivotal decade of the 1670s, in particular with the theoretical promotion of the "je ne sais quoi," we witness an astonishing attempt to integrate the theory of the marvelous and *phantasia* into the mechanism of representation that constitutes simultaneously its pinnacle and its immanent interrogation. The "je ne sais quoi" is precisely the key operator of such an integration, which *betrays*, in all senses of the term, the persistence, the insistence of the question of the sublime as an aesthetic motif that calls into question aesthetics itself—it is the destination and the suspense of art. Still according to my hypothesis, this is revealed by the remarkable semantic operation—already noted in connection with the sublime itself—that takes place with the substantification of the adjective. Here we have the substantification of a phrastic utterance, that is, the transformation of a sentence—a "je ne sais quoi," *signifying* a limit or indeterminate knowledge, i.e., a judgment articulating a state of the theoretical subject—into a noun that raises that state to the dignity of an essence, i.e., a nominal idea, to a term that designates a substance and thereby acquires in language, and in language alone, a determined ontological and semantic status: a truly "marvelous," extraordinary way of presenting, through and in representation, its unrepresentable, the blind spot of knowledge and meaning.

Before coming to Bouhours and the *Entretiens d'Ariste et*

d'Eugène, I should like to propose by way of epigraph, and perhaps as an emblem for this study, two well-known portraits of La Rochefoucauld, one a self-portrait and the other by his intimate enemy, the cardinal de Retz.

The phrase "je ne sais quoi" appears nowhere in La Rochefoucauld's text, but his self-portrait brings to light the logical and semantic structure of that substantive in the "representation" of the subject. La Rochefoucauld constructs his self-portrait one distinctive feature—physical, moral, or intellectual—at a time. The general structure of "neither . . . nor" "informs," as it were, each lineament of his being (he is neither tall nor short, his nose is neither fat nor pointed, and so on). This structure of the *neuter* is not that of an indefinite in general; on the contrary, it defines an interval to which no name corresponds, one that can only be characterized—or so it seems—by the double negation of extreme limits (or limits posited as such) of each feature. By that very token, the representation effect or the portrait effect is that of an accumulation of unique traits that constitute, through an imaginary totalization, an absolutely unique, exceptional, uncategorizable being, a being in its infinite singularity, the "I" itself.

Retz, on the contrary, begins his portrait of La Rochefoucauld with the following statement: "There has always been something undefinable [du je ne sais quoi] in M. de La Rochefoucauld overall." Perhaps he is saying the same thing about La Rochefoucauld that La Rochefoucauld is saying about himself, but he makes a substantive of La Rochefoucauld's singular "I" by making a substantive of "je ne sais quoi," that is, of his own inability to paint La Rochefoucauld's portrait, to trace the lines and lineaments of that portrait, to capture La Rochefoucauld's own distinctive form through those lines; thus the indeterminate, the indefinite, becomes through the global substantifying operation ("always," "overall"), the principal substantial attribute of La Rochefoucauld's being. La Rochefoucauld *is* an indeterminate entity, a sort of psychological and moral ectoplasm. Very schematically, one might say that the confrontation between the two portraits traces, in the mechanism of representation of the subject of representation, the operation of substantification of the utterance "je ne sais quoi," or that it describes the operator "je ne sais quoi" simultaneously in the constitution of the mimetic representation, on its limits and in its effects. It opens up a path for investigation—a path that is at once historical and theoretical—into the "sublime" presentation (which is the very question of the sublime) of the unrepresentable in the representational mechanism.

Let us stop here a moment to consider this process of substantification. Let us begin with the statement "I do not know something," analyzed as an admission, the recognition of ignorance about an object or a domain of objectivity. Actually, this statement hides a paradox that has been well known since Plato's day: how can I know *what* I do not know? (Hence all the philosophical theories, from ideas about the intelligible nether-world rediscovered through an originary anamnesis to the Stoics' prenotions, and so on.) From this standpoint, Montaigne's famous "Que sais-je?" ("What do I know?") constitutes the skeptical relativist formulation of the paradox: I do not know nothing, I do not know everything, I know neither nothing . . . nor everything. Still, the interrogative phrasing destabilizes learned ignorance, and with it the position of a theoretical subject: I do not know whether I know what I know; I do not know whether I am ignorant of what I do not know.

Turning now to the statement "je ne sais quoi," "I know not what," an examination of its occurrences in sentences like "There is—I know not what—over there," "there is I know not what that is affectionate, deep," would show the power of "there is," "there are," before any perceptive, cognitive, or volitional determination, the "there is" of things, of Being in general before the constitution, the construction, of the subject-object relation of representation, a "there is" that I have tried to rediscover as the basis for the theory of judgment in the *Grammaire générale* and in the *Logique de Port-Royal*, through the surreptitious position of which it is assured, without any metaphysical psychological deduction, the exact coextensivity of language and of being and its epistemological validation—its veridiction. From this standpoint, the expression "I know not what" marks the recognition of a "there is," but each time related to a *virtual* knowledge and to a specific realm of experience. It is easy to relate all these remarks to Kant's thinking about the free *Bild* anterior to all images, all representations, the nonfigurative *Bild* that Kant calls a schema in the first *Critique* and that we find again in the third *Critique* with aesthetic judgment: play of the reflection of the imagination (the motif of representation "presenting itself"), when it schematizes without concepts, that is, when the world that forms itself, that manifests itself, is not a universe of objects, but only a schema (a schema that constitutes a world). A schema is a figure (*skhēma* in Greek), but the imagination that figures without concepts figures "nothing." It is a nothing that is not nothing, but that is the first impulse of a form that gives itself form. In short, we recognize the sublime here as the limitless, the in-finite, as the movement of nonlimitation that takes place on the edge of limits, of shapes, of forms: that is, beauty itself.

With the substantification of the utterance, or even of the adverb, we witness a power play of language, a linguistic act of violence, since the indeterminate is given a name, and is thereby determined as indeterminate. The passage to the name, to the noun, unseats the subject from its position of indetermination, of affect-effect of indetermination: "I" is henceforth the part of a noun that the "I" constitutes in constituting itself as subject.

It will be up to Pascal to thematize the threat that appears with the sentence "I know not what," the threat that the noun "I know not what" "covers" (but that it does not suppress) by its logothetic creation. For example, in a passage from fragment 113 of the *Pensées* we observe that, for Pascal, the nominalization of the "I know not what" only *shows* the operation of any nomination: "A town or a landscape from afar off is a town and a landscape, but as one approaches it becomes houses, trees, tiles, leaves, grass, ants, ants' legs, and so on *ad infinitum. All that is comprehended in the word 'landscape.'*"[1]

We come at last to Bouhours and his *Entretiens d'Ariste et d'Eugène*, in which these operations, at once theoretical and ideological, seem to me perfectly recognizable so long as we notice that the fifth *entretien*, entitled "Le je ne sais quoi," "The I Know Not What," only reflects (pseudo-theoretically) what the six *entretiens* taken together establish.

Bouhours's book opens with a conversation entitled "The Sea" and closes with the very long sixth conversation, "Devices" (pertaining to heraldic devices), preceded by "The I Know Not What" and, before that, "The Fine Wit," "The Secret," and "The French Language." Here let me simply mark my working hypothesis concerning the "I know not what" as an operator of integration of the *phantasia* in *mimesis* or of the *marvelous* in *representation*, by evoking the starting point and the end point of the trajectory of the *entretiens* (without being able to demonstrate it, of course: these are merely suggested directions for study and discussion).

"The Sea" is, if one may say so, the presentation of the "there is" itself. Surprising, marvelous, admirable, the sea always appears new, since it is never in the same state: an immense expanse, calm or agitated. Here at the very beginning of the conversation Bouhours articulates the opposition between the beautiful and the sublime in connection with the storm of which the motif of the "I know not what" is an integral part: a "terrible *and* pleasant spectacle" that inspires "*I know not what horror accompanied by pleasure.*" Animated by the ebb and flow of the waves, changing colors from one moment to the next, mingling an infinite number of different faces, an infinite number of colors, the sea is a natural painting that art cannot imitate; the sea is the limitless aspect of nature, the very indeterminacy of its perceptible presentations, not quantitatively but qualitatively: its infiniteness is less a matter of "spatial" expanse than of variety, a variety such that the mind, the theoretical subject, cannot discover its law or its rules. This impossibility of producing the law of diversity is emblematized by the long discussion on ebb and flow, an "abyss where the human mind loses itself," a veritable carousel of philosophical or physical theories that is developed in a sort of skeptical jubilation of the "theoretical" variety: "not one [theory] explains what is singular in ebb and flow." The ideological presuppositions of the competing theories are easy to observe (the opposition between the aristocrat and the scholar), and so are the philosophical presuppositions: a skeptical relativism about knowledge and theory opens up the more or less autonomous field of an *aesthetics* of variety, of singularity, that is, of infinity in representation, and its objective *ratio* in which it would sink if that field were not, at this initial stage, immediately covered over by two motifs in reciprocal tension, that of a practical philosophy of the useful, of commerce, of interest properly understood (see the end of the *entretien*), and that of a metaphorics and a symbolics in which the sea ceases to be a thing, the "there is an infinity" of singularities, and becomes the image, itself contradictory, of God and the World. This double motif should be pursued in a study of the subsequent *entretiens*, not only the ones entitled "The Fine Wit" and "The Secret," but even more particularly the one on "the French language," one key to which, it seems to me, consists in articulating, or even identifying, the idiomatic singularity of a language (French) with the rational-natural universality of a linguistic order.

The sea is a marvel; but it is not a question of dissipating the "marvel" by constructing the representation, the ideal and rational order of Nature that would explain the marvelous effects of its diversity. It is a question of introducing the marvel into the mechanism of representation by a linguistic power play, by a tactical stroke of language and thought: this will be an operation that the conversation on "the I know not what" will *reflect* before finding its culmination in the conversation titled "Devices."

The "I know not what" names the indefiniteness of variety, of singularities: the typology of versions of "I know not what" attempts a purely descriptive taxonomy, an open grid whose entries are themselves of an interminable diversity, the essential factor being that through the operation of language, through nomination itself multiplied by a jubilatory description, the indeterminate is *uttered* as *indeterminate*—so that one can rejoice in it—without *being known* (in the sense of explaining), for knowledge and theory would cause the object itself, the object to be known, to disappear, as one of the interlocutors points out. Better still, it is an object whose "reality" exists only because one cannot say what that reality is, or more precisely, which wins its status as reality through a name that states the impossibility of knowing it: "One can explain it only by admiration and silence." And we shall not be surprised to observe that the conversation about the "I know not what" is broken off when Nature itself presents its own unrepresentability, through a storm.

The conversation about "devices" closes the circle that had been opened—broken into—by the one titled "The Sea": it closes the circle of representation that encloses, in its turning and returning, the marvel, the sublime of the marvel in the harmonized double gesture of language and image.

From the beginning, it is expressly noted that the discourse on devices will respond in some way to the discourse on the sea and, in particular, to the discussion on ebb and flow. It does respond, but as a reversed image in a mirror. In fact, whereas the dialogue on the ebb and flow of the sea had manifested the theoretical collapse of a rational knowledge of the diversity, the indefiniteness, the shapelessness of varieties and circumstances, Ariste's discourse seeks to define, as precisely and as rigorously as possible, the rules for constructing devices—that is to say, beyond devices (devices being limited in this instance to the device of representation), the rules of representation, of metaphor as representation and of representation as metaphor, rules which, in an immanent way, constitute the legitimacy of representation, its "objective" validity: the domain of mimesis; "the device is, properly construed, a metaphor of proportion that represents one object by another to which it has some resemblance." And we shall not be surprised that the example chosen to illustrate what a regular device is—that is, a "rationally, legitimately regulated" device—is that of the Sun King. It is on the basis of this Aristotelian definition of metaphor that there will be true devices and false ones, even if the latter are sometimes ingenious and brilliant.

The device is the conjunction of an image—a figure—and a word, a *concetto*, a *moto*. Bouhours concentrates on the regulation of these two parts and their "metaphorical" articulation, and once that has been achieved, once the rigorous system of rules and law legitimizing representation has been constructed, then the marvelous can make its appearance, the marvelous that, *alone*, makes a *perfect* device: it is added to representation only to bring it to completion; it is the pinnacle of representation. Now, what is the marvelous? It is "the union of two thoughts and two terms that seem contrary and incompatible"; but this contradiction in thought and language must be not only plausible, as with the marvelous of epic poetry, but also based on truth itself. Bouhours goes on to explain by way of an example. The marvelous or the sublime in representation? Let us listen to Bouhours:

> The marvelous results, as you see, from a figure, which causes both astonishment and pleasure at once. Thus to introduce it into the device, one must choose bodies which, however natural they may be in themselves, have that semblance of qualities above nature. However, for this it is not always necessary to seek extraordinary and surprising figures. . . . It suffices [therefore] to find properties in ordinary figures that no one has yet discovered; for one cannot see without surprise something rare and exquisite in an object that seemed to have only common qualities. The secret of art consists in discovering these new lights, and it is in this that the one I regard as the master of the others in this matter excels.

And soon afterward we are going to see the conjunction of all the motifs that we have attempted to recognize in our study, the sublime and/or the marvelous and the "I know not what." What is the perfect idea for the device? "One must conceive simultaneously of I know not what mysterious aspect and I know not what clear aspect, or rather something that is neither too clear nor too obscure." This uniting of contrary features is accomplished in an instant, as if by lightning; its effect is the blinding, the astonishment of an irresistible I know not what: the marvelous, the sublime is closer here to what will be the Romantic lightning stroke of the *Witz*. But Bouhours will attempt to spell out the means for producing the sublime and marvelous "lightning stroke," once again within the rigorously rule-governed representation of the device.

The lightning stroke of the *Witz* can only be that of a singularity, of the difference that distinguishes the person who bears the device from all others, *absolutely*: its pure presentation belongs to itself alone. "This particular convention has as its basis the special individual circumstances that distinguish one person from others. The first of these circumstances is the very *Name* of the person. . . . The second, that of the person's arms, his blazon, the third his individual actions," and so forth. Ariste goes on to conclude that the perfect device, that is, the one that is totally regular, because it is ruled by the laws of representation, has not been and will perhaps never be produced. "This science is infinitely above me."

And just as the device appeared to us as the device of "classical" representation itself, the particular mechanism that best exhibits its construction *and* its deconstruction, the work of the question of the sublime, of *phantasia* in mimesis, and of the marvel in the classical order of discourse and image, in the same way the science of the device will be given by Bouhours as the paradigm for a knowledge and an acquaintance in which are simultaneously accomplished and undone the knowledge of and acquaintance with the natural, rational *universality* of man and the world. Here we would need to read the closing pages of the conversation. I shall draw from them only this: the science of devices is the rare and exquisite science of the prince, lover, and conqueror, of courtisans, of brave and gallant knights, that of delicate scholars whom schooling has not spoiled and whom the world has polished, the universal *and* singular science of the courtier, that is, the man whose entire being falls within the jurisdiction of an inexplicable, indiscernible difference—indeterminate, indefinite—the sublime I know not what of the distinction of the spirit in the circumstantial tactics of its acts of language and image: the opening, in the space closed off by representation, of a sociohistorical field whose impossible theorization it will fall to Kant to propose, in the waning years of the Enlightenment.

Appendix 1

Presented below is the outline for the work Louis Marin planned to write called *Sublime Poussin*, an outline drawn up in 1988. This document will allow the reader to situate the collection of studies offered here within the general landscape of Poussin's work as Louis Marin surveyed it in the course of his own studies, encountering in its diverse aspects the motif of the sublime.

For the "digressions" that were to punctuate this itinerary, certain texts published by Louis Marin with which the developments of the projected work might have resonated are indicated in brackets.

SUBLIME POUSSIN

Introduction

For a genealogy of the sublime: from Kant to Longinus
—a limit-notion: the sublime and the sublime style
—the presentation of the unrepresentable: fulfillment and excess

Digression I: Giorgione's *Tempesta*

[See "Les fins de l'interprétation ou les traversées du regard dans une tempête," in *De la représentation* (Paris: Hautes Etudes–Seuil-Gallimard, 1994), pp. 179–203.]

Chapter I

The sublime: figure I: the tempest in landscapes
1. Instantaneous difference or representation astonished: lightning and thunder
Landscape—A Calm (Art Institute of Chicago) and *Landscape—A Storm* (Rouen, Musée des Beaux-Arts)
Landscape with Pyramus and Thisbe (Frankfurt)
2. The indiscernible blend or the landscape swallowed up: the cataract and the whirlwind
Winter or the Flood—The Four Seasons (Louvre)

Digression II: Leonardo da Vinci's *Floods*

[See "Mimésis et description," in *De la représentation,* pp. 251–66]

Chapter II

The sublime: figure II: the colossal or the shock of ostentation
1. The variation of scale and the architectural ruin
The Coliseum and the Tower of Babel (*Pyramus and Thisbe* II)
2. The giant and nature
Orion blind and the sun, *Landscape with Orion* (New York)
Polyphemus and the mountain, *Landscape with Polyphemus* (Saint Petersburg)
Hercules, Cacus, and the den, *Hercules and Cacus* (Moscow)
The monstrous and the shock of terror
The snake, earth, and water
Landscape with a Man Killed by a Snake (National Gallery, London)
Landscape with Two Nymphs and a Snake (Chantilly)

Digression III: Dante, Noah, and Nimrod: the sublime and the question of language

Chapter III

The sublime: figure III: violence or the absolute of force
The Plague at Ashdod (Louvre)
War, *The Capture of Jerusalem by Titus* (Vienna)
Rape, *The Rape of the Sabines* (Louvre–New York)

the minute infinity of death
Et in Arcadia ego (Louvre)
The Ashes of Phocion Collected by his Widow (Knowley Hall, Lancashire)

Digression IV: Medusa or the "tense" of the sublime

Conclusion

The "between-painting" or the sublime of variation in Poussin.
The two self-portraits (Berlin, Louvre)

Appendix 2

Letter to Chantelou
Rome, 28 April 1639

Monsieur, I shall wait until God grants me the privilege of being with you to repay my obligations, not merely with words, but with deeds, if you find me worthy of so doing. At the moment I shall not bore you with long discourses; I shall only inform you that I am sending you your picture of *The Manna* via Bertholin, the Lyon courier: I crated it carefully and believe that you will receive it in good condition. Accompanying it is another little one which I am sending to M. Debonaire, since this is the only chance I have of getting it to him. Kindly permit him to take it, since it is his.

When you receive yours, I beg of you, if you like it, to provide it with a small frame; it needs one so that, in considering it in all its parts, the [rays of the] eye shall be retained and not dispersed beyond the limits of the picture by receiving impressions [?] of objects which, seen pell-mell with painted objects, confuse the light.

It would be very suitable if the said frame were gilded simply with dull gold, as it blends very softly with the colors without clashing. Furthermore, if you can remember the first letter I wrote you concerning the movements of the figures which I promised to depict, and if you consider the picture at the same time, I think you will be able to recognize with ease which figures languish, which ones are astonished, which are filled with pity, perform deeds of charity, are in great need, seek consolation, etc. The first seven figures on the left side will tell you everything that is written here, and all the rest is much to the same effect: study [read] the story and the picture in order to see whether each thing is appropriate to the subject.

And if after having studied the picture more than once, you find some satisfaction in it, write it to me if you please, without hesitation so that I may be happy to think that I had been able to please you on the first occasion that I had the honor of serving you. If you are not satisfied, we hold ourselves ready to make any improvement you desire. Begging you to remember once more that the spirit is willing and the flesh is weak . . . [1]

I have written to Monsieur Le Maire about the principal circumstance that keeps me here this summer; thus I beg you, Sir, with him, to make my excuses to Monseigneur de Noyers so that, putting this courtesy along with the others that I receive from you daily, I shall be more obliged to serve you my entire life than anyone in the world.

I shall write to Monsieur Stella, who I believe is in Lyon, that as soon as the painting arrives he should get it to you. Before you exhibit your picture, it would be highly appropriate to embellish it a little. It must be hung very little above eye level, if not a little below.

Appendix 3

Letter to Chantelou
24 November 1647

This will serve as answer to your last two letters, one dated 23 October and the other dated the first of this month. I am keeping the promise I made you. That is, I shall not use my brushes for anyone but you, until I have finished your "Seven Sacraments," and, consequently, after sending you the "Last Supper," which is the sixth, I have set my hand to the last, which is the one that you say you like the least. I promise myself however that it will be no less a success than the one of the six that pleases you the most.

I have been paid for the last painting I sent you by a clerk working for Monsieur Gierico, as you will have seen by the bill of exchange that you have received and the one I wrote you about sending the painting in question, which I am certain you will have received before the present one. I have resolved to serve Monsieur de Lisle since you command me to do so, even though I had decided I would henceforth do something as it were for myself, without subjecting myself further to the whims of others, and chiefly of those who see only through others' eyes. The gentleman in question will nevertheless have to reconcile himself to something difficult for a Frenchman, that is, patience. I have given your distinguished greetings to Monsieur le Chevalier du Puis, who returns them to you with his customary courtesy. Concerning what you wrote me in your last letter, it is easy to relieve you of the suspicion you have that I honor you less and that I have less love for you than for some other person. If that were the case, why would I have preferred you, over the last five years, to so many persons of worth and quality who have very ardently desired that I do something for them, and who have offered me their purses? For [what] reason have I contented myself with such a modest price that I have not wanted to take what you yourself have offered me? Why is it that, after having sent you the first of your paintings composed of only sixteen or eighteen figures, and when I could make the others in the same number, or even decrease the number, to come more quickly to the end of such a long and tiring enterprise, I have enriched them with more, without thinking of any interest other than that of earning your good will?

Why have I spent so much time, run so much here and there, in hot weather and cold, for your other private services, if it was not to show you how much I honor you? I do not wish to say more about this: I should have to give up the terms of the servitude I have sworn to you. Believe assuredly that I have done for you what I shall do for no living person, and that I shall always continue in the determination to serve you with all my heart. I am not a flighty man, nor changeable in my affection when I have invested it in a subject.

If you feel affection for the picture of *Moses Found in the Waters of the Nile*, which belongs to M. Pointel, is that a proof that I made it more lovingly than I did yours? Do you not see that, along with your own disposition, in the nature of the subject lies the cause of this effect, and that the subjects which I am treating for you have to be done in a different manner? All artifice in painting depends upon this. Pardon me the liberty that I take in saying that you have shown yourself hasty in the judgment you have made of my works. To judge well is very difficult, if one does not possess both the theory and the practice of this art. Not only our compulsions, but our reason should judge.

That is why I wish to bring to your attention one important thing that will teach you what to observe in the subjects depicted.

Our wise ancient Greeks, inventors of all beautiful things, found several Modes by means of which they produced marvellous effects.

This word "Mode" means actually the rule or the measure and form, which serves us in our productions. This rule constrains us not to exaggerate by making us act in all things with a certain restraint and moderation; and, consequently, this restraint and moderation is nothing more than a certain determined manner or order, and includes the procedure by which the object is preserved in its essence.

The Modes of the ancients were a combination of several things put together; from their variety was born a certain difference of Mode whereby one was able to understand that each one of them retained in itself a subtle variation; particularly when all the things which entered into combination were put together in such a proportion that it was made possible to arouse the soul of the spectator to various passions. Hence the fact that the ancient sages attributed to each style its own effects. Because of this they called the Dorian Mode stable, grave, and severe, and applied it to subjects which are grave and severe and full of wisdom.

And proceeding thence to pleasant and joyous things, they used the Phrygian Mode, in which there are more minute modulations than in any other mode, and a more clear-cut aspect. These two styles and no others were praised and approved of by Plato and Aristotle, who deemed the others superfluous; they considered this [Phrygian Mode] intense, vehement, violent, and very severe, and capable of astonishing people.

I hope, before another year is out, to paint a subject in this Phrygian Mode. The subject of frightful wars lends itself to this manner.

They [the ancients] also decided that the Lydian Mode lends itself to tragic subjects because it has neither the simplicity of the Dorian nor the severity of the Phrygian.

The Hypolidian Mode contains a certain suavity and sweetness which fills the souls of the spectators with joy; it lends itself to subjects of divine glory, and paradise.

The ancients invented the Ionic, with which they represented bacchanalian dances and feasts in order to achieve a festive effect.

The good poets used great care and marvelous artifice in order to fit the words to the verses and to dispose the feet in accordance with the usage of speech, as Virgil did throughout his poem, where he fits the sound of the verse itself to all his three manners of speaking with such skill that he really seems to place the things of which he speaks before your eyes by means of the sound of the words, with the result that in the portions where he speaks of love, one finds that he has skillfully chosen such words as are sweet, pleasant and very delightful to hear; whereas, if he sings of a feat of arms or describes a naval battle or a storm, he chooses hard, rasping, harsh words, so that when one hears or pronounces them, they produce a feeling of fear. Therefore, if I had made you a picture in which such a style were adhered to, you would imagine that I did not like you.[1]

If it would not amount to composing a book rather than a letter, I would call to your attention several important things that must be considered in painting, so that you should know fully to what extent I devote myself to serving you well. For, even though you are intelligent in all things, I fear that the company of all the mindless and ignorant people that surround you may corrupt your judgment by contagion.

Reference Matter

Notes

Chapter 1

Lecture given at a colloquium in Saint-Maximin, published as "Lire un tableau en 1639 d'après une lettre de Poussin" in *Pratiques de la lecture*, ed. Roger Chartier (Marseille: Rivages, 1983; repr. Paris: Payot & Rivages, 1993), pp. 101–124.

1. Meyer Schapiro, *Words and Pictures: On the Literal and the Symbolic in the Illustration of a Text* (The Hague: Mouton, 1973), p. 9.
2. Nicolas Poussin, *Lettres et propos sur l'art*, ed. Anthony Blunt (Paris: Hermann, 1964), pp. 35–36; partial translation in *A Documentary History of Art*, ed. Elizabeth Gilmore Holt, vol. 2 (Garden City, N.Y.: Doubleday, 1958), pp. 146–147. Cf. my "La lecture du tableau d'après Poussin," in *Cahiers de l'Association internationale des études françaises* 24 (1972): 251–266; Françoise Siguret, "Lisez l'histoire avec le tableau," *Etudes françaises* 14 (1975): 21–24. For a more complete bibliography on this topic and on Poussin's painting, see Anthony Blunt, *Nicolas Poussin: A Critical Catalogue* (London: Phaidon, 1966), p. 18, no. 21.
3. Paul Klee, *Notebooks*, vol. 1: *The Thinking Eye*, trans. Ralph Manheim (London: Lund Humphries; New York: G. Wittenborn, 1961), pp. 89–90.
4. Louis Richeome, *Tableaux sacrés des figures mystiques du très auguste sacrement et sacrifice de l'Eucharistie* (Paris: Sounie, 1601). See also Louis Richeome, *La peinture spirituelle, ou l'art d'admirer, aimer et louer Dieu en toutes ses oeuvres* (Lyon: Pierre Rigaud, 1611).
5. A remarkable confirmation of this point is found in Pierre Coton's

preface to his *Sermons sur les principales et plus difficiles matières de la foi . . . réduits par lui-même en forme de méditations* (Paris, 1617). See also Marc Fumaroli's commentary in *L'age de l'éloquence. Rhétorique et "res literaria" de la Renaissance au seuil de l'époque classique* (Geneva: Droz, 1980), p. 264.

6. Richeome, *Tableaux sacrés*. See also Henri Bremond, *Histoire littéraire du sentiment religieux en France depuis la fin des guerres de religion jusqu'à nos jours*, 11 vols. (Paris: Bloud & Gay, [1915–1936] 1967–1971, pp. 35ff.; Fumaroli, *Age de l'éloquence*, p. 258.

7. André Félibien, *6e conférence de l'Académie royale de peinture pendant l'année 1667* (Paris: D. Mortier, 1668), n.p. (emphasis added).

8. Poussin, *Lettres et propos sur l'art*, pp. 62–63.

9. See Denis Mahon, "Poussiniana," *Gazette des beaux-arts*, July–August 1962, pp. 95, 107.

10. Poussin, *Lettres et propos sur l'art*, p. 184. Regarding the term "lineament" in this passage, the following definition is found in Antoine Furetière's lexicon of the language of seventeenth-century France: "Feature or delicate line that is observed in something and especially on the face, and that composes its delicacy, that causes its image to be retained, that causes its relation or resemblance to some other." The lineament is thus the feature, the character, of the object-to-be-painted, the object inasmuch as it is destined to be painted. The problem that arises between the citation from Félibien's text and Poussin's letter to Chantelou is the problem of the relation between lineament and movement, or, to remain within the scriptural analogy, between an isolated letter of the alphabet and the same letter used in a composition.

11. Poussin, *Lettres et propos sur l'art*, pp. 121–125; partial translation in Holt, ed., *Documentary History of Art*, pp. 154–156. See also Appendix 3 in this volume.

12. Charles Le Brun, *Conférence sur l'expression générale et particulière* (Paris: E. Picard, 1698); reprinted in *Nouvelle revue de psychanalyse* 21 (spring 1980): 93–121 (special issue entitled "La passion"); in English as *A Method to Learn to Design the Passions* (n.p., 1734), Augustan Reprint Society, nos. 200–201 (Los Angeles: William Andrews Clark Memorial Library, UCLA, 1980).

13. It is a process, too, in which the relation between painted figures and "real" emotions is one of homonymy; cf. Aristotle, *Categories* 1.1: "When things have only a name in common and the definition of being which corresponds to the name is different, they are called *homonymous*.

Thus, for example, both a man and a picture are animals. These have only a name in common and the definition of being which corresponds to the name is different" (*Aristotle's "Categories" and "De Interpretatione,"* trans. J. L. Ackrill [Oxford: Clarendon Press, 1963], p. 3).

14. They are in the foreground or front of the painting, as opposed to the ones in the distance, as theoreticians and painters say. In other words, taking into account the illusory hollowing out of the painting's surface by a prospective depth on the basis of the plane of representation, the foreground is nearest to the spectator.

15. Hence the composition or the conjunction of a proximity of visibility in the pictorial space (the foreground is the place closest to the spectator) and a priority of readability in the written field (all occidental reading begins with the left-hand portion and the first line at the top of the page); here the "left-hand" part of the reading is conjugated in the "foreground" of vision with a double exclusion of the higher (left-hand) zone of the painting and of the central and right-hand parts (of the foreground) of the painting.

16. This dimension, which lies between an engraved painting (the brush, mute painting) and a speaking painting (words, the narrated), is what Louis Richeome called (spiritual) signification.

17. But between the Parisian "baroquism" of Richeome, Coton, or Binet, that of the court Jesuits at the beginning of the century, and Poussin's "classicism" (of which *Manna* would be something like the Roman manifesto in painting), an essential displacement of the notion of allegory and symbolic meaning occurs.

18. This scene is represented frequently in the plastic arts of antiquity and, more recently, from the early sixteenth century on. Most often, however, the young woman's starving father is the one saved from death. Both versions of the anecdote are recounted by Valerius Maximus in his collection of *exempla*, in a chapter on filial piety; see Valerius Maximus, *Dictorum factorumque memorabilium libri*, vol. 5 (Anvers, 1614). On the motif of *Caritas romana*, see W. Waldemar Deonna, "La légende de Pero et Micon et l'allaitement symbolique," *Latomus* 13 (1954): 140–166, 356–375; Elfriede Regina Knauer, "Caritas Romana," *Jahrbuch der Berliner Museen* 6 (1964): 9–23; Andreas Pigler, *Barockthemen* (Budapest, 1974), vol. 2.

19. Cf. Félix Thürleman, "La fonction de l'admiration dans l'esthétique du XVIIe siècle, à propos de la charité romaine dans *La Manne* de Poussin" (unpublished ms., 1976); René Descartes, *Les passions de l'âme*,

in *Oeuvres philosophiques* (Paris: Garnier, 1973), vol. 3 (in English as *The Passions of the Soul*, trans. Stephen Voss [Indianapolis: Hackett, 1989]); Le Brun, *Conférence sur l'expression générale et particulière*. We may note that, even though in his lecture Le Brun begins the list of the passions he is defining with admiration, the first drawing illustrating the lecture depicts tranquillity; it is followed by drawings depicting attention, esteem, and admiration. It would be interesting to analyze the reason for this divergence between the lecture (the readable) and the drawings (the visible). In a philosophical analysis of the passions, there is nothing to say about tranquillity, which is a "non-passion." On the contrary, for the painter, the various passions, including admiration itself, can be rendered visible or shown only through modifications of the parts of the calm face, chiefly the eyes and eyebrows on one side, the mouth and lips on the other.

20. Letter to Jacques Stella, 1637, in Poussin, *Correspondance*, p. 27. Emphasis added.

21. Cf. Thomas Aquinas (attributed): "Non enim intelligendum est eum habuisse cornua ad litteram, sicut quidam eum pingunt; sed dicitur cornuta propter radios, qui videbantur esse quasi quaedam cornuta" (For we must not think that he literally had horns, as some [artists] paint him; but he is said to be horned because of the beams of light that seem to be almost like horns).

22. See also Siguret, "Lisez l'histoire."

23. Exodus 16:14–15; cf. Richeome, *Tableaux sacrés*. See also Jacques Vanuxem, "Les 'tableaux sacrés' de Richeome et l'iconographie de l'Eucharistie chez Poussin," in *Nicolas Poussin*, ed. André Chastel (Paris: CNRS, 1960), 1: 151–162; and John Shearman, "Les dessins de paysages de Poussin," trans. Françoise Vitale, in ibid., pp. 176–188 (cited by Thürleman in "Fonction de l'admiration").

Chapter 2

First published as "La description de l'image: A propos d'un paysage de Poussin" in *Communications* 15 (1970): 186–208.

1. Editors' note: "Récit pictural et récit mythique chez Poussin," lecture given at Urbino at a colloquium on narrative analysis, 1968.

2. Cf. Jean-Louis Schefer, *Scénographie d'un tableau* (Paris: Seuil, 1969).

3. On this subject, see Anthony Blunt's critique of Guy de Tervarent,

"Le véritable sujet du *Paysage au serpent* de Poussin à la National Gallery de Londres," *Gazette des beaux-arts* 2 (1952): 343–350.

4. "Landscape with a Man Killed by a Snake," in Blunt, *Poussin: A Critical Catalogue*, p. 143.

5. See Pierre Francastel, *La figure et le lieu* (Paris: Gallimard, 1967). See also the discussion of the notion of pictorial reading in my "Eléments pour une sémiologie picturale," in *Etudes sémiologiques* (Paris: Klincksieck, 1971), pp. 17–45.

6. Editors' note: For the text of Fénelon's imaginary dialogue between Leonardo and Poussin, and for the three texts by Félibien, see pp. 62–64. For more on Baudet's engraving, see G. Georges Wildenstein, "Les graveurs de Poussin au XVIIe siècle," *Gazette des beaux-arts*, July–August 1955, pp. 73ff.

7. Cf., for example, Ernst Hans Gombrich, "The Renaissance Theory of Art and the Rise of Landscape," in *Norm and Form* (London: Phaidon, 1966), pp. 107ff.

8. See Blunt, "Véritable sujet du *Paysage au serpent*," pp. 290ff., for a reference to the situation that prevailed in Poussin's day.

9. Gottfried Wilhelm Leibniz, *Philosophical Papers and Letters*, trans. Leroy E. Loemker (Dordrecht: D. Reidel, 1969), p. 292.

10. Definitions of the word *titre* are taken from Emile Littré, *Dictionnaire de la langue française* (Paris: Hachette, 1881).

11. Félibien's notation is very brief and stereotypical: "The situation of the place in the painting is marvelous."

12. The term *l'aire* is used by François Hédelin, the abbé d'Aubignac, in *La pratique du théâtre*, ed. Pierre Martino (Paris, 1657; repr. Algiers: Jules Carbonel, 1927), p. 101; in English as *The Whole Art of the Stage* (London, 1684; repr. New York: Benjamin Blom, 1968), book 3, p. 100.

13. D'Aubignac, *Whole Art of the Stage*, book 3, p. 86

14. Moreover, this beginning of a code could be refined or made more specific by a more discreet opposition that Fénelon's text implicitly brings to light: the drama represented on stage brings together three characters in a linked action. The decor, as the environment of the staged place, envelops a multitude of characters, among whom certain groups—the people playing, the fishermen—appear to be the significant elements in the decor on the intermediate level. Thus there is an opposition between the drama woven among three characters, on the one hand, and the numerous figurative silhouettes belonging to the decor that signify an "atmosphere" or an ambiance, on the other; or an oppo-

sition between the concentration of the dramatic action and the dissolving of the hero, through the sheer weight of numbers, into an element of the decor. Cf. the controversy between Andrea Sacchi and Pietro da Cortona at the Accademia di S. Luca in Rome; on this topic, see Denis Mahon, *Studies in Seicento Art and Theory* (London: Warburg Institute, 1957); and Rudolf Wittkower, *Art and Architecture in Italy 1600–1750* (Harmondsworth, Eng.: Penguin Books, 1965), p. 171.

15. Symbol: there must still be the trace of the break in a split piece of metal or stone, once the two pieces are put back together, otherwise there would only be a piece of metal and not a sign of recognition.

16. D'Aubignac, *Whole Art of the Stage*, book 3, p. 87.

17. One last observation will conclude this rapid analysis of the descriptive part of Fénelon's description: the fictitious character of Fénelon's discourse must be stressed. His discourse, a dialogue between two dead men, Leonardo da Vinci and Poussin, has one peculiar feature: da Vinci has not seen Poussin's painting; he is able to view it only owing to Poussin's words. Thus we are dealing with a dual representation: a verbal description ("Picture a rock [on] the left side of the painting," says Poussin to da Vinci) and the pictorial representation, itself a second staging, in which the "expressed" visual elements of the painting function as symptoms of an emotional state or an internal physiological condition ("his frightful face represents a cruel death"), or, to put it more concisely, the visual elements ("frightful face," "livid flesh," for example), to the extent that they are expressed in the dramatic description, appear as the signifiers of a signified: "cruel death." Thus in the painting described, the frightful face and the livid flesh are to death what Poussin's discourse is to da Vinci's representation, in the text describing the painting. The invisibility of Poussin's painting for da Vinci (this is a fiction Fénelon used to make the description necessary) is like the invisibility of the signified "death" for Poussin the painter. And Poussin's discourse in his description allows the painting to be seen, just as, in the discourses that describe—and constitute—them, the figures allow meaning to be seen. Thus, owing to the impossibilities built into Fénelon's fiction (Poussin's interlocutor could not see the painting; between da Vinci and Poussin there can have been no prior visual connivance; the entire painting has to come across within the discursive space allotted to it), the *Dialogue des morts* allows fine connections to be made between the descriptive discourse as a representation of the painting and the painting as a described-represented representation, in discourse.

18. Editors' note: *Correspondance de Poussin*, ed. Charles Jouanny (Paris: F. de Nobele, 1968), letter to Chantelou, 28 April 1639, p. 21 (cf. pp. 228–29).

19. See, for example, the Cartesian theory of deduction in the *Regulae* or certain analyses of the unexpressed in the *Logique de Port-Royal* by Antoine Arnauld and Pierre Nicole; in English as *Logic; or, The Art of Thinking* (Cambridge: Cambridge University Press, 1996).

20. I am borrowing this remarkable expression from Roland Barthes.

21. "Know that I turned neither to your books nor to the paintings of the past century to inform myself; I turned to the ancient bas-reliefs that you have studied as well as I," Poussin says to Leonardo da Vinci at the end of Fénelon's dialogue. On this point, see Anthony Blunt, *Nicolas Poussin* (London: Phaidon, 1966), pp. 102ff.

22. On this subject, see Ernst Kris and Abraham Kaplan, "Aesthetic Ambiguities," in *Psychoanalytic Explorations in Art* (New York: International Universities Press, 1952), pp. 243–264.

23. Roman Jakobson, *Selected Writings*, vol. 3 (The Hague: Mouton, 1981), p. 27.

24. This analysis should be related to those undertaken in Freud's *The Interpretation of Dreams*, chapter 6, "The Dream-Work," in *The Standard Edition of the Complete Psychological Works of Sigmund Freud*, trans. James Strachey, vols. 4–5 (London: Hogarth Press, 1953), pp. 277–508.

25. *Mourre* is a popular Italian game for two players. Each holds up a certain number of fingers, then guesses how many fingers the other player has raised.

Chapter 3

First published as "La description du tableau et le sublime en peinture: A propos d'un paysage de Poussin et de son sujet" in *Communications* 34 (1981): 61–84.

In the original, Marin included the following statement:

> The study presented here is part of a larger work devoted to the sublime in painting, and more precisely to the representation of storms, which are viewed as one of the "natural" expressions of the sublime.
>
> Giorgione's *Tempesta* was my initial area of research interest. [See "Les fins de l'interprétation ou les traversées du regard dans le sublime d'une tempête," in *De la représentation* (Paris: Gallimard, 1994), pp. 180–203.] The reasons

need not concern us here, but the fact must be pointed out nevertheless, for here and there in what follows the reader will spot traces that this earlier trajectory has left in the text.

The project raises an initial question: How does the painted picture represent what may seem to be unrepresentable—a "natural" challenge to all representation—in this case, the sublime?

This question is coupled with another: How does discourse describe (represent) a painting?

In other words, the storm, or the unrepresentable in pictorial representation: the sublime in painting. Or again, painting, or the unrepresentable in descriptive discourse: the sublimity of painting of the sublime.

Ten years ago, *Communications* kindly agreed to publish my study entitled "La description de l'image: A propos d'un paysage de Poussin" [see Chapter 2 in this volume]. By publishing today, and in the same journal, a work whose title echoes the earlier one, I should be pleased, without presuming too much, if the resonances of this echo should mark the coherence of a passage from one of Poussin's landscapes to another.

1. Nicolas Poussin, letter to M. de Chambray, 1 March 1665, in Holt, ed., *Documentary History of Art*, p. 158.

2. Poussin, *Lettres et propos sur l'art*, p. 160.

3. Victor Goldschmidt, *Le système stoïcien et l'idée de temps* (Paris: J. Vrin, [1953] 1977), p. 178.

4. Ibid., p. 180.

5. Ibid., pp. 180–181.

6. Claude Imbert, "Stoic Logic and Alexandrian Poetics," in *Doubt and Dogmatism: Studies in Hellenic Epistemology*, ed. Malcolm Schofield, Myles Burnyeat, and Jonathan Barnes (Oxford: Oxford University Press, 1980), pp. 206–207. [Editors' note: This is an early English-language version of "La logique stoïcienne et la construction du récit," in *Phénoménologies et langues formulaires* (Paris: Presses Universitaires de France, 1992), chap. 3.]

7. Ibid., pp. 210–211.

8. Ibid., p. 212.

9. Ibid., pp. 213–214.

10. This quotation and those that follow are from Ovid, *Metamorphoses*, trans. Mary M. Innes (Harmondsworth, Eng.: Penguin Books, [1955] 1986), pp. 95–98 (book 4, lines 54–165).

11. Goldschmidt, *Système stoïcien*, pp. 43–44.

12. Imbert, "Stoic Logic," p. 183 (citing Longinus, *On the Sublime* 15.1).

13. Marcus Aurelius, *The Meditations*, trans. G. M. A. Grube (Indianapolis: Hackett, 1983), pp. 53 (6.25), 56 (6.37), 68 (7.49), 110 (11.1).

14. Seneca, *Ad Lucilium epistulae morales*, trans. Richard M. Gummere (London: William Heinemann; New York: G. P. Putnam's Sons, 1925), p. 359 (53.11).

15. Goldschmidt, *Système stoïcien*, pp. 96–98.

16. Ibid., pp. 180–181.

Chapter 4

First published as "Panofsky et Poussin en Arcadie" in *Erwin Panofsky: Cahiers pour un temps* (Paris: Centre Georges Pompidou, 1983), pp. 151–166.

1. Editors' note: This short text appeared in *Première livraison (Strasbourg)* 12 (1977); we have chosen to include it as an epigraph.

2. See the excellent bibliography of Panofsky's works published as an appendix to the French translation of *Gothic Architecture and Scholasticism* by Pierre Bourdieu, *Architecture gothique et pensée scolastique* (Paris: Editions de Minuit, 1967), pp. 185–197.

3. See Erwin Panofsky, "*Et in Arcadia ego*: On the Conception of Transience in Poussin and Watteau," in *Philosophy and History: Essays Presented to Ernst Cassirer*, ed. Raymond Klibansky and H. J. Patton (New York: Harper & Row, [1936] 1963), pp. 223–252.

4. Erwin Panofsky, "*Et in Arcadia ego* et le tombeau parlant," *Gazette des beaux-arts*, ser. 6, 19 (1938): 305–306.

5. Erwin Panofsky, "*Et in Arcadia ego*: Poussin and the Elegiac Tradition," in *Meaning in the Visual Arts: Papers in and on Art History* (Garden City, N.Y.: Doubleday Anchor Books, 1955), pp. 295–320.

6. In this connection, see "Three Decades of Art History in the United States: Impressions of a Transplanted European," in *Meaning in the Visual Arts*, pp. 321–322 (reprint of "The History of Art," in Franz L. Neumann et al., *The Cultural Migration: The European Scholar in America*, ed. W. R. Crawford [Philadelphia: University of Pennsylvania Press, 1953], pp. 82–111).

7. Panofsky, *Meaning in the Visual Arts*, p. v.

8. Erwin Panofsky, "Introductory," in *Studies in Iconology: Humanistic Themes in the Art of the Renaissance* (Oxford: Oxford University Press, 1939; repr. New York: Harper & Row, 1962), pp. 3–31. In what follows I

cite the reprint edition as well as the reprinted essay in *Meaning in the Visual Arts*, pp. 26–54, there titled "Iconography and Iconology: An Introduction to the Study of Renaissance Art."

Regarding "*Et in Arcadia ego*" as an application of this construction, "Three Decades" (reprinted in *Meaning in the Visual Arts*, pp. 321–346, from Franz L. Neumann et al., *The Cultural Migration: The European Scholar in America*, ed. W. R. Crawford [Philadelphia: University of Pennsylvania Press, 1953]) warrants close analysis. As to 1914 marking the beginning of his practice of art history, see the first work published by Panofsky, his thesis, *Die theoretische Kunstlehre Albrecht Dürers (Dürers Aesthetik)* (Berlin: G. Reimer, 1914), p. 61; published in English as *The Life and Art of Albrecht Dürer* (Princeton: Princeton University Press, 1955).

9. In this connection, one can only note France's astounding lag in translating Panofsky's work (and that of the Warburg School in general). The first translation, in 1967, was done by Pierre Bourdieu, with a very important theoretical and methodological afterword on Panofsky; see *Architecture gothique*, pp. 135–167.

10. The cardinal in question is Giulo Cardinal Rospigliosi, who later became Pope Clement IX (1600–1669). See Panofsky, *Meaning in the Visual Arts*, p. 305, n. 29, for essential information about the great humanist prelate; see also the appendix to the 1936 essay in *Philosophy and History*, pp. 252–254. It has nevertheless occurred to me that in studying the theme in *Et in Arcadia ego*, and especially for the precise description of the Chatsworth and Louvre paintings, Panofsky may not have given enough weight to Rospigliosi's role as sponsor of *A Dance to the Music of Time* (Wallace collection, London) and *Time Saving Truth from Envy and Discord* (a painting that has been lost; an engraving of it was published by J. Dughet, 1667–1669). See further remarks on this subject in Louis Marin, *To Destroy Painting*, trans. Mette Hjort (Chicago: University of Chicago Press, 1995), pp. 91–94.

11. Regarding the "theory-history" of art: in combining in a single expression the title and subtitle of Hubert Damisch's *Théorie du nuage: Pour une histoire de la peinture* (Paris: Seuil, 1972), I am asserting my view that art history and art theory are inseparable. . . . A history of art can be achieved only through the simultaneous construction of a theory of art, just as a theory of art can be achieved only as a history of the theory (of art).

12. This evolution is perfectly clear in "Aims and Limits of Iconol-

ogy," the introduction to Ernst Hans Gombrich's *Symbolic Images: Studies in the Art of the Renaissance*, vol. 2 (London: Phaidon, 1972), pp. 1–25, with the application of the "principle of the primacy of genres": "Without the existence of such genres in the traditions of Western art the task of the iconologist would indeed be desperate" (p. 5). In the same text (pp. 4–5), Gombrich summarizes the important work of E. D. Hirsch, *Validity in Interpretation* (New Haven: Yale University Press, 1967).

13. Upon close examination of the painting in the Louvre, we may wonder whether the inscription is actually half-effaced. On the theoretical importance of what is apparently a detail, in particular for the interpretation of the formula *Et in Arcadia ego*, see *To Destroy Painting*, pp. 86–87.

14. On mode in painting, see Poussin's well-known letter of 24 November 1647 to Chantelou, in Poussin, *Lettres et propos sur l'art*, pp. 121–125. Cf. the commentary in Blunt, *Nicolas Poussin*, pp. 225–227 and the literature cited there. For an interpretation of the theory of modes, see my article on Poussin's self-portraits, "Variations sur un portrait absent: Les autoportraits de Poussin, 1649–1650," *Corps écrit* 5 (1983): 90–91 (special issue entitled "L'autoportrait") [editors' note: Chapter 9 in this volume], concerning the notion of the "principle of variation" and that of the "sound of words," two notions that are not foreign to the fiction of a voice (from the grave?) in Panofsky's study.

15. Panofsky, "*Et in Arcadia ego*: On the Conception of Transience in Poussin and Watteau," in *Philosophy and History*, p. 224; emphasis added.

16. Here I am closely following Panofsky's study "Iconography and Iconology," in *Meaning in the Visual Arts*, pp. 38–39.

17. Cf. Ernst Cassirer, *The Philosophy of Symbolic Forms*, trans. Ralph Manheim, 3 vols. (New Haven: Yale University Press, 1953–1966).

18. Let us note here that Panofsky does not go very far at all toward developing or using the idea of a history of types. It would be interesting to retrace the genealogy of the notion of type in Panofsky, in particular in relation to Max Weber and his concept of ideal types.

19. "*Et in Arcadia ego*," in *Meaning in the Visual Arts*, p. 296.

20. Ibid., p. 297.

21. I feel obliged here to correct some errors in the French translation of the English text: "Finally, I shall try to fix the ultimate responsibility for this change," Panofsky writes, "which was of paramount importance for modern literature, not on a man of a letters but on a great painter" (ibid., pp. 296–297). The responsibility for the change—a responsibility

whose importance has been paramount for modern literature—thus belongs not to a man of letters but to a great painter; cf. the French translation: "I shall try finally to establish what was at the origin of this change—whose importance for modern culture was paramount through its consequences not on a man of letters but on a great painter" (p. 281). It is excessive, but doubtless significant, to translate "modern literature" by "modern culture," all the more so because Panofsky displaces the responsibility for the change from a man of letters onto a painter. It is incorrect, and at the limit of meaninglessness, to make this great painter, whose name is not pronounced, the "object" of the consequences of a change the responsibility for which Panofsky attributes to him (in a problematic form, it is true, at this stage of his argument).

22. "*Et in Arcadia ego*," in *Meaning in the Visual Arts*, p. 296.

23. Ibid. Neither in 1936 nor in 1955 did Panofsky have linguistic instruments of analysis at his disposal (or perhaps he simply did not use them) for dealing rigorously with the semantic problems posed by the formula *Et in Arcadia ego*. The first of these problems concerns the meaning of *et*, which to be sure as an adverb signifying "also" bears upon the word or verb group that immediately follows: "Also in Arcadia I"; but which, as a coordinating conjunction used in isolation or taken with adversative value, can perfectly well bear upon the whole of the sentence that follows. For example, Cicero, *De provinciis consularibus* 13.32: "Et ea victoria contentus . . . " (And [but] satisfied with that victory . . .). The second problem concerns the absence of a verb. In the 1955 essay, Panofsky fleshes out his argument a bit by giving some examples of expressions that he calls elliptical, that is, in which he supposes that the verb is implied—*Summum jus, summa injuria pluribus unum*, for example, or *Nequid nimis*, or *Sic semper Tyrannis*—whereas the relevant category is that of nominal sentences whose quite specific functioning in Greek and Latin was demonstrated by Emile Benveniste in "The Nominal Sentence," in *Problems in General Linguistics*, trans. Mary Elizabeth Meek (Coral Gables, Fla.: University of Miami Press, 1971), pp. 131–144; and in my own *To Destroy Painting*, pp. 84–87. On the other hand, one of the examples Panofsky gives, this time in order to recognize the possibility of an implied verb in the future tense, is "Neptune's famous *Quos ego*" ("*Et in Arcadia ego*," in *Meaning in the Visual Arts*, p. 306). Here indeed *ego* appears, but we do not have a nominal sentence of the proverbial type, we have instead an interrupted sentence, precisely a rhetorical figure of interruption, and it is not astonishing that this figure strikes

Panofsky as an exception. The third problem, and doubtless the most difficult one, is the status of *ego.* I have attempted to address its use in the expression *Et in Arcadia ego* in *To Destroy Painting*, pp. 79–90. My analysis is directly derived from two articles by Benveniste: "Relationships of Person in the Verb," in *Problems*, pp. 195–204; and "L'antonyme et le pronom en français moderne," *Bulletin de la Société de linguistique de Paris* 55, fasc. 1 (1965: 71–87; reprinted in *Problèmes de linguistique générale* (Paris: Gallimard, 1974), 2:197–214. Let me add that the study of the Daphnis epitaph in Virgil's fifth *Eclogue*, cited by Panofsky, does not allow him to solve the problem definitively, either, especially since in 1955 he settles (p. 302) for reproducing Dryden's translation, whereas in 1936 he stressed the key words in Latin: "Daphnis ego in Silvis, hinc *usque ad sidera notus, formosi pecoris custos, formosior ipse.*" In fact, in Virgil, *ego* explicitly bears a name, Daphnis; this is not the case for *Et in Arcadia ego.* But whatever difficulties arise in the analysis, the absence of any theory of enunciation seems to me to render Panofsky's conclusions very fragile, whereas that same theory finds a particularly fruitful field of application in Guercino's painting as well as in Poussin's.

24. Arthur O. Lovejoy and George Boas, *A Documentary History of Primitivism and Related Ideas*, vol. 1: *Primitivism and Related Ideas in Antiquity* (Baltimore: Johns Hopkins University Press, 1935).

25. It is undeniable that that historical and cultural determination poses real problems and encounters great theoretical difficulties; the fact remains that, for Cassirer, the notion of the transcendental schema lies at the heart of the Kantian construction from the first *Critique* to the third, which he considers to be "a consequence of the elaboration of the transcendental schematism." See Cassirer, *Kant's Life and Thought*, trans. James Haden (New Haven: Yale University Press, 1981), p. 273; also pp. 306–307, 314, 351–355. The same thesis is found in *Das Erkenntnisproblem in der Philosophie und Wissenschaft der neueren Zeit*, vol. 3 (1920; Berlin: B. Cassirer, 1974) (in English as *The Problem of Knowledge: Philosophy, Science, and History since Hegel*, trans. William H. Woglom and Charles W. Hendel [New Haven: Yale University Press, 1950]), including the introduction to the third volume in which the *Critique of Judgment* is considered an "advance over the abstract schematism" of the *Critique of Pure Reason.* The treatment of the problem of art is one of the most remarkable of these advances toward the concrete. In this connection, two passages from *Kant's Life and Thought* show the power of Cassirer's thought compared to the Panofsky of the 1936 essay: "The work of

art is something singular and apart, which is its own basis and has its goal surely within itself, and yet at the same time in it we are presented with a new whole and a new image of reality and of the mental cosmos itself" (p. 307). And "the aesthetic consciousness possesses in itself that form of concrete realization through which, wholly abandoned to its temporary passivity, it grasps in this very fleeting passivity a factor of purely timeless meaning" (p. 310). Panofsky's study of *Et in Arcadia ego* and on "the conception of transience in Poussin and Watteau" evidently constitutes both a gloss on and a particular development of Cassirer's theses. See also, in *Meaning in the Visual Arts*, "The History of Art as a Humanistic Discipline," with Panofsky's reference, p. 11, n. 9, to Edgar Wind,"Zur Systematik der künstlerischen Probleme," *Zeitschrift für Aesthetik und allgemeine Kunstwissenschaft* 18 (1925): 438ff.

26. On Panofsky's distinction between "document" and "monument," see *Meaning in the Visual Arts*, pp. 10–11, and the reference to delight as the goal of painting for Poussin.

27. "*Et in Arcadia ego*," in *Philosophy and History*, pp. 232–233.

28. We must nevertheless note that, as much in 1955 as in 1936, the description of Guercino's painting remains not only cursory but very uncertain on a point that is essential to Panofsky's argument. It seems to me in fact difficult to consider that "the Arcadian shepherds are not absorbed in lasting contemplation, but are interrupted in their walk by the sudden sight of a death's head gnawed by a mouse (a time-honoured and very well-known symbol for all-devouring time)" ("*Et in Arcadia ego*," in *Philosophy and History*, p. 233). The posture of the shepherd on the left leaning on his rod seems to me to rule out a sudden halt. This remark might lead to a reexamination not only of pre-iconographic description in Panofsky, but also more generally of the problem of the description—and its semantic and pragmatic categories—of paintings with figures. But while the two shepherds in Guercino's painting are contemplating the death's head in an intense and prolonged way, the death's head is not facing them: it is situated in the lower right-hand corner of the canvas, facing the viewer at whom it "looks" with its empty sockets, like the death's head in Honthorst's *Vanitas* (Palazzo Corsini, Rome), a reproduction of which is provided by Panofsky with his 1936 essay. The meditative contemplation of death has three poles: the shepherds at left, the death's head at right, and, finally, the viewer, outside the painting. Thus on the iconographic level one cannot follow Panofsky when he posits that Guercino's painting is a synthesis between the painting of *Vanitas* with a fem-

inine figure personifying the "contemplazione della Morte" and the *narrative* image of a "dramatic encounter between death and some mischievous young people." The comparison with Honthorst's painting is revealing. It is not the *narrative* that Guercino is displacing into Arcadia, as Panofsky writes, but a *Vanitas* with figures in a landscape and an outdoor decor named in the inscription: Arcadia. Moreover, the effects on description of the absence of a "theory of enunciation" become clear; such a theory necessarily implies a positioning of the viewer which is all the more required here not only by the *ego* in the painting, but *by the very place* of the inscription on the stonework that is offered to the viewer for reading, whereas the figures in the painting, the shepherds, cannot see it.

29. "*Et in Arcadia ego*," in *Philosophy and History*, p. 232.

30. "*Et in Arcadia ego*," in *Meaning in the Visual Arts*, p. 311.

31. "*Et in Arcadia ego*," in *Philosophy and History*, p. 240. Cf. Ernst Cassirer's reflection on "genius," based on Goethe's conception, in *Das Erkenntnisproblem*, vol. 3, and in *The Philosophy of the Enlightenment*, trans. Fritz C. A. Koelin and James P. Pettegrove (Princeton: Princeton University Press, 1951); also Panofsky, "Artist, Scientist and Genius: Notes on the Renaissance-Dämmerung," in *The Renaissance: Symposium* (New York: Metropolitan Museum of Art, 1952), pp. 77–93.

32. "*Et in Arcadia ego*," in *Philosophy and History*, p. 240.

33. On Fragonard in general, and more especially for a commentary on *Le baiser*, see Jacques Thuillier, *Fragonard*, trans. Robert Allen (Geneva: Skira, 1967), "Lofty Lyric Accents," pp. 113–128, and especially "'Romantic' Passion," pp. 129–139.

34. "*Et in Arcadia ego*," in *Meaning in the Visual Arts*, pp. 319–320.

35. "*Et in Arcadia ego*," in *Philosophy and History*, p. 251.

36. Ibid.

37. For a related approach, see Rudolf Wittkower, "Giorgione and Arcady," in *Umanesimo europeo ed umanesimo veneziano* (Florence, 1963); reprinted in *Idea and Image: Studies in the Italian Renaissance* (London: Thames & Hudson, 1978), pp. 161–173.

Chapter 5

Lecture delivered at a colloquium at the University of Saint-Etienne in November 1983; published as "Le sublime classique: Les 'tempêtes' dans quelques paysages de Poussin" in *Lire le paysage, lire les paysages: Travaux* 42 (1984): 201–220.

1. The *Littré* dictionary gives three basic definitions of the word "landscape": (1) an expanse of countryside seen from a single perspective; (2) a genre of painting that has as its object the representation of rural sites; (3) a painting that represents a landscape. The dictionary entry goes on to make distinctions among landscapes characterized as historical, ancient, mixed, ideal, or heroic.

2. Cf. Immanuel Kant, *Critique of Judgment*, trans. Werner S. Pluhar (Indianapolis: Hackett, 1951), sec. 26. See the commentary by Jacques Derrida in *The Truth in Painting*, trans. Geoff Bennington and Ian McLeod (Chicago: University of Chicago Press, 1987), pp. 125–126.

3. Cf. Louis Marin, "La description du tableau et le sublime en peinture: A propos d'un paysage de Poussin et de son sujet," in *Communications* 34 (1981): 61–84 (special issue entitled "Les ordres de la figuration"); and the references to Goldschmidt, *Système stoïcien*; and Imbert, "Stoic Logic and Alexandrian Poetics" (see Chapter 3 in this volume). See also John Onians, *Art and Thought in the Hellenistic Age: The Greek World View, 350–50 B.C.* (London: Thames & Hudson, 1979).

4. Cf. Gombrich, "Renaissance Theory of Art," pp. 107–121. The bibliography on landscapes in painting is obviously vast. In preparing this study, I consulted Kenneth Clark, *Landscape into Art* (New York: Harper & Row, 1976); Henry V. S. Ogden and Margaret S. Odgen, *English Taste in Landscape in the Seventeenth Century* (Ann Arbor: University of Michigan Press, 1955); Max J. Friedlander, *Über die Landschaftsmalerei und andere Bildgattungen* (The Hague: A. A. M. Stols, 1947); Otto Pächt, "Early Italian Nature Studies and the Early Calendar Landscape," in *Journal of the Warburg and Courtauld Institutes* 13 (1950): 13–47; *Relations artistiques entre les Pays-Bas et l'Italie à la Renaissance* (Rome and Brussels, 1980); *Il paesaggio nella pittura fra Cinque e Seicento a Firenze*, catalogue (Florence, 1980); *Il paesaggio nel disegno del Cinquecento europeo*, catalogue (Rome, 1972–1973); Wolfgang Stechow, *Dutch Landscape Painting of the Seventeenth Century* (London: Phaidon, 1966). See also Svetlana Alpers, *The Art of Describing: Dutch Art in the Seventeenth Century* (Chicago: Chicago University Press, 1983).

5. Cf. the reference to Joachim Patinir in the note of 5 May 1521, in *Dürer's Journal*, cited by Gombrich, "Renaissance Theory of Art."

6. Friedlander, *Über die Landschaftsmalerei*, pp. 58ff.

7. On this topic, see Edgar Wind, *Giorgione's "Tempesta" with Comments on Giorgione's Poetic Allegories* (Oxford: Clarendon Press, 1969); and also Salvatore Settis, *Giorgone's Tempest: Interpreting the Hidden Sub-*

ject, trans. Ellen Bianchini (Chicago: University of Chicago Press, 1990); see also my own article cited above, note 3. It should be noted that the term for "storm" is *fortuna*.

8. Cf. Gombrich, "Renaissance Theory of Art," pp. 109–110.

9. Cf. Leon Battista Alberti, *On the Art of Building in Ten Books*, trans. Joseph Rykwert, Neil Leach, and Robert Tavernor (Cambridge, Mass.: MIT Press, 1989), book 4, chap. 4; Leonardo da Vinci, *Treatise on Painting*, ed. A. P. McMahon II (Princeton: Princeton University Press, 1956), fol. 51; Irma A. Richter, ed., *Paragone: A Comparison of the Arts* (London: Oxford University Press, 1949), pp. 51ff; Vitruvius Pallio, *The Ten Books on Architecture*, trans. Morris Hicky Morgan (New York: Dover, 1960), p. 153 (book 5, chap. 8).

10. Giovanni Paolo Lomazzo, *Trattato dell'arte della pittura, scultura ed archittetura*, book 6, chap. 42; cited by Gombrich, "Renaissance Theory of Art," p. 120.

11. On the influence of Leonardo, see Jan Bialostocki, "Une idée de Léonard réalisée par Poussin," *Revue des arts* 4 (1954): 130–136.

12. Pliny the Elder, *Natural History*, trans. H. Rackham, 10 vols. (Cambridge, Mass.: Harvard University Press; London: William Heinemann, 1969–1989), book 35, chap. 96 (in vol. 9).

13. On the "sublation" of landscape painting in Poussin, the indispensable work is naturally Blunt, *Nicolas Poussin*, in particular chapters 9, "Landscape"; 11, "The Late Mythological Landscapes"; and 12, "The Last Synthesis: *The Four Seasons* and the *Apollo and Daphné*." See also, by the same author, "The Heroic and the Ideal Landscape of Nicolas Poussin," in *Journal of the Warburg and Courtauld Institutes* 7 (1944): 154–168. Still, in my judgment, only the questioning that the sublime introduces makes it possible to interpret this sublation, in particular with the figures of the "shapeless," the "giant," the "snake," or the "tempest." The task that remains, then, is to rearticulate Blunt's impressive work through a new problematics that would be at once historical, iconographic, and philosophical but also formal and plastic.

14. On Giorgione's *Tempesta*, see my "Les fins de l'interprétation ou les traversées du regard dans le sublime d'une tempête," in *Les fins de l'homme: A partir du travail de Jacques Derrida* (Paris: Galilée, 1981), pp. 317–344. [Editors' note: reprinted in *De la représentation* (Paris: Seuil-Gallimard, 1994), pp. 179–203.]

15. Longinus, *On the Sublime*, trans. James A. Arieti and John H. Crossett (New York: E. Mellen, 1985), p. 9 (1.3).

16. André Félibien, *Entretiens sur les vies et ouvrages des plus excellens peintres anciens et modernes*, 5 vols. (Paris: D. Mortier, 1666–1688). I am citing the reprint edition (London, 1705).

17. On the question of the schematism of variation in its relation to the unrepresentable, see my "Variations sur un portrait absent" [editors' note: Chapter 9 in this volume].

18. For critical documentation on the two paintings, see the catalogue *Nicolas Poussin, 1594–1665* (Rome: Villa Medicis, 1977), pp. 207–214. Cf. Jacques Thuillier, "Poussin et le paysage tragique: *L'orage Pointel* au Musée des beaux-arts de Rouen," *Revue du Louvre et des musées de France* 5–6 (1976): 345–355; Clovis Whitfield, "Nicolas Poussin's *Orage* and *Temps calme*," *Burlington Magazine*, Jan. 1977, pp. 4–12. See also Blunt, *Poussin: A Critical Catalogue*, nos. 216–217, notices prepared before the two originals were rediscovered, *Landscape—A Storm* in 1975 (now at Rouen, Musée des Beaux-Arts) and *Landscape—A Calm* in 1976 (now at Art Institute of Chicago).

19. On the notion of *ekphrasis*, or description, historically related both to painting and to landscape as far back as the Second Sophistic, see the invaluable text by Ernst Robert Curtius, *European Literature and the Latin Middle Ages*, trans. Willard R. Trask (New York: Harper Torchbooks, 1953), especially p. 69 and all of chapter 10, "The Ideal Landscape," pp. 183–202. The prototype of *ekphrasis* and its paradigm is of course the famous description of Achilles' shield in the eighteenth book of the *Iliad*.

20. Cf. Poussin, *Lettres et propos sur l'art*, p. 149.

21. Félibien, *Entretiens*, 3:41–45. In what follows, quotations describing this event are from this page span unless otherwise indicated.

22. Ibid., p. 34.

23. Ibid.

24. Cf. the first meaning of the term "landscape" in the *Littré* dictionary, and the following passage from Fontenelle's "Eloge de Monsieur Varignon," in *Oeuvres complètes*, vol. 7 (Paris: Fayard, 1996), pp. 19–31: "A landscape of which one sees all the parts one after the other will not, however, have been seen; it must be viewed from fairly high up, from a place where all the formerly dispersed objects are gathered together in a single gaze." This element, which has a very long history, is clearly essential in the constitution of the very notion of "landscape."

25. The zigzagging line in the represented space is also a noteworthy element of the "landscape" mechanism in the Renaissance and afterward.

26. This point is crucial both for a theory and a history of *ekphrasis* and for the constitution of the perspective mechanism. See my remarks on this subject in *To Destroy Painting.*

27. Gombrich, "Renaissance Theory of Art," p. 117. See also his *Art and Illusion,* 3d ed. (London: Phaidon, 1962), chap. 2.

28. Félibien, fifth *entretien,* in *Entretiens,* 3:5.

29. Ibid. The painting Félibien mentions is now in the Ashmolean Museum in Oxford. See Blunt, *Poussin: A Critical Catalogue,* p. 12. The painting was done for Jacques Stella in 1654. Cf. Félibien, *Entretiens,* 3:39.

30. Félibien, *Entretiens,* 3:40–41.

31. Ibid., p. 40.

32. Ibid., p. 42–43. Let us note that the descriptions of the landscape bring sounds into play in language: the noise of the fountains in *Temps calme,* the great commotion of thunder in *Orage.* The painted picture cannot, of course, do the same thing in its own "language." Hence the search, among seventeenth-century art theorists (and some of their predecessors), for equivalences in the field of painting, especially with the notions of consonance and dissonance.

33. Félibien, *Entretiens,* 3:42–43.

34. Ibid., p. 43.

35. It would be appropriate—though not possible here—to spell out as rigorously as possible the procedures of transformation and transposition between the respective syntactic organizations of a discourse and a painting.

36. Félibien, *Entretiens,* 3:43.

37. Ibid.

38. The pathetic effects of sublimity always imply a theatricalization of the sublime "object." Let us note that in Longinus's treatise, the first examples of the "sublime" are always drawn from tragedies and even from passages in which a character on stage is describing a sublime object that is off stage, thereby inscribing a second imaginary scenography within the first. It will fall to Kant, at the end of the eighteenth century, to propose the philosophical theory of this theatricalization; see in particular his *Critique of Judgment,* sec. 28.

39. Félibien, *Entretiens,* 3:44. Cf. the reference to Pliny, above, which would offer a guiding thread for a rereading and interpretation of representation (*phantasia*) as it has been elaborated by middle Stoicism and the Second Sophistic.

40. Nicolas Poussin, letter to M. de Chambray, 1 March 1665, in Holt, ed., *Documentary History of Art*, p. 158. See Anthony Blunt's commentary and especially the comparisons he makes with Poussin's *observations* as reported by Bellori, dating from the 1640s (in Poussin, *Lettres et propos sur l'art*, pp. 169–174).

41. Félibien, *Entretiens*, 44–45.

42. It would be useful to distinguish, on the theoretical level, between the notions of variation (and schematism of variation) and transformation (and group or law of transformation): they belong to two different levels, the second more abstract and more general than the first. It is not surprising, then, to find Hubert Damisch applying the notion of transformation group to the mechanism of perspective. See Damisch, "Les voir, dis-tu; et les décrire," in *Versus* (Milan) 29 (May–August 1989): 15–49; see also the notion of variation schema in my own work, cited above, on Poussin's self-portraits or in the essay on Signorelli concerning the figures and scenes decorating the cupola.

43. Félibien, *Entretiens*, 3:23.

44. *Landscape with Orpheus and Eurydice*, no. 170 in *Poussin: A Critical Catalogue*, was done in 1650, according to Anthony Blunt and Denis Mahon. It is now in the Louvre.

45. *Landscape with Polyphemus* (ibid., no. 175), currently in the Hermitage Museum in Saint Petersburg, was painted in 1649; *Landscape with Hercules and Cacus* (ibid., no. 158), currently in the Pushkin Museum in Moscow, was painted around 1655, according to Blunt, in 1659, according to Mahon.

46. *Spring*, or *The Earthly Paradise* (ibid., no. 3), currently in the Louvre, was painted in 1660–1664; *Landscape with Orion* (ibid., no. 169), today in the Metropolitan Museum of Art, New York, was painted in 1658. A different approach to the sublime in Poussin, one linked to the figures of the colossus and the monster, would give rise to the series of works that I have just evoked.

47. On the simultaneity of the too-distant and the too-close, again see Kant, *Critique of Judgment*, sec. 26. On the systematic search for that effect in Caravaggio, a search Poussin denounced, see my own *To Destroy Painting*.

48. Cf. Poussin's well-known letter on musical modes, to Chantelou, 24 November 1647 [editors' note: see Appendix 3], and his hesitation as to the definition of the Phrygian mode.

49. On the distinction Poussin himself made between prospect and aspect, see his letter to Sublet des Noyers (*Lettres et propos sur l'art*, pp. 62–63). The letter is undated, but we may presume it was written during the artist's stay in Paris.

50. On the distinction between the order of places and the process of spaces, see Michel de Certeau, *The Practice of Everyday Life*, trans. Steven F. Rendall (Berkeley: University of California Press, 1984), chap. 9, "Spatial Stories," including numerous bibliographical references.

51. The reference to the Stoic theory of passion and its relation to time is unavoidable here, especially regarding the status of the present. Cf. Goldschmidt, *Système stoïcien*, pp. 43–44, 180–181; and my "La description du tableau et le sublime en peinture" [editors' note: see Chapter 3 in this volume].

52. Félibien, *Entretiens*, 3:44.

53. It could well be that the counterpart to the "figure of theory" found in the *Landscape with Pyramus and Thisbe* in the mirror-lake of the second level is, in *Le temps calme*, the absence of any reflection, in the central lake, of the smoke-cloud that foreshadows *L'orage*. This observation, which was made to me during the colloquium, would warrant—if it proves to be correct, which is very likely—a lengthy analysis on the formal and plastic level and on the theoretical level, since a breakdown of representation in one of its most compelling figures—that of the "natural" mirror represented—would refer both to a lacuna in the reflective dimension of the representative mechanism, thus to a theoretical "syncope" (contemplation and speculation), and to an intrusion of one of the essential secondary characteristics of the sublime—the excess of representation over itself, its "overfullness"—in the very picture of beauty, but figured as absence or negativity. From this standpoint, not only through the figures that anticipate the storm, the smoke-cloud, and the rider carried away on his galloping horse, but also in its very center (the mirror-lake), *Le temps calme* would be caught up in the variation in which the unrepresentable presents itself, namely, the sublime.

Chapter 6

First published as "Fragments d'un parcours dans les ruines de Poussin," in "Les Ruines," special issue, *Oracl* 23/24 (1988): 20–26.

Chapter 7

First published as "A l'éveil des métamorphoses: Poussin (1625–1635)" in *Corps écrit* 7 (1983): 31–43.

1. Torquato Tasso, *Gerusalemme liberata*, 14.65–67, ed. Lanfranco Caretti, 2d ed. (Milan: Mondadori, 1988); translation from *Jerusalem Delivered*, trans. Ralph Nash (Detroit: Wayne State University Press, 1987).

Chapter 8

First published as "Récompenses d'un regard, ou Moïse tiré des eaux" in *Corps écrit* 4 (1982): 123–132.

Chapter 9

First published as "Variations sur un portrait absent: Les autoportraits de Poussin, 1649–1650" in *Corps écrit* 5 (1983): 87–107.

1. Poussin, *Correspondance*, pp. 357–358.
2. Nicolas Poussin, letter to Chantelou, 7 April 1947, in Holt, ed., *Documentary History of Art*, p. 154.
3. *Lettres et propos sur l'art*, p. 117.
4. Ibid., p. 118.
5. Letter to Chantelou, 24 November 1647, in Holt, ed., *A Documentary History of Art*, p. 155 [editors' note: see Appendix 3].
6. Editors' note: Technical examinations done on the occasion of the 1994 Poussin exhibit at the Grand Palais in Paris showed that the inscription *De lumine et colore* was added after the painting was finished. The restorers were thus justified in removing it, but Louis Marin's interpretation turns out to be oddly reinforced by this addition that has now disappeared.
7. Letter to Chantelou, 24 November 1647, ibid., p. 155.
8. Letter to M. de Chambray, 1 March 1665, ibid., p. 159.
9. Letter to Chantelou, 7 April 1647, in *Lettres et propos sur l'art*, p. 118.
10. Blaise Pascal, *Pascal, Pensées*, trans. A. J. Krailsheimer (Harmondsworth, Eng.: Penguin Books, 1966), p. 107 (fragment 260).

Chapter 10

This text first appeared as a talk given at a meeting of the Association of Seventeenth-Century French Studies in Baton Rouge, Louisiana; it was published as "Le sublime dans les années 1670: Un je-ne-sais-quoi?" in *Actes de Bâton-Rouge, Biblio 17: Papers on French Seventeenth-Century Literature* (Paris, Seattle, Tübingen, 1986), pp. 185–201.

1. *Pascal Pensées*, p. 48 (65).

Appendix 2

1. The passage from the beginning of the letter to this point is quoted from Holt, ed., *Documentary History of Art*, pp. 146–147.

Appendix 3

1. The passage beginning at "If you feel affection for the picture of *Moses Found in the Waters of the Nile* . . . " to this point is quoted from ibid., pp. 154–156.

Works Cited

Alberti, Leon Battista. *On the Art of Building in Ten Books*. Trans. Joseph Rykwert, Neil Leach, and Robert Tavernor. Cambridge, Mass.: MIT Press, 1989.

Alpers, Svetlana. *The Art of Describing: Dutch Art in the Seventeenth Century*. Chicago: Chicago University Press, 1983.

Aristotle. *Aristotle's "Categories" and "De Interpretatione."* Trans. J. L. Ackrill. Oxford: Clarendon Press, 1963.

Arnauld, Antoine, and Pierre Nicole. *Logic; or, The Art of Thinking*. Cambridge: Cambridge University Press, 1996.

Aurelius, Marcus. *The Meditations*. Trans. G. M. A. Grube. Indianapolis: Hackett, 1983.

Benveniste, Emile. "L'antonyme et le pronom en français moderne." *Bulletin de la Société de linguistique de Paris* 55, fasc. 1 (1965): 71–87. Reprinted in *Problèmes de linguistique générale*, 2:197–214. Paris: Gallimard, 1974.

———. "The Nominal Sentence." In *Problems in General Linguistics*, pp. 131–144.

———. "Relationships of Person in the Verb." In *Problems in General Linguistics*, pp. 195–204.

———. *Problems in General Linguistics*. Trans. Mary Elizabeth Meek. Coral Gables, Fla.: University of Miami Press, 1971.

Bialostocki, Jan. "Une idée de Léonard réalisée par Poussin." *Revue des arts* 4 (1954): 130–136.

Blunt, Anthony. "The Heroic and the Ideal Landscape of Nicolas Poussin." *Journal of the Warburg and Courtauld Institutes* 7 (1944): 154–168.

———. *Nicolas Poussin*. London: Phaidon, 1967.

———. *Nicolas Poussin: A Critical Catalogue*. London: Phaidon, 1966.

———. "Le véritable sujet du *Paysage au serpent* de Poussin à la National Gallery de Londres." *Gazette des beaux-arts* 2 (1952): 343–350.

Bouhours, Dominique. *Entretiens d'Ariste et d'Eugène*. Paris: Sebastien Mabre-Cramoisy, 1671.

Bremond, Henri. *Histoire littéraire du sentiment religieux en France depuis la fin des guerres de religion jusqu'à nos jours*. 11 vols. Paris: Bloud & Gay, [1915–1936] 1967–1971.

Cassirer, Ernst. *Das Erkenntnisproblem in der Philosophie und Wissenschaft der neueren Zeit*. Vol. 3. Berlin: B. Cassirer, 1974.

———. *Kant's Life and Thought*. Trans. James Haden. New Haven: Yale University Press, 1981.

———. *The Philosophy of the Enlightenment*. Trans. Fritz C. A. Koelin and James P. Pettegrove. Princeton: Princeton University Press, 1951.

———. *The Philosophy of Symbolic Forms*. Trans. Ralph Manheim. 4 vols. New Haven: Yale University Press, 1953–1996.

———. *The Problem of Knowledge: Philosophy, Science, and History since Hegel*. Trans. William H. Woglom and Charles W. Hendel. New Haven: Yale University Press, [1920] 1950.

Certeau, Michel de. *The Practice of Everyday Life*. Trans. Steven F. Rendall. Berkeley: University of California Press, 1984.

Chastel, André, ed. *Nicolas Poussin*. Vol. 1. Paris: CNRS, 1960.

Cicero. *De provinciis consularibus*. In *Cicero*, vol. 13. Trans. R. Gardner. Cambridge, Mass.: Harvard University Press; London: Heinemann, 1937.

Clark, Kenneth. *Landscape into Art*. New York: Harper & Row, 1976.

Coton, Pierre. *Sermons sur les principales et plus difficiles matières de la foi . . . réduits par lui-même en forme de méditations*. Paris, 1617.

Curtius, Ernst Robert. *European Literature and the Latin Middle Ages*. Trans. Willard R. Trask. New York: Harper Torchbooks, 1953.

Damisch, Hubert. *Théorie du nuage: Pour une histoire de la peinture*. Paris: Seuil, 1972.

———. "Les voir, dis-tu; et les décrire." *Versus* (Milan) 29 (May–August 1989): 15–49.

d'Aubignac, abbé [Hédelin, François]. *La pratique du théâtre*. Ed. Pierre Martino. Paris, 1657; repr. Algiers: Jules Carbonel, 1927. In English as *The Whole Art of the Stage*. London, 1684; repr. New York: Benjamin Blom, 1968.

Deonna, W. Waldemar. "La légende de Pero et Micon et l'allaitement symbolique." *Latomus* 13 (1954): 140–166, 356–375.
Derrida, Jacques. *The Truth in Painting.* Trans. Geoff Bennington and Ian McLeod. Chicago: University of Chicago Press, 1987.
Descartes, René. *Les passions de l'âme.* In *Oeuvres philosophiques*, vol. 3. Paris: Garnier, 1973. In English as *The Passions of the Soul.* Trans. Stephen Voss. Indianapolis: Hackett, 1989.
Félibien, André. *Entretiens sur les vies et ouvrages des plus excellens peintres anciens et modernes.* 5 vols. Paris: D. Mortier, 1666–1688. Repr. London, 1705.
———. *Sixième conférence de l'Académie royale de peinture pendant l'année 1667.* Paris: D. Mortier, 1668.
Fontenelle, M. de Bernard le Bouvier. "Eloge de Monsieur Varignon." In *Oeuvres complètes*, 7:19–31. Paris: Fayard, 1996.
Francastel, Pierre. *La figure et le lieu.* Paris: Gallimard, 1967.
Freud, Sigmund. "The Dream-Work." In *The Standard Edition of the Complete Psychological Works of Sigmund Freud*, vols. 4–5: *The Interpretation of Dreams*, pp. 277–508. Trans. James Strachey. London: Hogarth Press, 1953.
Friedlander, Max J. *Über die Landschaftsmalerei und andere Bildgattungen.* The Hague: A. A. M. Stols, 1947.
Fumaroli, Marc. *L'age de l'éloquence. Rhétorique et "res literaria" de la Renaissance au seuil de l'époque classique.* Geneva: Droz, 1980.
Goldschmidt, Victor. *Le système stoïcien et l'idée de temps.* Paris: J. Vrin, [1953] 1977.
Gombrich, Ernst Hans. "Aims and Limits of Iconology." In *Symbolic Images: Studies in the Art of the Renaissance*, 2:1–25. London: Phaidon, 1972.
———. *Art and Illusion.* 3d ed. London: Phaidon, 1962.
———. "The Renaissance Theory of Art and the Rise of Landscape." In *Norm and Form*, pp. 107–121. London: Phaidon, 1966.
Hirsch, E. D. *Validity in Interpretation.* New Haven: Yale University Press, 1967.
Imbert, Claude. "La logique stoïcienne et la construction du récit." *Phénoménologies et langues formulaires.* Paris: Presses Universitaires de France, 1992.
———. "Stoic Logic and Alexandrian Poetics." In *Doubt and Dogmatism: Studies in Hellenic Epistemology*, ed. Malcolm Schofield, Myles

Burnyeat, and Jonathan Barnes, pp. 182–216. Oxford: Oxford University Press, 1980.

Jakobson, Roman. *Selected Writings*. Vol. 3. The Hague: Mouton, 1981.

Kant, Immanuel. *Critique of Judgment*. Trans. Werner S. Pluhar. Indianapolis: Hackett, 1951.

Klee, Paul. *Notebooks*. Vol. 1: *The Thinking Eye*. Trans. Ralph Manheim. London: Lund Humphries; New York: G. Wittenborn, 1961.

Knauer, Elfriede Regina. "Caritas Romana." *Jahrbuch der Berliner Museen* 6 (1964): 9–23.

Kris, Ernst, and Abraham Kaplan. "Aesthetic Ambiguities." In *Psychoanalytic Explorations in Art*. New York: International Universities Press, 1952.

Le Brun, Charles. *Conférence sur l'expression générale et particulière*. Paris: E. Picard, 1698. Reprinted in *Nouvelle revue de psychanalyse* 21 (spring 1980): 93–121 (special issue entitled "La passion"). In English as *A Method to Learn to Design the Passions*. London: J. Huggonson, 1734. Reprinted Augustan Reprint Society, nos. 200–201. Los Angeles: William Andrews Clark Memorial Library, UCLA, 1980.

Leibniz, Gottfried Wilhelm. *Philosophical Papers and Letters*. Trans. Leroy E. Loemker. Dordrecht: D. Reidel, 1969.

Leonardo da Vinci. *Treatise on Painting*. Ed. A. P. McMahon II. Princeton: Princeton University Press, 1956.

Longinus. *On the Sublime*. Trans. James A. Arieti and John H. Crossett. New York: E. Mellen, 1985.

Lovejoy, Arthur O., and George Boas. *A Documentary History of Primitivism and Related Ideas*. Vol. 1: *Primitivism and Related Ideas in Antiquity*. Baltimore: Johns Hopkins University Press, 1935.

Mahon, Denis. "Poussiniana." *Gazette des beaux-arts*, July–August 1962, pp. 1–138.

———. *Studies in Seicento Art and Theory*. London: Warburg Institute, 1957.

Marin, Louis. *De la représentation*. Paris: Hautes Etudes/Seuil/Gallimard, 1994.

———. "La description du tableau et le sublime en peinture: A propos d'un paysage de Poussin et de son sujet." *Communications* 34 (1981): 61–84 (special issue entitled "Les ordres de la figuration").

———. "Eléments pour une sémiologie picturale." In *Etudes sémiologiques*, pp. 17–45. Paris: Klincksieck, 1971.

———. "ET." *Première livraison* (Strasbourg) 12 (1977). N.p.
———. "Les fins de l'interprétation ou les traversées du regard dans le sublime d'une tempête." In *Les fins de l'homme: A partir du travail de Jacques Derrida*, pp. 317–344. Paris: Galilée, 1981. Reprinted in *De la représentation*, pp. 179–203.
———. "La lecture du tableau d'après Poussin." *Cahiers de l'Association internationale des études françaises* 24 (1972): 251–266.
———. "Mimésis et description." In *De la représentation*, pp. 251–66.
———. "Récit pictural et récit mythique chez Poussin." Lecture, Urbino, 1968.
———. "Variations sur un portrait absent: Les autoportraits de Poussin, 1649–1650." *Corps écrit* 5 (1983): 87–107 (special issue entitled "L'autoportrait").
Nicolas Poussin, 1594–1665. Catalogue. Rome: Villa Medicis, 1977.
Ogden, Henry V. S., and Margaret S. Ogden. *English Taste in Landscape in the Seventeenth Century*. Ann Arbor: University of Michigan Press, 1955.
Onians, John. *Art and Thought in the Hellenistic Age: The Greek World View, 350–50 B.C.* London: Thames & Hudson, 1979.
Ovid, *Metamorphoses*. Trans. Mary M. Innes. Harmondsworth, Eng.: Penguin Books, [1955] 1986.
Pächt, Otto. "Early Italian Nature Studies and the Early Calendar Landscape." *Journal of the Warburg and Courtauld Institutes* 13 (1950): 13–47.
Il paesaggio nel disegno del Cinquecento europeo. Catalogue. Rome, 1972–1973.
Il paesaggio nella pittura fra Cinque e Seicento a Firenze. Catalogue. Florence, 1980.
Panofsky, Erwin. *Architecture gothique et pensée scolastique*. Trans. Pierre Bourdieu. Paris: Editions Minuit, 1967.
———. "Artist, Scientist, and Genius: Notes on the Renaissance-Dämmerung." In *The Renaissance: Symposium*, pp. 77–93. New York: Metropolitan Museum of Art, 1952.
———. "*Et in Arcadia ego*: On the Conception of Transience in Poussin and Watteau." In *Philosophy and History: Essays Presented to Ernst Cassirer*, ed. Raymond Klibansky and H. J. Patton, pp. 223–252. New York: Harper & Row, [1936] 1963.
———. "*Et in Arcadia ego*: Poussin and the Elegiac Tradition." In *Meaning in the Visual Arts*, pp. 295–320.

———. "*Et in Arcadia ego* et le tombeau parlant." *Gazette des beaux-arts*, ser. 6, 19 (1938): 305–306.

———. "The History of Art." In Franz L. Neumann et al., *The Cultural Migration: The European Scholar in America*, ed. W. R. Crawford, pp. 82–111. Philadelphia: University of Pennsylvania Press, 1953. Reprinted as "Three Decades of Art History in the United States: Impressions of a Transplanted European" in *Meaning in the Visual Arts*, pp. 321–346.

———. "The History of Art as a Humanistic Discipline." In *Meaning in the Visual Arts*, pp. 1–25

———. "Introductory." In *Studies in Iconology: Humanistic Themes in the Art of the Renaissance*, pp. 3–31. Oxford: Oxford University Press, 1939; repr. New York: Harper & Row, 1962. Reprinted as "Iconography and Iconology: An Introduction to the Study of Renaissance Art" in *Meaning in the Visual Arts*, pp. 26–54.

———. *Meaning in the Visual Arts: Papers in and on Art History*. Garden City, N.Y.: Doubleday Anchor Books, 1955.

———. *Die Theoretische Kunstlehre Albrecht Dürers (Dürers Aesthetik)*. Berlin: G. Reimer, 1914. In English as *The Life and Art of Albrecht Dürer*. Princeton: Princeton University Press, 1955.

Pascal, Blaise. *Pascal, Pensées*. Trans. A. J. Krailsheimer. Harmondsworth, Eng.: Penguin Books, 1966.

Pigler, Andreas. *Barockthemen*. Vol. 2. Budapest, 1974.

Pliny the Elder. *Natural History*. Trans. H. Rackham. 10 vols. Cambridge, Mass.: Harvard University Press; London: William Heinemann, 1969–1989.

Poussin, Nicolas. *Correspondance de Nicolas Poussin*. Ed. Charles Jouanny. Paris: F. de Nobele, 1968.

———. *Lettres et propos sur l'art*. Ed. Anthony Blunt. Paris: Hermann, 1964.

———. "Nicolas Poussin: Letter to Chantelou." In *A Documentary History of Art*, ed. Elizabeth Gilmore Holt, 2:141–159. Garden City, N.Y.: Doubleday, 1958.

Relations artistiques entre les Pays-Bas et l'Italie à la Renaissance. Rome and Brussels, 1980.

Richeome, Louis. *La peinture spirituelle, ou l'art d'admirer, aimer et louer Dieu en toutes ses oeuvres*. Lyon: Pierre Rigaud, 1611.

———. *Tableaux sacréz des figures mystiques du très-auguste sacrifice et sacrement de l'Eucharistie*. Paris: Laurens Sonnius, 1609.

Richter, Irma A. ed. *Paragone: A Comparison of the Arts.* London: Oxford University Press, 1949.
Schapiro, Meyer. *Words and Pictures: On the Literal and the Symbolic in the Illustration of a Text.* The Hague: Mouton, 1973.
Schefer, Jean-Louis. *Scénographie d'un tableau.* Paris: Seuil, 1969.
Seneca. *Ad Lucilium epistulae morales.* Trans. Richard M. Gummere. London: William Heinemann; New York: G. P. Putnam's Sons, 1925.
Settis, Salvatore. *Giorgone's Tempest: Interpreting the Hidden Subject.* Trans. Ellen Bianchini. Chicago: University of Chicago Press, 1990.
Shearman, John. "Les dessins de paysages de Poussin." Trans. Françoise Vitale. In *Nicolas Poussin,* ed. André Chastel, 1:176–188. Paris: CNRS, 1960.
Siguret, Françoise. "Lisez l'histoire avec le tableau." *Etudes françaises* 14 (1975): 21–24.
Stechow, Wolfgang. *Dutch Landscape Painting of the Seventeenth Century.* London: Phaidon, 1966.
Thuillier, Jacques. *Fragonard.* Trans. Robert Allen. Geneva: Skira, 1967.
———. "Poussin et le paysage tragique: *L'orage Pointel* au Musée des beaux-arts de Rouen." *Revue du Louvre et des musées de France* 5–6 (1976): 345–355.
Thürleman, Félix. "La fonction de l'admiration dans l'esthétique du XVIIe siècle, à propos de la charité romaine dans *La Manne* de Poussin." Unpublished ms., 1976.
Valerius Maximus. *Dictorum factorumque memorabilium libri.* Vol. 5. Anvers, 1614.
Vanuxem, Jacques. "Les 'tableaux sacrés' de Richeome et l'iconographie de l'Eucharistie chez Poussin." In *Nicolas Poussin,* ed. André Chastel, 1:151–162. Paris: CNRS, 1960.
Vitruvius Pallio. *The Ten Books on Architecture.* Trans. Morris Hicky Morgan. New York: Dover, 1960.
Whitfield, Clovis. "Nicolas Poussin's *Orage* and *Temps calme.*" *Burlington Magazine,* Jan. 1977, pp. 4–12.
Wildenstein, G. Georges. "Les graveurs de Poussin au XVIIe siècle." *Gazette des beaux-arts,* July–August 1955, pp. 75–371.
Wind, Edgar. *Giorgione's "Tempesta" with Comments on Giorgione's Poetic Allegories.* Oxford: Clarendon Press, 1969.
———. "Zur Systematik der künstlerischen Probleme." *Zeitschrift für Aesthetik und allgemeine Kunstwissenschaft* 18 (1925): 438ff.

Wittkower, Rudolf. *Art and Architecture in Italy, 1600–1750*. Harmondsworth, Eng.: Penguin Books, 1965.

———. "Giorgione and Arcady." *Umanesimo europeo ed umanesimo veneziano*. Florence, 1963. Reprinted in *Idea and Image: Studies in the Italian Renaissance*, pp. 161–173. London: Thames & Hudson, 1978.

MERIDIAN

Crossing Aesthetics

Louis Marin, *Sublime Poussin*

Aris Fioretos, *The Gray Book*

Deborah Esch, *In the Event: Reading Journalism, Reading Theory*

Winfried Menninghaus, *In Praise of Nonsense: Kant and Bluebeard*

Giorgio Agamben, *The Man Without Content*

Giorgio Agamben, *The End of the Poem: Essays in Poetics*

Theodor W. Adorno, *Sound Figures*

Philippe Lacoue-Labarthe, *Poetry as Experience*

Jacques Derrida, *Resistances of Psychoanalysis*

Marc Froment-Meurice, *That Is to Say: Heidegger's Poetics*

Francis Ponge, *Soap*

Philippe Lacoue-Labarthe, *Typography: Mimesis, Philosophy, Politics*

Giorgio Agamben, *Homo Sacer: Sovereign Power and Bare Life*

Emmanuel Levinas, *Of God Who Comes to Mind*

Bernard Stiegler, *Technics and Time, 1: The Fault of Epimetheus*

Werner Hamacher, *pleroma—Reading in Hegel*

Serge Leclaire, *Psychoanalyzing: On the Order of the Unconscious and the Practice of the Letter*

Serge Leclaire, *A Child Is Being Killed: On Primary Narcissism and the Death Drive*

Sigmund Freud, *Writings on Art and Literature*

Cornelius Castoriadis, *World in Fragments: Writings on Politics, Society, Psychoanalysis, and the Imagination*

Thomas Keenan, *Fables of Responsibility: Aberrations and Predicaments in Ethics and Politics*

Emmanuel Levinas, *Proper Names*

Alexander García Düttmann, *At Odds with AIDS: Thinking and Talking About a Virus*

Maurice Blanchot, *Friendship*

Jean-Luc Nancy, *The Muses*

Massimo Cacciari, *Posthumous People: Vienna at the Turning Point*

David E. Wellbery, *The Specular Moment: Goethe's Early Lyric and the Beginnings of Romanticism*

Edmond Jabès, *The Little Book of Unsuspected Subversion*

Hans-Jost Frey, *Studies in Poetic Discourse: Mallarmé, Baudelaire, Rimbaud, Hölderlin*

Pierre Bourdieu, *The Rules of Art: Genesis and Structure of the Literary Field*

Nicolas Abraham, *Rhythms: On the Work, Translation, and Psychoanalysis*

Jacques Derrida, *On the Name*

David Wills, *Prosthesis*

Maurice Blanchot, *The Work of Fire*

Jacques Derrida, *Points . . . : Interviews, 1974–1994*

J. Hillis Miller, *Topographies*

Philippe Lacoue-Labarthe, *Musica Ficta (Figures of Wagner)*

Jacques Derrida, *Aporias*

Emmanuel Levinas, *Outside the Subject*

Jean-François Lyotard, *Lessons on the Analytic of the Sublime*

Peter Fenves, *"Chatter": Language and History in Kierkegaard*

Jean-Luc Nancy, *The Experience of Freedom*

Jean-Joseph Goux, *Oedipus, Philosopher*

Haun Saussy, *The Problem of a Chinese Aesthetic*

Jean-Luc Nancy, *The Birth to Presence*

Library of Congress Cataloging-in-Publication Data

Marin, Louis
[Sublime Poussin. English]
Sublime Poussin / Louis Marin ; translated by Catherine Porter.
p. cm. — (Meridian, crossing aesthetics)
Includes bibliographical references.
ISBN 0-8047-3476-3 (cloth). — ISBN 0-8047-3477-1 (pbk.)
1. Poussin, Nicolas, 1594?–1665—Criticism and interpretation.
2. Sublime, The, in art. I. Poussin, Nicolas, 1594?–1665.
II. Title. III. Series: Meridian (Stanford, Calif.)
ND553.P8M3413 1999
759.4—dc21 99-11562

Original printing 1999.
Last figure below indicates date of this printing:
07 06 05 04 03 02 01 00 99

Typeset by James P. Brommer in 10.9/13 Garamond
and Lithos display

The authorized representative in the EU for product safety and compliance is:
Mare Nostrum Group
B.V Doelen 72
4831 GR Breda
The Netherlands

www.ingramcontent.com/pod-product-compliance
Lightning Source LLC
LaVergne TN
LVHW091033080826
845145LV00002B/477
* 9 7 8 0 8 0 4 7 3 4 7 7 6 *